EVENTS AND ECONOMIC DEVELOPMENT

Events of all shapes and sizes play an important part in all of our lives. They are fun, frivolous, and often allow us to escape from our everyday lives – and they are also fascinating to study and examine in a more serious way, to understand what they mean and do for us – individually and collectively. *Events and Economic Development*, therefore, explores the economic impact and developmental implications of designing, planning, and delivering events – cultural events like the Notting Hill Carnival and Day of the Dead, to sporting events like the Olympics to the Super Bowl.

This book comprises 24 chapters, each addressing various diverse and interconnected topics related to the economic and developmental implications of hosting events. Each chapter follows a consistent structure, beginning with the aim and learning objective(s), followed by theoretical focuses and the significance of these perspectives. Similarly, practical focuses and their significance are also outlined. The main body of each chapter consists of an 800 to 2000-word argument. Following the argument, chapters include managerial, policy, and/or research implications, explicitly mapping how they relate to the UN Sustainable Development Goals. Each chapter concludes with a series of quizzes to test knowledge and debate questions to engage learners in discussing and interrogating the argument.

Some of the topics covered include:

- Nation Branding through Events
- Urban Transformation via Events
- Commercialization of Culture and Events
- Crisis and Resilience in Event Management
- Sustainability in Event Hosting
- Cultural Identity and Heritage Preservation
- Globalization of Sports and Festivals
- Media and Narrative Evolution
- Ethics and Sponsorship in Events
- Community Impacts and Gentrification.

This innovative, topical, engaging, and comprehensive book is an essential reading and teaching resource for all students and lecturers in events that are easy to integrate into educational programmes.

Mike Duignan is a Professeur at the Sorbonne, University of Paris 1, France, and the Director of Research, Intelligence, and Education at Trivandi, UK. Since 2021, Mike has been the Editor-in-Chief of the leading peer-reviewed journal for the study and analysis of events: *Event Management Journal*. Formerly, he was a tenured Associate Professor at the University of Central Florida, USA; the Director of the UK Olympic Studies Centre; and a Reader and Head of Department at the University of Surrey, UK.

Routledge 'How Events Transform Society' Series

Events of all shapes and sizes are witnessing significant growth – locally, regionally, nationally, internationally – shaping our lives, economies, and society-at-large in profound and complex ways.

Books in this series are cutting edge and intellectually stimulating, with a balance between theory and application. Titles are accessible and content is easily digestible for students, academics, and practitioners. Taking a flip classroom approach, these can easily be integrated as a week of teaching, with interactive activities such as classroom quizzes, debate questions, and further reading to situate theory in real-life practices.

Each book in the series includes approximately 30 carefully crafted case studies written by leading academics and practitioners globally, that present complex scholarly arguments as concise and accessible chapter-based articles. Each short topical chapter explores a critical issue or debate based on real-life events related to the overarching theme, and contextualises this within the key theoretical debates, managerial and policy implications, and links to SDGs.

Events and Society
Bridging Theory and Practice
Edited by Mike Duignan

Events and Economic Development
Bridging Theory and Practice
Edited by Mike Duignan

For more information about this series, please visit: www.routledge.com/tourism/series/RPISEF

EVENTS AND ECONOMIC DEVELOPMENT

Bridging Theory and Practice

Edited by Mike Duignan

Routledge
Taylor & Francis Group
LONDON AND NEW YORK

Designed cover image: Getty Images

First published 2025
by Routledge
4 Park Square, Milton Park, Abingdon, Oxon OX14 4RN

and by Routledge
605 Third Avenue, New York, NY 10158

Routledge is an imprint of the Taylor & Francis Group, an informa business

British Library Cataloguing-in-Publication Data
A catalogue record for this book is available from the British Library

ISBN: 978-1-032-79057-2 (hbk)
ISBN: 978-1-032-79055-8 (pbk)
ISBN: 978-1-003-49032-6 (ebk)

DOI: 10.4324/9781003490326

Typeset in Berthold Akzidenz Grotesk
by Newgen Publishing UK

This book is dedicated to my wonderful boy and canine companion, Milo, who passed away on March 3, 2023.

CONTENTS

FIGURES

TABLES

CONTRIBUTORS

Taylor Aucoin, University of Edinburgh, UK.
Becky Ashworth, Sheffield Hallam University, UK.
Richard Baka, Victoria University, Australia.
Brendan Barratt, University of Osaka, Japan.
John Bryson, University of Birmingham, UK.
Thomas Burelli, Ottawa University, Canada.
Jo Clarke, Sheffield Hallam University, UK.
Christopher T. Conner, University of Missouri, USA.
Ralph Crane, University of Tasmania, Tasmania.
Leon Davis, Teeside University, UK.
Marie Dykukha, Ottawa University, Canada.
Nicole Ferdinand, Oxford Brookes University, UK.
Lucy Gill-Simmen, Royal Holloway: University of London, UK.
Katerina Girginova, University of Pennsylvania, USA.
Ben Green, Griffith University, Australia.
Todd Green, Brock University, Canada.
John Harris, independent scholar.
Danielle Hidalgo, University of Missouri, USA.
Kirsten Holmes, Curtin University, Australia.
Robin Ireland, University of Glasgow, UK.
Haoran Liu, Ottawa University, Canada.
Leonie Lockstone-Binney, Griffith University, Australia.
Pascale Jossart-Marcelli, San Diego State University, USA.
Thor Kerr, Curtin University, Australia.
Brendon Knott, Cape Peninsula University of Technology, South Africa.
Judith Mair, University of Queensland, Australia.
Dan Plumley, Sheffield Hallam University, UK.
Mathew Sandoval, Arizona State University, USA.
Gary Sinclair, Dublin City University, Ireland.
Tracy Taylor, RMIT, Australia.
Julie Tinson, University of Stirling, UK.

John Varano, Worley, UK.
Irfan Wahyudi, Universitas Airlangga, East Java.
John Weldon, Victoria University, New Zealand.
Sam Whiting, University of South Australia, Australia.
Ling Xiao, Royal Holloway: University of London, UK.

FOREWORD

Prof Holger Preuss, University of Mainz, Germany

Events hold a remarkable place in our lives, offering moments of joy, cultural immersion, and an escape from the everyday. Yet, their significance extends far beyond entertainment. From iconic celebrations like the Notting Hill Carnival and the Day of the Dead, to mega-sporting events like the Olympics and the Super Bowl, events serve as powerful platforms for economic development, cultural preservation, and societal transformation. They are engines of change, shaping economies, communities, and identities in profound and lasting ways. This book, ***Events and Economic Development***, explores the multifaceted impacts of events, shedding light on their potential to drive progress and foster sustainability.

Events have increasingly been recognized as tools for urban development, nation branding, and advancing the United Nations' Sustainable Development Goals (SDGs). Their influence extends beyond the immediate excitement they generate, creating opportunities for long-term legacies that encompass structural changes, economic growth, and social cohesion. By drawing from an interdisciplinary approach, this book bridges the gap between theory and practice, integrating insights from disciplines such as economics, sociology, anthropology, and political science. It provides readers with a holistic understanding of events as transformative phenomena with implications for individuals, communities, and nations alike.

The diversity of topics covered in this book highlights the complexity of the event industry and its far-reaching implications. Chapters explore themes such as the commercialization of culture, ethics and sponsorship, crisis management, and the globalization of festivals and sports. Other pressing issues, including community impacts, urban gentrification, and the sustainability of hosting events, are also examined in detail. For instance, how events like the FIFA World Cup or the Commonwealth Games redefine urban landscapes or promote cultural heritage illustrates the strategic potential of events to foster long-term development.

A unique strength of this book lies in its structure, designed to deepen understanding while encouraging active engagement. Each chapter begins with clear objectives, followed by theoretical insights and practical applications that highlight their relevance. Arguments are presented with depth and rigor, while implications for management, policy, and research ensure a grounded perspective. Quizzes and debate questions at the end of each chapter challenge readers to think critically and apply their knowledge, making the book a dynamic resource for students, educators, and practitioners alike.

Central to the book's exploration is the concept of 'legacy', which underscores the dual potential of events. It is less important how the event is than what the event changes in our society. Research in this area of legacy reveals that, depending on how they are managed, events can either catalyze sustainable development or exacerbate existing challenges. The nuanced discussion of legacy permeates the chapters, urging readers to consider both the immediate benefits and the enduring consequences of hosting events. This perspective invites reflection on how events can be leveraged responsibly to create meaningful and lasting impact.

By weaving together rigorous academic analysis, practical case studies, and critical insights, ***Events and Economic Development*** offers a comprehensive exploration of the transformative power of events. It challenges readers to view events not merely as spectacles, but as catalysts for positive change, equipping them with the tools to navigate the complexities of event management in a rapidly evolving world. Whether you are a student, researcher, or practitioner, this book provides invaluable perspectives on the profound ways events shape our societies and economies.

ACKNOWLEDGEMENTS

I want to thank all the authors for submitting their interesting work in events, their contribution to the production of this book, for being open to feedback, and for being part of a diverse set of chapters that honour the power and potential of events for economic and development purposes.

INTRODUCTION

Events and festivals are powerful instruments for economic growth and development, serving as platforms for nation branding, urban renewal, cultural celebration, and societal transformation. Across various forms and scales, these events demonstrate their potential to reshape perceptions, foster tourism, stimulate local economies, and create legacies that endure beyond their immediate timelines. However, their efficacy hinges on strategic planning, sustained investment, and the ability to navigate complex sociopolitical and economic landscapes.

Mega-events like the FIFA World Cup, the Olympics, and the Africa Cup of Nations illustrate how countries, particularly emerging economies, use these platforms to enhance their global image. Such events offer opportunities to showcase cultural richness, infrastructure development, and political stability to a global audience. For instance, nations such as Qatar, Brazil, and South Africa have used these events to redefine their international standing, often leveraging them to attract investment and tourism. Yet, these efforts also reveal inherent challenges, including the risks of over-commercialization, limited local benefits, and controversies surrounding governance and ethics.

At the urban level, events act as catalysts for revitalization and economic stimulation. Festivals such as Dark Mofo in Hobart and initiatives in regions like Banyuwangi, Indonesia, highlight how localized cultural celebrations can transform cities and regions. By harnessing their unique identities and heritage, these events have driven tourism growth, urban development, and cultural vibrancy, fostering pride and economic resilience in their communities. Similarly, large-scale sporting events, such as the Commonwealth Games in Birmingham, exemplify the dual role of such occasions in attracting global attention while

DOI: 10.4324/9781003490326-1

addressing local priorities, such as sustainable urban planning and infrastructure upgrades.

Cultural festivals further underscore the intricate interplay between tradition, globalization, and commercialization. Celebrations like Día de los Muertos in Mexico, and migrant-driven carnivals such as London's Notting Hill Carnival, demonstrate the economic potential of culturally rooted events. These festivals not only preserve and promote heritage, but also face pressures of commodification, which can dilute authenticity and challenge community ownership. Events centered on food, music, and art often contribute to urban gentrification, raising questions about inclusivity and equity as they draw new economic opportunities and displace existing communities.

Despite their benefits, the sustainability of events is an ongoing concern, particularly in light of rising costs, environmental impacts, and evolving consumer expectations. Efforts to integrate eco-friendly practices and prioritize meaningful legacies are becoming critical, as exemplified by plans for the 2032 Brisbane Olympics and growing resistance to harmful sponsorships in events like Euro 2024. The adaptability of events to crises, such as climate disruptions or post-pandemic recovery, further underscores their need for innovative and resilient frameworks.

The rise of digital platforms and social media has also redefined how events are experienced and perceived. By enabling alternative narratives and democratizing participation, digital advancements have expanded the reach of events while raising challenges around controlling and shaping their legacies.

Ultimately, the power of events lies in their ability to unite people, promote economic growth, and serve as platforms for cultural and social expression. However, their success requires balancing short-term gains with long-term development, ensuring inclusivity, authenticity, and sustainability. These considerations are essential for events to remain relevant and impactful in an increasingly interconnected and scrutinized world.

The key economic and development themes addressed across this book include:

Nation Branding through Events: Mega-events serve as platforms for nations to enhance global image, attract investment, and foster unity, with mixed results.

Urban Transformation via Events: Events drive urban renewal, boosting tourism, infrastructure, and local economies, while highlighting challenges of sustainability and inclusivity.

Commercialization of Culture and Events: Events face tensions between cultural authenticity and economic interests, shaping their role in society and raising ethical concerns.

Crisis and Resilience in Event Management: Climate change, economic shifts, and audience behavior disrupt events, requiring innovative planning and adaptive strategies for future stability.

Sustainability in Event Hosting: Increasing emphasis on cost-effective, eco-friendly practices challenge traditional hosting models, focusing on meaningful legacies and climate-positive outcomes.

Cultural Identity and Heritage Preservation: Events celebrate cultural heritage while navigating globalization, commercialization, and community displacement, balancing authenticity with broader appeal.

Globalization of Sports and Festivals: Events expand inclusivity and engagement while reflecting power dynamics, commercialization, and evolving societal expectations.

Media and Narrative Evolution: Social media reshapes event storytelling, offering diverse perspectives while amplifying traditional media narratives for wider global reach.

Ethics and Sponsorship in Events: Sponsorships raise health, social, and ethical concerns, prompting debates about prioritizing financial gains versus public wellbeing.

Community Impacts and Gentrification: Events can transform neighborhoods in cities, but often risk displacing communities, necessitating equitable and inclusive urban strategies.

This book comprises 24 chapters, each addressing various diverse and interconnected topics related to the economic and development implications of hosting events. Each chapter follows a consistent structure, beginning with the aim and learning objective(s), followed by theoretical focuses and the significance of these perspectives. Similarly, practical focuses and their significance are also outlined. The main body of each chapter consists of an 800–2000-word article. Following the article, chapters include managerial, policy, and/or research implications, explicitly mapping how they relate to the UN Sustainable Development Goals. Each chapter concludes with a series of quizzes to test knowledge, and debate questions to engage learners in discussing and interrogating the argument.

The abstracts for all chapters are provided below:

Chapter 1: (Re)branding a nation through a sport mega-event

Since 2000, emerging nations, notably the BRICS, have pursued sport mega-events for nation-branding. Examples include Brazil (2014 FIFA, 2016 Olympics), Russia (2018 FIFA, 2014 Winter Olympics), and Qatar (FIFA 2022). South Africa's 2010 World Cup achieved positive nation branding, despite initial doubts about safety. Hosting strategies like media engagement, local support mobilization, and partnerships boosted perceptions. Future hosts should recognize that mega-events alone do not guarantee branding success; sustained strategic actions are essential to reinforce positive legacies amidst potential pre-event skepticism.

Chapter 2: How 'Dark Mofo' Transformed Hobart
Dark Mofo, Hobart's midwinter festival launched in 2013, has significantly transformed the city, both culturally and economically. Embracing Tasmania's long, dark nights and gothic aesthetic, the festival draws large crowds through avant-garde programming, unique venues, and community involvement. Supported by MONA's David Walsh and local government, Dark Mofo has revitalized Hobart's winter tourism and inspired urban renewal projects like 'In the Hanging Gardens'. Even during its 2024 'pause', the festival's impact continues, highlighting its lasting value for Hobart.

Chapter 3: Nation-Building and the African Cup of Nations: A case study of Cameroon
This chapter examines Cameroon's hosting of the 2021 Africa Cup of Nations (AFCON), highlighting the event's role in nation branding and unity amid political and social unrest. Delayed by COVID-19, AFCON allowed Cameroon to showcase extensive infrastructure investments and cultural diversity to a global audience, with hopes of fostering tourism and investment. Domestically, the tournament provided short-term unity, but underscored long-standing civil conflicts, particularly in Anglophone regions, revealing the limits of sports as a unifying force in the face of deep-seated issues.

Chapter 4: Symbolic and significant: Qatar delivers a huge 2022 FIFA World Cup to propel a future legacy of sporting events in the Middle East
The Qatar 2022 FIFA World Cup showcased the complex intersection of sport, politics, and nation branding, as Qatar leveraged the event to enhance its international image amid controversies over human rights, corruption, and sportswashing. Despite global criticism, Qatar's massive investments resulted in record-breaking attendance and engagement, potentially transforming its geopolitical standing. The tournament highlighted the cultural tensions between East and West, with scholars debating its legacy on national identity, public diplomacy, and the future of mega-event hosting in the Gulf region.

Chapter 5: Buying and Selling Day of the Dead: A History of the Holiday's Commercialization
Día de los Muertos has long been commercialized, from its early adaptation by the Catholic Church to modern marketing through tourism and merchandise. While

some Latinos express concern over recent consumer trends, the holiday's economic dimension has historically shaped its widespread appeal. Commercialization continues to increase participation across generations, with cultural products like Disney's Coco sparking interest among younger Latinos. Thus, Día de los Muertos remains a deeply significant yet commercially supported cultural celebration.

Chapter 6: From Rebellion to Revenue: Dance Music Reckonings
This chapter explores the commodification of Electronic Dance Music (EDM) culture, highlighting its shift from egalitarian values (peace, love, unity, and respect) toward consumerism and individualism. While EDM originated as a countercultural movement supporting social causes, commercialization and sensationalism reshaped it. Notably, political stances, once central, are now often muted or exploited. Recent resistance efforts emphasize that reclaiming EDM's values requires addressing systemic issues within the industry, but the future of these restorative efforts remains uncertain.

Chapter 7: Events and Unhealthy Sponsorship: An Analysis of Euro 2024.
Transnational corporations have long leveraged mega-events like the FIFA World Cup and the Olympics for brand exposure, with sponsorship deals driving economic models for events like UEFA's Euro 2024. While sport sponsorship boosts corporate profits, it often promotes unhealthy products such as junk food, alcohol, and gambling, raising public health concerns. Despite athlete-led protests against harmful sponsorships, event organizers prioritize financial gain over health. As gambling ads surge, alongside junk food and alcohol promotions, the ethical implications of such partnerships merit serious reconsideration.

Chapter 8: No More Hunger Games: From Olympic Legacy to Livability Olympics
Mega-sporting events like the Olympics often burden host cities with high costs and long-term facility maintenance challenges, while delivering mixed local benefits. The 2012 London and 2020 Tokyo Games, for example, show limited community impact amid soaring expenses. With declining bids, the International Olympic Committee's sustainability initiatives aim to attract hosts, but questions persist about whether such events truly enhance urban life. Alternative approaches, such as a 'Livability Olympics Ranking' focused on housing, poverty, and well-being, could refocus global competition toward quality of life.

Chapter 9: Gastrodevelopment and Gentrification: How Food Promotes Urban Development and Displacement
Foodie culture has transformed overlooked neighborhoods into trendy food destinations, often rebranding working-class, immigrant, and ethnic areas as 'vibrant

and diverse'. In San Diego's City Heights, ethnic restaurants and food markets attract affluent visitors, fueling gentrification and displacing long-time residents. Food-driven development, celebrated for promoting multiculturalism and economic growth, often prioritizes newcomers over community needs. This 'urban food machine' erases local stories, replacing authentic food cultures with commodified experiences. As a result, food revitalization projects risk exacerbating inequality under the guise of cultural celebration.

Chapter 10: Livable Cities and the Infra-ordinary versus the Extraordinary: Commonwealth Games 2022 and Birmingham's Urban Transformation
While Birmingham's 2022 Commonwealth Games drew global attention and significant investment, the city's broader transformation has deep roots, shaped by strategic urban planning since the 19th century. Innovations like tax increment financing and infrastructure upgrades have attracted major businesses, enhanced urban connectivity, and improved quality of life. Today, Birmingham prioritizes sustainable development with initiatives like the 'Our Future City Plan', aiming to create livable neighborhoods within a 15-minute city framework, blending extraordinary events with everyday urban improvement.

Chapter 11: How do festivals catalyze growth in Banyuwangi, Indonesia?
Banyuwangi Regency, on Java's eastern tip, exemplifies how local government-backed festivals can transform a regional economy. From 2011 to 2018, tourism grew fivefold, bolstered by festivals showcasing local culture and boosting economic resilience. While the COVID-19 pandemic paused Banyuwangi's growth, festivals and tourism rebounded quickly by 2022, with the event calendar expanding further in 2024. Supported by new development projects, including heritage sites, Banyuwangi's model highlights how festivals can fuel urban transformation and post-crisis recovery.

Chapter 12: Australia and the Olympic Games: An outline of participation and Games hosting
Australia has a proud Olympic and Paralympic history, participating in every Summer Olympics since 1896 and achieving significant success, including 566 Summer and 1240 Paralympic medals. It has hosted the Olympics twice, in Melbourne (1956) and Sydney (2000), and is set to host the 2032 Brisbane Games under a cost-efficient model prioritizing sustainability. While Australia excels in global rankings, the rising costs and environmental impacts of hosting and participating in the Olympics present challenges, prompting debates about balancing elite sports funding with sustainability goals.

Chapter 13: Leaner, cost-effective, practical: How the 2032 Brisbane Games could revolutionize the Olympics

The 2032 Brisbane Olympics present a strategic opportunity to showcase Brisbane and accelerate urban development across South-East Queensland (SEQ). Unlike previous Olympics, Brisbane's bid, informed by the IOC's 'New Norm', emphasizes temporary venues, regional event distribution, and existing urban plans. This sustainable approach anticipates a budget of A$7 billion. Key challenges include costly transport infrastructure and achieving a climate-positive event. Effective legacy planning is essential for long-term benefits, potentially setting a model for future Olympics in sustainable event hosting and regional development.

Chapter 14: When Festivals Fail: Patterns, Causes, and Implications

In 2023, the Burning Man Festival faced a wash-out due to unseasonal rains, leaving 70,000 attendees stranded in Nevada's Black Rock Desert. This incident highlights a growing issue of festival failures, driven by weather, poor planning, and management deficiencies. While Burning Man's longevity defies the trend of short-lived events, external shocks like storms and heatwaves, exacerbated by climate change, pose increasing risks. Addressing these challenges requires improved planning, site selection, and contingency strategies, alongside potential legislative protection for festival goers against event cancellations.

Chapter 15: Crisis or transition: Understanding the wave of Australian music festival cancellations.

The Australian music festival market faces significant post-COVID-19 challenges, with major events like Groovin' the Moo and Splendour in the Grass canceled due to rising costs, climate disruptions, slower ticket sales, and evolving youth interests. Compounded by inflation and shifting audience demographics, these issues threaten the sustainability of the sector. To stabilize and adapt, the industry may need new approaches, such as government-backed insurance, climate resilience measures, and fiscal reforms. A federal inquiry into live music will provide critical recommendations for the future.

Chapter 16: Media Events 2.0: How social media developments impact event narratives.

The 2024 Paris Olympics illustrate the evolving nature of media events, highlighting the interplay between traditional broadcasters, official narratives, and citizen-driven social media content. Social media now mirrors television in global engagement, enabling alternate storytelling and counter-narratives, yet often reinforcing broadcasters' dominance. The IOC has increasingly institutionalized content, partnering with platforms like TikTok while regulating athlete-generated posts. This chapter explores how modern Olympics rely on media for their reach and legacy, emphasizing the complexities of communication in an era of fragmented narratives and evolving technology.

Chapter 17: Australian Music Festivals: Is the current crisis a perfect storm or a passing shower?
The Australian music festival industry faces a crisis marked by over 20 cancellations since 2020 due to COVID-19 impacts, cost-of-living pressures, and extreme weather events. Changes in ticket-buying behavior, particularly among 18–24-year-olds, have destabilized revenue models, while rural festival locations amplify logistical and financial challenges. Climate change and rising costs exacerbate risks for promoters and attendees alike. Calls for government intervention grow, but long-term solutions may involve revising festival models, reconsidering remote locations, and addressing audience fragmentation in an increasingly volatile landscape.

Chapter 18: Esports and the Olympic Games: Hopeless marriage or obvious pairing?
Esports, a $1.38 billion industry captivating millions, has drawn interest from the International Olympic Committee (IOC) as a tool to engage younger audiences and modernize the Olympics. Encompassing games from FIFA to first-person shooters, esports challenge traditional notions of sport, with players demonstrating significant physical and mental skills. Despite hurdles like intellectual property rights and compatibility with Olympic values, the IOC has taken steps toward inclusion, signaling a transformative opportunity to unite innovation and tradition in the global sporting arena.

Chapter 19: Are major sports events worth hosting? A closer look
Once highly desired for prestige and economic benefits, hosting major sports events is now met with caution in Western economies, due to escalating costs and risks. Conversely, emerging economies view these events as valuable tools for economic growth and global recognition, despite similar financial burdens. This chapter explores these dynamics, highlighting cost overruns, as seen in Tokyo 2020 and Sochi 2014, and the strategic interest from emerging nations, underscoring the complex, often cautionary, considerations facing potential host nations.

Chapter 20: The Rugby World Cup: A major event in an odd-shaped world
The Rugby World Cup (RWC) has evolved into a globally recognized event since its 1987 debut, transitioning from an amateur competition to a professional, highly commercialized tournament. Southern hemisphere nations dominate, with New

Zealand and South Africa leading in titles. Despite expansion efforts, including awarding hosting rights to Japan (2019) and the USA (2031), the sport remains controlled by core nations. Future growth focuses on women's rugby, Olympic Rugby Sevens, and sustainability initiatives. The RWC's transformation reflects rugby's ongoing globalization and commercialization.

Chapter 21: Global Migrant Festivals: London Notting Hill Carnival versus the West-Indian American Parade Day
Global events extend beyond mega-sporting events to include cyclical and single-issue celebrations, such as Live Aid. Trinidad-style carnivals, like London's Notting Hill Carnival and New York's West Indian Parade, highlight the adaptability of migrant festivals in expressing cultural identity globally. Three strategies – fusion, second-generation, and immigrant-initiated festivals – enable cultural expression through local adaptations, each with distinct benefits and challenges. These models offer valuable insights for organizers in balancing authenticity with global appeal, particularly in preserving heritage while fostering inclusivity.

Chapter 22: Commonwealth Games: Civic Sponsorship of Festive Football in Medieval and Early Modern Britain
Sports and festivals have a deep historical relationship, especially evident in medieval British Shrovetide celebrations. Originally, Shrove Tuesday was marked by communal sports, notably football, which involved both townspeople and officials. Football games were organized along communal lines, uniting guilds and newlyweds in celebrations that embodied communal ideals. Despite opposition due to the game's disorder, officials often supported these events, recognizing their role in fostering civic pride and community bonds. Shrovetide football thus reflected shared values of communal benefit and civic identity.

Chapter 23: The Super Bowl: The Risk of Inauthentic Brand Storytelling
Authentic brand storytelling draws on theories like self-congruity, narrative transportation, and the elaboration likelihood model, to build meaningful consumer connections. Inauthentic stories, however, can damage trust, as seen in recent brand controversies like Peloton's and Bud Light's. By focusing on immersive, narrative-driven strategies – such as VR experiences showcasing genuine sustainability efforts – brands can bypass accusations of virtue signaling. Rather than relying on overt value-based messaging, brands should leverage narrative immersion to foster trust and deep, emotional, resonance with audiences.

Chapter 24: Socially responsible live music: Do fans/consumers care?
Live music events have become highly commercialized in the digital era, with booming revenues exemplified by Taylor Swift's billion-dollar Eras Tour, and Live

Nation's record-breaking $22.7 billion in 2023. While historically countercultural movements used music events to champion social justice, modern festivals often prioritize commercial interests. Efforts to align music with social causes face challenges, as fans demand authenticity, and often resist being preached to during leisure time. Successful initiatives, such as eco-friendly tours by Jack Johnson and Coldplay, require genuine connections between causes, performances, and fan experiences.

I EVENT-LED DESTINATION DEVELOPMENT

1 (RE)BRANDING A NATION THROUGH A SPORT MEGA-EVENT

Brendon Knott

AIM

To identify examples of how an emerging nation can leverage a sport mega-event as a nation branding opportunity, with a focus on the impact of the 2010 FIFA World Cup for South Africa.

LEARNING OBJECTIVES

1. To identify nation branding ambitions of emerging nations through hosting sport mega-events.
2. To reflect the perceived nation branding gains from the 2010 FIFA World Cup for South Africa.
3. To propose practical leveraging activities that can be adopted by future sport mega-event hosts to achieve a positive nation branding impact.

DOI: 10.4324/9781003490326-3

THEORETICAL FOCUS AND SIGNIFICANCE

Theoretically, this chapter focuses on nation-branding, through the hosting of sport mega-events, within the context of emerging nations. The focus on a successful example of nation branding through a sport mega-event by an emerging nation is of significance when contrasted with more recent examples and future event-hosting aspirations of emerging nations.

PRACTICAL FOCUS AND SIGNIFICANCE

This chapter identifies three practical leveraging activities that assisted the successful nation branding impact of the 2010 FIFA World Cup for South Africa. The chapter argues that the leveraging activities identified can be applied to future mega-event hosting contexts.

ARTICLE

Since the turn of the millennium, emerging nations, and especially the BRICS nations, have increasingly bid for and hosted sport mega-events (Knott & Tinaz, 2021). For example, Brazil hosted the 2014 FIFA World Cup and 2016 Olympic Games; Russia hosted the 2018 FIFA World Cup and 2014 winter Olympic Games; India hosted the 2010 Commonwealth Games; China hosted the 2008 summer and 2022 winter Olympic Games; and South Africa hosted the 2010 FIFA World Cup. The middle east has similarly made its hosting ambitions clear, with Qatar hosting FIFA 2022 and Saudi Arabia linked to a bid for the 2034 FIFA World Cup. A common objective driving each of these emerging nations, is their desire to leverage the sport mega-events for global recognition and reputation enhancement – more commonly referred to as 'nation branding'.

While the perception abounds that hosting a sport mega-event will reap branding benefits for the host nation, research emanating from these events suggests it is not an automatic achievement. In the case of South Africa, nation branding has proved to be a positive legacy outcome for the country from the hosting of the 2010 FIFA World Cup. A variety of studies conducted before, during, and up to eight years after the event, indicated that stakeholders, representing residents, tourists, government agencies, the tourism and event sector, and event sponsors, viewed the overall reputational gains for the country as positive and enduring (e.g., Swart, Moyo & Hattingh, 2019).

What is often forgotten amidst this positivity, is that South Africa experienced serious doubts and concerns over its ability to host the event. While this included some general 'Afro-pessimism', there was also global media highlighting a high crime rate in the nation, cautioning that it was not safe for visitors. From my study of the event visitor perceptions, crime was the top-rated negative perception pre-event among a study of event visitors. Yet, post-event, this perception was far reduced. Importantly for the developing nation, limited perceptions of South African cities, people, technology, and general development prior to the event, were replaced by improved awareness of the nation, its people, and cities. Hosting the event clearly helped to shift many incorrect perceptions relating to the perceived segregation in the country, the lack of development of its cities, and high association with crime, to an image more welcoming of visitors, embracing of diversity, with a competent and capable industry (see Knott, Fyall & Jones, 2013).

Unfortunately, many nations assume that just hosting an event will automatically lead to branding gains. However, this is not so. For example, it is questionable whether the large resident protest around FIFA corruption in 2014 in Brazil aided Brazil's attempts to free itself from corruption-linked political perceptions. Similarly, with strong global perceptions linked to human rights or global politics, it is uncertain the impact of positive nation branding gains for countries like Russia and China from the mega-events they have hosted.

For Qatar, host of the FIFA World Cup 2022, global media focused on perceived human rights abuses suffered by migrant workers in the lead up to the event. Widespread western sentiment viewed the event as a means of 'sportswashing' – an attempt by the host nation to gloss over a lack of civil freedoms and links to terrorist sponsorship. Several teams lodged various protests, such as wearing rainbow-colored armbands – an action later banned by FIFA, along with any form of public protest during the event. Nonetheless, the event is hailed as a (re)branding success for the nation, with primary research also confirming that visitors associated the country with technological advancement, hospitality, and safety – and in general, a more nuanced understanding of the nation, its culture, history, and development (Knott *et al.*, 2024).

Let us return to the case of South Africa to identify potential lessons in leveraging nation branding benefits from mega-event hosting. Studies post the 2010 mega-event investigated the activities of event and nation-brand stakeholders that had led to the positive nation-brand legacy. From the 27 stakeholders and key-informants interviewed after the event, it was clear that specific, strategic activities and focus assisted in leveraging the event's opportunities (see Knott, Fyall & Jones, 2017).

For example, I wish to highlight three key focus areas: Firstly, hosting the global media (including new media). In order to portray accurate reflections of the country in the lead up to the event, media tours were offered to showcase the host cities and stadium development. A great effort was made to assist the media to showcase key areas of the nation brand image, through being located in iconic areas or with views of city symbols or heritage sites. Even the new and social media, often neglected, were accommodated, and facilitated in their access to information and, importantly, provided with positive news stories surrounding the event. With an estimated 18,000 media personnel attending the event, this was sure to have an impact on informing more factual opinions of the nation.

Secondly, mobilizing the local population to support the event. Creating and promoting specific songs, dances, and campaigns – such as 'Football Friday', where residents were encouraged to wear the national team's football jersey – led to a social cohesion impact even before the event kicked off. Besides the internal brand impact, this also provided a welcoming environment for visitors to enjoy, and a greater sense of security for visitors and residents alike.

The third key strategic focus was leveraging partnerships to cooperate and align strategically around their messaging and branding. Stakeholders claimed that the event created opportunities for different government levels, the tourism industry, and the private sector, to partner and align far better than they had done before. Nation-branding is not solely the responsibility or concern of merely one department or entity. It is built on the multiple acts of communication and activities by a broad array of private and public sector stakeholders, media, and citizens. It is regrettable that it often takes a mega-event to create the impetus for such cooperation. The respondents implored that such partnerships should be sustained post the event.

What then can future sport mega-event hosts learn from the South African experience? Firstly, countries should be encouraged that pre-event negative media issues usually surround any mega-event yet, they often give way to more balanced and factual reporting once the sporting action takes center stage, and the global media and sport tourists arrive in person.

Most importantly, future hosts need to acknowledge that a sport mega-event, in itself, is no guarantee of leaving a positive nation-branding legacy. It will take strategic leveraging actions that are sustained over time, even long past the event, to do so. While South Africa clearly benefited from the mega-event, stakeholders acknowledged that negative global perceptions of South Africa, primarily linked with corruption and politically-led 'state-capture' in the years that followed, has diminished this effect to an extent. This is a reminder that while nation-branding portrays a strategic vision for how a country would like to be perceived, this image does need to be consistently reinforced by actions aligned with this image over time.

MANAGERIAL IMPLICATIONS

Identify strategic leveraging activities to sustain positive nation branding from hosting a sport mega-event, before, during, and post the event.

POLICY IMPLICATIONS

Future host nations need to acknowledge that a sport mega-event is no guarantee of leaving a positive nation-branding legacy. Strategic cooperation with multiple stakeholders before, during, and after the event is essential to ensure this.

RESEARCH IMPLICATIONS

As an increasing number of emerging nations host sport mega-events, alternate geo-political contexts are brought into the public focus. Researchers should consider more nuanced and multi-faceted approaches to assessing nation branding through sport mega-events, as well as the popular rhetoric around 'sportswashing'.

QUIZ QUESTIONS

1. List five sport mega-events hosted in emerging nations since 2008.
2. What is nation branding and why is it important for emerging nations?
3. Why could hosting a sport mega-event be a successful means of achieving nation branding?

DEBATE QUESTIONS

1. What makes South Africa a perceived successful case of nation branding gains from hosting a sport mega-event?
2. Select one of the other examples mentioned in the chapter, and motivate for any perceived nation branding gains not mentioned in the chapter.
3. What is the difference between 'sportswashing' and leveraging nation branding through hosting a sport mega-event?

ALIGNMENT TO UNITED NATIONS SUSTAINABLE DEVELOPMENT GOALS

Goal	How
1. No Poverty	
2. Zero Hunger	
3. Good Health and Wellbeing	
4. Quality Education	
5. Gender Equality	
6. Clean Water and Sanitation	
7. Affordable and Clean Energy	
8. Decent Work and Economic Growth	The hosting of sport mega-events, particularly in emerging nations, is viewed as part of a country's sustainable development objectives. This is predicated on driving economic growth and providing jobs. Within this context, nation branding plays a pivotal role in attracting future investment and global engagement.
9. Industry, Innovation, and Infrastructure	
10. Reduced Inequalities	
11. Sustainable Cities and Communities	
12. Responsible Consumption and Production	
13. Climate Action	
14. Life Below Water	
15. Life on Land	
16. Peace, Justice, and Strong Institutions	
17. Partnerships for the Goals	

REFERENCES

Knott, B., Fyall, A., & Jones, I. (2013). The nation-branding legacy of the 2010 FIFA World Cup for South Africa. *Journal of Hospitality Marketing & Management*, 22(6), 569–595. https://doi.org/10.1080/19368623.2012.663155.

Knott, B., Fyall, A., & Jones, I. (2017). 'Sport Mega-events and nation branding: Unique characteristics of the 2010 FIFA World Cup South Africa', *Journal of Contemporary Hospitality Management*, 29(3), 900–923. https://doi.org/10.1108/IJCHM-09-2015-0523.

Knott, B., Swart, K., Althawadi, O., & Zeyad Ali, Y. (2024). Nation-branding opportunities through sport mega-events: tourism impact from FIFA World Cup in South Africa 2010 and Qatar 2022. *Proceedings of the 7th International Conference on Tourism Research (ICTR)*, Cape Town, 17–19 March, 149–156. https://papers.academic-conferences.org/.

Knott, B. and Tinaz, C. (2022) The legacy of sport events for emerging nations. *Frontiers in Sports and Active Living* 4, 926334. doi: 10.3389/fspor.2022.926334

Swart, K., Moyo, L.G., & Hattingh, C. (2019). Brand image legacies of the 2010 FIFA World Cup: a long-term assessment. *Sport in Society*, 22(11), 1848–1863. https://doi.org/10.1080/17430437.2019.1619322.

2 HOW 'DARK MOFO' TRANSFORMED HOBART

Ralph Crane

AIM

To show how the Dark Mofo winter festival has transformed the city of Hobart.

LEARNING OBJECTIVES

1. To describe Hobart's Dark Mofo Festival.
2. To show the cultural and economic impact of the festival on Hobart.
3. To show how Dark Mofo has led to urban renewal and redevelopment in Hobart.

DOI: 10.4324/9781003490326-4

THEORETICAL FOCUS AND SIGNIFICANCE

The theoretical focus of this chapter is on the relationship between the festival organisers, the artists and the audiences, and the use of urban space. A discussion of these issues allows us to consider the ways an urban festival can enrich the life of a city.

PRACTICAL FOCUS AND SIGNIFICANCE

To provide a case study which focuses on a city festival and its urban geography, in order to show how a festival can shape the cultural and urban development of a city. Understanding the way a festival can contribute to the urban development of a city will enable better cultural and economic planning in the future.

ARTICLE

For decades South Australia has advertised itself as 'The Festival State' – with the state's motor vehicle number plates embossed with the slogan between 1981 and 2008 to promote the claim. The Adelaide Festival of Arts and the Adelaide Writers' Week both boast strong lineages and have set a high standard for comparable festivals around Australia. Like Adelaide, the capital cities of Brisbane (Queensland), Sydney (New South Wales), Melbourne (Victoria), Perth (Western Australia), and Darwin (Northern Territory) all host annual arts festivals, while Tasmania is home to a biennial international arts festival, Ten Days on the Island. Other festivals, too, including writers' festivals, film festivals, music festivals, food festivals, and more, crowd the calendars of every Australian state and territory.

With a glut of festivals across Australia, any new festival must offer something new or different if it is going to attract an audience. Against this background Dark Mofo was launched in Tasmania's capital city, Hobart, in 2013. In its own words:

> Dark Mofo is a midwinter festival in Hobart that celebrates the dark through large-scale public art, food, music, fire, light, and noise, underpinned by the longest night of any Australian capital city. Delving into centuries-old rituals, Dark Mofo explores the links between ancient and contemporary mythology, humans and nature, religious and secular traditions, darkness and light, birth, death, and renewal.[1]

The festival was by no means embraced by everyone in its first year. In the build-up to the festival, and following a series of complaints, Tasmania Police advised the organisers that 'the Nude Solstice swim is contrary to the public decency provision of the *Police Offences Act*',[2] which led to the swim being withdrawn from the programme before agreement was reached and the event went ahead with about 200 participants. Indeed, a degree of controversy has been a vital feature of Dark Mofo each year, including: The initial threat to public decency offered by the nude swim (which by 2023 was attracting over 2,000 hardy souls[3]); the inverted red crosses which in 2018 caused offence to some Christians who chose to interpret them as Satanic symbols; the outrage which led to the cancellation of Santiago Sierra's *Union Flag* in 2021;[4] and the removal of the 'Welcome to Hell' sign promoting the festival in the arrivals area of Hobart's airport in 2023.[5]

By the third iteration of the festival in 2015 Hobartians had largely put any initial reservations aside and they, together with visitors from around the island and interstate, were virtually queuing for the latest offerings of David Walsh's Dark Mofo.

Pre-sale tickets for two concerts featuring Antony and the Johnsons with the Tasmanian Symphony Orchestra sold out in just three hours, several other events also quickly sold out, and tickets for the five-night Winter Feast of food, fire, and music sold fast. The dark partner of MONA's highly successful summer festival, Mona Foma (MOFO), had found its formula, and with that its audience.

In 2015, over the 11 days leading up to the winter solstice on 22 June, audiences were able to see artists from around the world bring some hitherto little used or improbable venues to life. Top international acts such as Antony and the Johnsons played at the historic Odeon Theatre; a midnight performance by Belgian cellist, composer, and singer Helen Gillet took place in the city's St David's Cathedral; the Rabble theatre company staged their cosmic, theatrical take on Virginia Woolf's *Orlando* at the Theatre Royal; and Patricia Piccinini and Peter Hennessey's *The Shadows Coming* took over the old Mercury (newspaper) building.

Dark Mofo has each year lured festival-goers into a series of unlikely venues and less-frequented parts of the city, and by its third year it was drawing large crowds of people out of their homes and into the wintery darkness. Also in 2015, the vast Macquarie Point industrial precinct on the waterfront, made its debut as the 'Dark Park'. Its various attractions included *Fire Organ*, a colossal structure created by Dutch chemo-acoustic engineer and sound artist Bastiaan Maris, and two large-scale immersive works by Anthony McCall, the light show *Solid Light Works*, and the fire performance *Landscape for Fire*. Elsewhere, McCall's *Night Ship* sailed up the Derwent River from Tinderbox to the city harbour each night for ten nights, directing its powerful searchlight onto the shore. And to coincide with the festival, the Museum of Old and New Art (MONA) launched a new major exhibition, Marina Abramovich's *Private Archaeology*. There was also a fresh iteration of the already popular Night Mass, a series of late-night party offerings that each year cater for those who want something even more avant-garde than the main Dark Mofo menu.

Since its inception the success of Dark Mofo has largely been down to the inspired vision of its Creative Director, Leigh Carmichael, whose programmes have consistently challenged boundaries and faced audiences with new and often confronting experiences. Crucially, that success has been possible because of the staunch support provided by MONA's owner, David Walsh, and the backing of both the state government and the Hobart City Council, who early recognised the economic as well as the cultural value of the festival.

Dark Mofo's success is also due to in no small part to its location: Hobart is Australia's most southern capital city. While the festival builds on the wintery darkness of Hobart's long southern nights, it also tunes in to the gothic aesthetic that is a consequence of both the state's isolated geography and its grim colonial history, and which has long permeated Tasmania's creative industries, as well as its tourism industry.

Winter festivals may be commonplace, but Dark Mofo excels, not only because it embraces the aesthetics of darkness, but also because of the way the people of Hobart have embraced the event. It is not only that over a decade Carmichael has made terrific use of some extraordinary locations, but because the distance between those myriad locations is never great. Consequently, as the festival-goers move between venues, the revelry transforms the whole area it into one big art space. This is not always true of similar events in larger capital cities in Australia or elsewhere. As a visitor to Paris's celebrated Nuit Blanche some years ago, I found the festival fever faded during the lengthy treks between the various curated installations. The Nuit Blanche concept has, of course, been around since Helsinki established its Night of the Arts in 1989, and continues to gather pace. In 2013 Melbourne held the first, very successful, White Night event in Australia. But by replacing the light with the dark, Carmichael *et al.* have curated something unique. As Leonard Cohen tells us, there is a crack in everything. In Hobart, that's how the dark gets in, and Dark Mofo has shown that the dark is very much in demand.

In an article about the way festivals can transform cities, Beth Perry and Rike Sitas write that:

> Festivals create exciting spaces to experience art, music, culture, and film. At their best, they perform a transformative role in society, celebrating traditions and powerfully expressing the meanings that places hold for people.

> Festivals can disrupt established ways of thinking about heritage. Taking place in streets, pubs, railway arches, houses, boats, and doorsteps, they can help residents explore different ways of belonging in cities, reengage with the past, and imagine the future.[6]

Moreover, as Andrew Smith, Guy Osborn, and Bernadette Quinn observe, 'Festivals are important features of contemporary cities that can be understood as celebrations or attractions, but also as agents of urban change'.[7] In Hobart Dark Mofo is a *celebration* of the darkness of midwinter, a major *attraction* in the state's tourist calendar, and over the last decade has been a *key agent of change in the city.*

This change is particularly evident in the development of In the Hanging Gardens, which was originally launched during Dark Mofo in 2019 and reopened later that year, and is a permanent fixture of Hobart's live music and dining scene. The enormous mixed-use live music, cultural, and dining precinct, which has taken over and re-vitalized almost a whole city block in the centre of Hobart, clearly demonstrates how a successful festival venture can lead to urban renewal or redevelopment.

In late 2023 the festival's new Artistic Director, Chris Twite, announced that Dark Mofo would be 'pausing' in 2024 before a full return in 2025.[8] However, such is the transformative impact the midwinter festival has had on Hobart as a community over the last decade, that to satiate demand both the winter feast and the nude solstice swim went ahead, as well as a line-up of music acts in the Hanging Gardens venue. And in 2024 the partial void left by the scaled-back art and music programme Dark Mofo was filled by Dark Fringe, which was first held in 2023. A decade on from its controversial beginnings Dark Mofo is an event that Hobart both wants and needs; it is an example of the way a festival can engage a local community, spawn new events, and bring both cultural and economic benefits to a city.

MANAGERIAL IMPLICATIONS

Managers may consider the way urban festivals shape public spaces, creating attractive public spaces and encouraging community use.

POLICY IMPLICATIONS

Policymakers may usefully consider the public value outcomes (including inclusivity), and the economic impacts of urban festivals – including the opportunities for urban renewal that can arise from the innovative use of urban spaces by festivals.

RESEARCH IMPLICATIONS

Moving forward researchers may consider specific projects that focus on the increasing number and significance of urban festivals, and their impact on urban geography and the perceived identity of a city.

QUIZ QUESTIONS

1. In what ways does Hobart's Dark Mofo festival differ from other urban festivals?
2. What specific aspects of its geography does the Dark Mofo festival embrace?
3. How has Dark Mofo influenced the urban development of Hobart?

DEBATE QUESTIONS

1. As key events, urban festivals can play a significant role in the urban renewal or revitalization of a city.
2. To be successful urban festivals need to continually challenge their audiences.
3. Urban festivals can bring enormous cultural and economic benefits to a city, but only if what they offer embraces the zeitgeist of the city.

ALIGNMENT TO UNITED NATIONS SUSTAINABLE DEVELOPMENT GOALS

Goal	How
1. No Poverty	
2. Zero Hunger	
3. Good Health and Wellbeing	
4. Quality Education	
5. Gender Equality	
6. Clean Water and Sanitation	
7. Affordable and Clean Energy	
8. Decent Work and Economic Growth	Supports employment in the arts and hospitality sectors.
9. Industry, Innovation, and Infrastructure	
10. Reduced Inequalities	
11. Sustainable Cities and Communities	Bringing neglected parts of the city back to life.
12. Responsible Consumption and Production	Dark Mofo has a zero-waste approach.
13. Climate Action	Dark Mofo has a zero-waste approach.
14. Life Below Water	
15. Life on Land	
16. Peace, Justice, and Strong Institutions	
17. Partnerships for the Goals	

NOTES

1 'About', https://darkmofo.net.au/about, accessed 3 April 2024.
2 'Support for Dark Mofo', 20 May 2013, www.police.tas.gov.au/news-events/media-releases/support-for-dark-mofo/, accessed 30 March 2024.
3 'Nude swimmers in Hobart celebrate passing of the longest night and end of Dark Mofo', www.abc.net.au/news/2022-06-22/tas-nude-swimmers-winter-solstice-dark-mofo/101172426, accessed 30 March 2024.
4 Annie McCann, 'Backlash over Dark Mofo's Union Flag proposal prompts internal review', www.themercury.com.au/news/tasmania/dark-mofo-debacle-prompts-broader-call-to-support-aboriginal-art/news-story/660ce8b42daebd91fb805e3666a435a2, accessed 30 March 2024.
5 Rob Inglis, 'Hobart airport removes Dark Mofo sign, organiser Leigh Carmichael labels move an "over-reaction"', www.themercury.com.au/news/tasmania/hobart-airport-removes-dark-mofo-sign-organiser-leigh-carmichael-labels-move-an-overreaction/news-story/635d8ca716e777178122b5943cd81ac4, accessed 30 March 2024.
6 Beth Perry and Rike Sitas, 'Festivals can transform cities by making space for overlooked people and cultures', https://theconversation.com/festivals-can-transform-cities-by-making-space-for-overlooked-people-and-cultures-121013, accessed 3 April 2024.
7 Andrew Smith, Guy Osborn, and Bernadette Quinn, 'Introduction: Festivalisation as a Contested Urban Strategy', in *Festivals and the City: The Contested Geographies of Urban Events*, ed. Andrew Smith, Guy Osborn, & Bernadette Quinn (London: University of Westminster Press, 2022), 1.
8 'Dark Mofo's "escalating costs" force 2024 cancellation as it pauses to "reshape"', www.sbs.com.au/news/article/dark-mofos-escalating-costs-force-2024-cancellation-as-it-pauses-to-reshape/h7l9apyi3, accessed 3 April 2024.

3 NATION-BUILDING AND THE AFRICAN CUP OF NATIONS

A case study of Cameroon

Jo Clarke and Becky Ashworth

LEARNING OBJECTIVES

AIM

The chapter aims to demonstrate how hosting a mega sporting event can put a country in the spotlight and showcase all it has to offer, and to sell the nation's brand. The use of nation branding is important for Cameroon on two fronts, firstly given the backdrop of civil unrest in Cameroon the tournament offered the opportunity to unite the nation. Secondly, hosting the AFCON was significant in relation to global nation branding which seeks to promote positive foreign public opinion of Cameroon.

To contribute to the literature of nation branding by extending the application of branding theory to emerging nations and identifying the strategic branding opportunities created in the context of a sport mega-event.

DOI: 10.4324/9781003490326-5

THEORETICAL FOCUS AND SIGNIFICANCE

The chapter focuses on the theoretical concept of nation branding. The theoretical significance of the chapter looks to explore the power of sport as a tool for national unity, whilst demonstrating its pivotal role of shaping global perceptions through strategic nation branding during a mega sport event.

PRACTICAL FOCUS AND SIGNIFICANCE

The practical focus of the chapter may assist with the prioritization and planning of event bidding and hosting sport mega-events in the future for Cameroon or nations with a similar profile. The practical significance of the chapter is that it provides deeper insights into a real-world case study which may help policymakers in Cameroon (or nations with a similar profile) reflect on their own experiences concerning the challenges, pitfalls, and future strategy for hosting mega sports events.

ARTICLE

This chapter presents the case study of Cameroon, hosts of the 2021 Africa Cup of Nations (AFCON, 2021), the biennial international men's football championship of Africa organized by the Confederation of African Football (CAF). The 2021 tournament took place a year later than planned due to COVID-19, and was hosted between January 9–February 6, 2022. The chapter aims to demonstrate how hosting a sporting mega-event can put a nation in the spotlight to showcase and promote the nation's brand through a harmonious narrative. The use of nation branding is important for Cameroon on two fronts, firstly given the backdrop of domestic civil unrest the tournament offered the opportunity to unite the nation, and secondly, hosting AFCON was significant in relation to global nation branding to promote positive foreign public opinion of the host nation.

Destination branding through sport events

Through hosting a sporting mega-event, many destinations utilize this opportunity as a re-positioning strategy with the expectation that the international media coverage of the event will contribute towards destination profiling and to increased prominence (Heslop *et al.*, 2013). Hosting in this way is a deliberate policy for many nations, most notably among emerging nations. Examples include South Africa (FIFA World Cup), Brazil (FIFA World Cup and Olympic/Paralympic Games), and Qatar (FIFA World Cup), which are known to have mobilized sport mega-events for nation branding benefits to positively change their image on the international stage. Linking to re-imaging benefits, Higham and Hinch (2009) suggest that national identity benefits are achieved through positive brand identity and positioning the nation as an interesting and unique place to host sport events. The notion of nation branding is typically framed in terms of impacts and attempts to engender positive legacies to the host city and nation (Ludvigsen *et al.*, 2022; Masikavanhu *et al.*, 2021; Nyikana & Tichaawa, 2020; Preuss, 2019).

The Cameroon sport brand

Sports such as football, boxing, wrestling, basketball, cycling, table tennis, netball and handball, hold prominent positions in the make-up of the Cameroon sport brand (Clarke & Ojo, 2016; Tichaawa & Hemmonsbey, 2022). Marathon running events, such as the Mount Cameroon Race for Hope, are also popular since they draw large numbers of participants and media attention. However, football is unquestionably the most popular sport in Cameroon, often referred to as the 'King' sport (Clarke & Ojo, 2016; Pannenborg, 2010). The desire for sporting success for Cameroon is immense, and hosting the 2021 edition of AFCON provided the ideal platform to shine a spotlight on Cameroon as a host nation, showcase all it had to offer, and sell the nation's brand through a harmonious narrative.

There was increasing pressure for Cameroon to host a successful tournament, both for on-pitch and off-pitch reasons. The last time the country hosted the showpiece continental football event was 50 years ago, and with Cameroon's youthful population there are few citizens who would have experienced such an event. Against the backdrop and expectations on the pitch, off the pitch there were continued concerns about ongoing domestic unrest in the country – which stem back to when Cameroon formed as an independent state, ending the French and British colonial legacy.

For decades, tensions have stemmed from the well-documented divide, where Anglophone Cameroonians, who compromise 20% of the population, feel marginalized and exploited by the Francophone-dominated state (Konings & Nyamnjoh, 1997, 2003). In recent years, a series of grievances have morphed into political demands, strikes, and riots. The government maintains it has a fair governance structure, yet English speaking Cameroonians still feel oppressed. Government powers and Anglophone separatists have engaged in increasingly brutal violence amid reprisals to lay down their weapons and return to community life. In addition, government authorities have detained opposition activists who pursue outright separation from Cameroon with a new state called 'Ambazonia'. This is a major challenge regarding national unity and security, especially given that francophone Cameroon dominates the country's most popular sport – football (Onwumechili & Akindes, 2014).

A turbulent build up

The significance of hosting a successful tournament was considerable on many levels. Internationally, media attention and speculation gathered pace. Cameroon was originally due to host the 2019 edition of the tournament, however, with months to go, the organizers (CAF) stripped the country of its hosting rights and gave the hosting rights to Egypt, citing a lack of confidence in Cameroon's readiness, based on its poor preparations and infrastructure. CAF's decision was a blow for Cameroon, and likely tarnished its international reputation, and affected the country's economy at the time. The short-term economic boost which is typically associated with big events is a surge in visitors, athletes, and media, who would have spent and injected money into the local economy, and this was lost.

There were further delays, with Cameroon finally given the hosting rights for the 2021 tournament by CAF. First, due to Cameroon's rainy season, the tournament had to be brought forward to January 2021, and then enforced delays moved the tournament to 2022 due to the COVID-19 pandemic. Amongst this, there were also rumors arising in December 2021 with concerns surrounding the threat of coronavirus affecting teams, incomplete building work, and organizational challenges. All of this prompted the president of CAF to arrive in Yaoundé to alleviate concerns.

As the hype of the tournament began, ex-professional Cameroonian football Samuel Eto'o had recently begun his presidency of the national football federation (FECAFOOT), bringing high expectations for Cameroon to perform well at AFCON as host nation.

In preparation for the tournament, the Cameroonian government had spent over 520 billion CFA (£680 million) renovating and upgrading infrastructure – roads, hospitals, airports, hotels – and on the development of the sports facilities. The new, 60,000-capacity Olembé Stadium in the capital, Yaoundé, used for the opening match, cost in the region of £222 million. In Douala, the country's economic capital and its second-largest city, the 50,000-seater Japoma Stadium cost £191 million. In Bafoussam and Limbé, two 20,000-capacity stadiums were built, while the one already in Garoua, with 25,000 seats, was renovated. The government funded a brand-new five-star hotel in Douala, where the official CAF delegation stayed. Eighty percent of the hotels where the teams, journalists, and tourists were staying were either new or had been renovated. The government pulled out all the stops, and the spending on this AFCON was higher than on previous editions. The new and upgraded infrastructure would provide a long-term legacy, while the global exposure of the tournament, being televised live to hundreds of countries, was expected to bring in substantial investment and tourism revenues. Economically, businesses in Cameroon all had their eyes on a revival and boost in revenue. And, off the field, a successful tournament was deemed vitally important from a political perspective – given ongoing domestic unrest, security issues, and a lack of national unity.

Uniting the nation

Within Cameroon, football is seen as the 'king sport'. The sport is seen amongst Cameroonians as something that is more than a sport, and argue that football *is* politics. Existing literature has shown that football is a major factor in fostering a sense of unity and building nationalism in Cameroon (Clarke & Ojo, 2016). This explains why the government often leverages football to maintain stability during times of political uncertainty. Unity and solidarity were called for by President Paul Biya prior to the tournament. Biya stated that 'We want it (AFCON) to be a great moment of brotherhood. Let us offer our guests the rich cultural diversity that has earned our country the nickname "Africa in miniature" '.

AFCON legacy

Early evidence indicates that hosting the AFCON was full of short-term wins for Cameroon. Globally, African Business (2022) estimate an increase of direct income from traveling supporters and tourists in 2022 at over £159 million (122 billion CFA). The increase in tourism indicates positive inroads to Cameroon's overall policy direction in pursuit of development, including tourism. Vision 2035 ultimately is working towards Cameroon becoming a middle-income and newly industrialized country (Ministry of Economy, Planning and Regional Development, 2009). Through the Vision 2035 policy, the Ministry of Tourism and Leisure aims to unite the people of Cameroon, along with the aims of the Cameroonian Government to aggressively push the tourism agenda in the Western Hemisphere, i.e., to attract one million foreign visitors to Cameroon by 2025 (Tichaawa & Hemmonsbey, 2022).

Domestically, there is evidence that the tournament proved a very welcome short-term relief from the lockdowns and political tensions, and helped in the short-term to create a sense of unity, by bringing together Cameroonians from different regions to celebrate the tournament (Nyikana & Tichaawa, 2024). Acha-Anyi (2023) emphasizes that in the future, the Cameroonian Government and sports event organizers need to include community representatives as part of the planning and delivery committee, to help foster long-term unity and community buy in.

However, there is a longer-term, more pressing issue of resolving a civil war, which is not going to be attained in the short-term through any nation branding strategies. The security situation remains highly volatile, particularly in the Anglophone north-west and south-west regions. During late 2023 and early

2024, armed clashes between government forces and separatist groups, as well as infighting among different separatist groups, continued to affect civilian populations, with over 2.2 million forcibly displaced persons living within Cameroon (UNICEF, 2023).

MANAGERIAL IMPLICATIONS

The implication for managers is that mega sport events pose many opportunities and challenges. The event provides a stage for improving nation branding and enhanced reputation. However, this is only possible through meticulous planning, ranging from managing political tensions to infrastructure development.

POLICY IMPLICATIONS

The policy implications that should be considered because of this chapter include:

1. More rigorous bidding criteria set by international federations.
2. Transparent bidding documents from bidding nations.
3. Demonstration of accountability and transparency.

QUIZ QUESTIONS

1. What were the primary motivations behind Cameroon's decision to host the AFCON despite domestic civil unrest and political tensions?
2. Outline the main challenges faced by Cameroon in preparing for hosting the AFCON 2021 tournament.
3. What were the short-term economic impacts of hosting the AFCON 2021 on Cameroon?
4. How did Cameroon leverage the AFCON 2021 tournament to enhance its national brand through football?

DEBATE QUESTIONS

1. Should countries that are experiencing high political tension and security challenges prioritize hosting mega sport events as a way to enhance their national brand?

2. How effective are nation branding efforts through mega sport events in reshaping global perceptions of host countries?
3. Should international sports governing bodies like CAF or FIFA take a more rigorous stance in assessing whether bidding countries meet specific criteria before awarding them the rights to host mega tournaments?

ALIGNMENT TO UNITED NATIONS SUSTAINABLE DEVELOPMENT GOALS

Goal	How
1. No Poverty	
2. Zero Hunger	
3. Good Health and Wellbeing	
4. Quality Education	
5. Gender Equality	
6. Clean Water and Sanitation	
7. Affordable and Clean Energy	
8. Decent Work and Economic Growth	Short term economic growth from hosting AFCON and longer-term growth in tourism.
9. Industry, Innovation, and Infrastructure	Building and upgrading infrastructure, e.g., – roads, hospitals, airports, hotels – and the development of sports facilities.
10. Reduced Inequalities	
11. Sustainable Cities and Communities	Attempt to alleviate political tensions (Anglophone crisis), through hosting of a mega sporting event.
12. Responsible Consumption and Production	
13. Climate Action	
14. Life Below Water	

Goal	How
15. Life on Land	
16. Peace, Justice, and Strong Institutions	
17. Partnerships for the Goals	

REFERENCES

Acha-Anyi, P.N. (2023). Sports events and community development: Analysis of the AFCON 2022 host cities in Cameroon. *Cogent Social Sciences*, *9*(1). https://doi.org/10.1080/23311886.2023.2195079

African Business. (2022). *AFCON is a winner for Cameroon.* Retrieved April 10, 2024, https://african.business/2022/03/trade-investment/afcon-is-a-winner-for-cameroon

Clarke, J., & Sunday Ojo, J. (2016). Sport policy in Cameroon. *International Journal of Sport Policy and Politics*, 9(1), 189–200.

Heslop, L.A., Nadeau, J., O'reilly, N., & Armenakyan, A. (2013). Mega-event and country co-branding: Image shifts, transfers and reputational impacts. *Corporate Reputation Review*, 16, 7–33.

Higham, J., & Hinch, T. (2009). *Sport and Tourism: Globalization, Mobility and Identity.* London: Routledge, pp. 1–314.

Konings, P., & Nyamnjoh, P. (1997). The anglophone problem in Cameroon. *The Journal of Modern African Studies,* 35(2), 207–229.

Konings, P., & Nyamnjoh, F. (2003). *Negotiating an Anglophone Identity.* Boston: Brill.

Lee Ludvigsen, J.A., Rookwood, J., & Parnell, D. (2022). The sport mega-events of the 2020s: Governance, impacts and controversies. *Sport in Society*, 25(4), 705–711.

Musikavanhu, R.R., Ladkin, A., & Sadd, D. (2021). The lasting social value of mega events: Experiences from Green Point Community in Cape Town, South Africa. *Journal of Sustainable Tourism*, 29(11–12), 1832–1849.

Nyikana, S., & Tichaawa, T. (2020). Revisiting sport and tourism interrelationships: The case of Cameroon. *Geojournal of Tourism and Geosites,* 29, 756–771.

Nyikana, S., & Tichaawa, T.M. (2024). Towards an integrated framework for sustainable sport tourism development in Central Africa. *Development Southern Africa*, 4, 1–15.

Onwumechili, C., & Akindes, G. (2014). *Identity and Nation in African Football: Fans Community and Clubs.* London: Palgrave Macmillan.

Pannenborg, A. (2010). Football in Africa: Observations about political, financial, cultural and religious influences. NCDO Publication Series Sport and Development. Available from: http://sportanddev.org/en/toolkit/latest_publications/?2718/1/Football-in-AfricaObservations-about-political-financial-cultural-and-religious-influences

Preuss, H. (2019). Event legacy framework and measurement. *International Journal of Sport Policy and Politics*, 11(1), 103–118.

Tichaawa, T. M., & Hemmonsbey, J. D. (2022). Destination branding though major sporting events: The case of the 2021 Africa Cup of Nations in Cameroon. *Geosport for Society*, 17(2), 142–156.

UNICEF. (2023). Humanitarian Action for Children report. Retrieved April 8, 2024, www.unicef.org/media/132001/file/2023-HAC-Cameroon.pdf

4 SYMBOLIC AND SIGNIFICANT

Qatar delivers a huge 2022 FIFA World Cup to propel a future legacy of sporting events in the Middle East

Leon Davis and Dan Plumley

AIM

The aim of this chapter is to begin to critically analyse the wider impact that the Qatar 2022 FIFA World Cup may have on the future hosting of mega sporting events.

LEARNING OBJECTIVES

1. Analyse the discourse prior to the event.
2. Analyse emergent research undertaken post-event.
3. Present our thoughts on the future of mega sport event hosting in light of the 2022 FIFA World Cup in Qatar.

DOI: 10.4324/9781003490326-6

THEORETICAL FOCUS AND SIGNIFICANCE

The theoretical focus is around the concept of 'sportwashing' and the use of the term in contemporary academic event literature as an advancement on Nye's concept of soft power. We argue that the sporting mega-event landscape has, and will, change following Qatar 2022, with wider objectives of legitimacy seeking and soft power projection replacing the traditional norms of event hosting. There are further implications linked to sport and geopolitics that are yet to surface, and are yet to be researched.

PRACTICAL FOCUS AND SIGNIFICANCE

The practical focus is on event organisers. The reasons why countries bid to host major sporting events may change in the future, and policymakers need to be aware of the discourse and landscape. Hosting major sporting events is a costly business. Linked to the practical focus on event holders, the significance is clear. It is a high-stakes and high-pressure industry, and real financial cost must be considered as a balance to any geopolitical narrative or influence. Many countries may actually be put off from hosting major sporting events in light of Qatar 2022, and both sides of the coin need to be considered.

ARTICLE

While sport and politics remain uneasy bedfellows for some, they can and do coexist – and the Qatar 2022 version of the FIFA World Cup is a perfect example. It was hoped that the 2022 FIFA (men's) World Cup in Qatar would be reflected on as being highly symbolic and significant. In many ways, Qatar silenced some of its critics in delivering a showcase tournament, boosted by one of the greatest finals the sport has arguably ever seen, and a fairytale World Cup ending for one of the game's greatest ever players, the Argentina captain, Lionel Messi. The tournament will never diminish the back story linked to the bidding process for the tournament and the accusations of corruption, sportswashing, and soft power, but it did prove that a mega-event can be successfully held within a gulf nation state – which is likely to prove the catalyst for further mega-events being held in the region.

Zidan (2022) highlighted 2022 as the potential 'year' of sportswashing, due to the number of events taking place in countries with authoritarian regimes, starting with the Winter Olympic/Paralympics Games in Beijing, China, and culminating with the FIFA men's World Cup 2022 in Qatar. The concept of 'sportswashing' advances Nye's concept of soft power (see Nye, 2004, 2021). It is a neologism that has begun to appear with increasing regularity in the English-language media (Skey, 2023). The term rose to the forefront of sport politics in the mid- to late-2010s, primarily due to the rise in nations with questionable human rights records hosting a variety of international sporting events (see Akhundova, 2015; Brannagan & Rookwood, 2016; Delgado, 2016; Grix *et al.*, 2023; Koch, 2018; Schausteck *et al.*, 2014). It became a contemporary term in the late 2010s, recognised initially in academia by the likes of Chadwick (2018a, 2018b, 2022). However, the term 'sportswashing' has been used for over a century in modern sporting events (see Boykoff, 2022; Davis *et al.*, 2023; Rosenberg, 2022), and has also been labelled as a 'new word for an old idea' (Menon, 2019).

When FIFA picked Qatar as the first Middle Eastern country to host the men's football World Cup in 2022, some considered it a bold gamble. Others thought it was a mistake – including former FIFA President Sepp Blatter. Controversy was never far away. There were allegations of bribery during the bidding process, and serious concerns raised about human rights, with particular focus on the migrant workers building the new stadia needed to deliver the tournament (see Berkeley, 2021; Blum, Harris & Dunbar, 2020; Millward, 2017).

As a result, Qatar 2022 will always be 'unique' in mega-event terms, and its legacy is one that will be studied for years to come. On a financial scale, it was like nothing we have ever seen before. No expense was spared in delivering the tournament, and much of the money invested was spent on infrastructure and transport projects in the country. Some of these were already planned, part of a much bigger strategy to put Qatar on the world's tourist map, with the tournament merely accelerating developments. Qatar was always playing the long game. Before the tournament, and despite the issues cited in the build-up, both Qatar and FIFA were bullish that millions of fans would travel to the Gulf from all over the world. Ultimately, they were both proved right. In-stadium spectators totalled 3.4 million – up from 3 million in 2018. Three matches at Lusail Stadium, including the Final, saw the highest attendance for a match registered at a FIFA World Cup since USA 1994. An estimated 5 billion people in total engaged with the tournament in some way across the globe (Inside FIFA, 2023). Again, such numbers are on a scale never seen before in men's World Cup tournaments.

A deeper post-mortem on the tournament has already begun in academic discourse and the tournament will likely provide a springboard for future research outlining the geopolitical and social impact of events in destinations not yet studied. As is perhaps to be predicted, the evidence is, and will remain, mixed. For example, Dubinksy (2023) discussed the clashing narratives around the Qatar 2022 FIFA men's World Cup through the lenses of nation branding, public diplomacy, and country image. Such narratives are argued to go beyond the athletic competition, and are centred around a cultural clash between East and West, or the Global North and the Global South. Naess (2023) argued that the tournament in Qatar is a key example of how soft power can become more precise as an analytical category in the context of sport and geopolitics. Abdeldayem (2023) cited the construction of hate speech linked to the tournament, which he suggests was constructed because of the invisible rejection from the western countries of Qatar winning the bid to host the World Cup, increasing the cultural tension of the event consequently. Jain (2023) focused on the debates surrounding the rights of migrant workers and the rights of the LGBTQIA+ community, and argued that while human rights advocacy had a notable impact in relation to the FIFA World Cup Qatar 2022, it is a tale full of cautions and lessons.

Others have proposed a more positive set of outcomes relating to the tournament. In a study seeking to analyse the correlation between sport, economy, politics, and religion in the context of the Qatar 2022 FIFA World Cup, Setiawati and Roziqin (2023) found that Qatar has implemented a comprehensive set of laws and policies to address national policy criticisms, and enhance its public soft power diplomacy. These measures include the establishment of an Islamic identity, the assertion of sovereignty, and the development of economic strength. The potentially negative perceptions surrounding the hosting of the 2022 FIFA World Cup were effectively mitigated, allowing for a successful outcome (Setiawati & Roziqin, 2023). Likewise, Brannagan *et al.* (2023) outlined how the tournament has transformed national and cultural identity in Qatar, and Hussain and Cunningham (2024) elucidate the positive changes happening due to the FIFA World Cup being hosted in Qatar, and the broader positive impact on the Muslim world and beyond. They also argue that a broader approach is warranted to understand the complexities of the region, and that there is a need for research on how sporting mega-events in the Arab world could be a source of transformational policy actions (Hussain & Cunningham, 2024). Additionally, Acheampong, Akwaa-Sekyi & Peprah-Yeboah (2023) outline fans lived experiences in the city of Doha during the tournament, with some describing it as 'the best FIFA World Cup ever'. They also report that there is a perceived image-rebranding strategy that worked successfully for the host nation.

It might never be possible to square the circle, but it is also impossible to ignore the numbers, and on that kind of measurement scale the Qatar 2022 FIFA men's World Cup will ultimately be viewed as a success story. Qatar needed this outcome, to push forward with the bigger picture. It was never about the money, or economic benefit. The gains that Qatar were seeking were non-commercial, with international relations at their heart. Early evidence suggests that they may have gone some way to swaying hearts and minds. Assuming the story remains positive, it is likely Qatar will aim to become a regular major player in the sports event hosting market. One would expect to see a bid to host a future Olympic

Games as an example. Money, again, will be no object. The primary objective will be that the rest of the world is watching the show. That is one objective that the 2022 FIFA World Cup undoubtedly delivered on.

RESEARCH IMPLICATIONS

More research is needed on the implications stemming from Qatar 2022, as cited in this chapter. Such future research could focus on a broader approach to understand the complexities of the region, and how sporting mega-events in the Arab world could be a source of transformational policy actions.

QUIZ QUESTIONS

1. Who was the winning captain of the Argentina team at the 2022 FIFA World Cup?
2. Which came first? Soft power or sportswashing?
3. In which year did FIFA select Qatar as the host of the 2022 World Cup?
4. In billions, how many people engaged with the 2022 FIFA World Cup?

DEBATE QUESTIONS

1. Is sportswashing an issue for the middle east only? Or is this a global issue?
2. Will the 2026 FIFA World Cup be marketed in the same way?
3. Are soft power and sportswashing actually different concepts?

ALIGNMENT TO UNITED NATIONS SUSTAINABLE DEVELOPMENT GOALS

Goal	How
1. No Poverty	
2. Zero Hunger	
3. Good Health and Wellbeing	
4. Quality Education	

Goal	How
5. Gender Equality	
6. Clean Water and Sanitation	
7. Affordable and Clean Energy	
8. Decent Work and Economic Growth	Explains migrant worker issues.
9. Industry, Innovation, and Infrastructure	Explains the way a country changes their industry and infrastructure for a mega-event.
10. Reduced Inequalities	
11. Sustainable Cities and Communities	How a city and community aim to become sustainable to host a mega-event.
12. Responsible Consumption and Production	
13. Climate Action	
14. Life Below Water	
15. Life on Land	
16. Peace, Justice, and Strong Institutions	Looking to allay issues to apparently promote peace and justice.
17. Partnerships for the Goals	Between the different organisations.

REFERENCES

Abdeldayem, F. (2023). Political employment of hate speech in sports coverage: Case study of Qatar 2022 World Cup. *Journal of Mass Communication Research, 64*(3), 1697–1724. https://jsb.journals.ekb.eg/index.php/FAQ/journal/journal/article_287610.html?lang=en

Acheampong, E.Y., Akwaa-Sekyi, E.K., & Peprah-Yeboah, A. (2023). Investments in sport: Fans' impressions of Qatar 2022. *Journal of Sport & Tourism*, 1–18. https://doi.org/10.1080/14775085.2023.2252405

Akhundova, G. (2015, June 12). Baku European Games 2015: A fearsome PR machine is using sport to sweep human rights under the carpet. *The Independent.* www.independent.co.uk/voices/comment/baku-european-games-2015-a-fearsome-pr-machine-is-using-sport-to-sweep-human-rights-under-the-carpet-10314316.html

Berkeley, G. (2021, March 28). Players wear shirts to voice human rights concerns in Qatar ahead of FIFA World Cup. *Inside the Games*. www.insidethegames.biz/articles/1105975/players-wear-human-rights-shirts-qatar

Blum, R., Harris, R., & Dunbar, G. (2020, April 20). FIFA officials 'received numerous bribes to vote for Russia and Qatar to host World Cup'. *The Independent.* www.independent.co.uk/sport/football/news/fifa-corruption-bribes-russia-2018-qatar-2022-world-cup-jack-warner-payments-a9451471.html

Boykoff, J. (2022). Toward a theory of sportswashing: Mega-events, soft power, and political conflict. *Sociology of Sport Journal, 39*(4), 342–351. https://doi.org/10.1123/ssj.2022-0095

Brannagan, P.M., & Rookwood, J. (2016). Sports mega-events, soft power and soft disempowerment: International supporters' perspectives on Qatar's acquisition of the 2022 FIFA World Cup finals. *International Journal of Sport Policy and Politics, 8*(2), 173–188. https://doi.org/10.1080/19406940.2016.1150868

Brannagan, P.M., Reiche, D., & Bedwell, L. (2023). Mass social change and identity hybridization: The case of Qatar and the 2022 FIFA World Cup. *Identities, 30*(6), 900–918. https://doi.org/10.1080/1070289X.2023.2203576

Chadwick, S. (2018a, August 24). Sports-washing, soft power and scrubbing the stains. Can international sporting events really clean up a country's tarnished image? *Policy Forum.* www.policyforum.net/sport-washing-soft-power-and-scrubbing-the-stains/

Chadwick, S. (2018b, July 25). How repressive states and governments use 'sportswashing' to remove stains on their reputation. *The Conversation.* https://theconversation.com/how-repressive-states-and-governments-use-sportswashing-to-remove-stains-on-their-reputation-100395

Chadwick, S. (2022, March 2). Why the 'Putinisation' of sport must no longer fool the world. *The Conversation.* https://theconversation.com/why-the-putinisation-of-sport-must-no-longer-fool-the-world-178150

Davis, L., Plumley, D., & Wilson, R. (2023). For the love of 'sportswashing'; LIV Golf and Saudi Arabia's push for legitimacy in elite sport. *Managing Sport and Leisure.* http://doi.org/10.1080/23750472.2022.2162953

Delgado, D.L. (2016). Opening ceremonies of international sports events: The other face of Chinese Soft Power. *International Journal of the History of Sport, 33*(5), 607–623. https://doi.org/10.1080/09523367.2016.1159200

Dubinsky, Y. (2023). Clashes of cultures at the FIFA World Cup: Reflections on Soft Power, Nation Building and Sportswashing in Qatar 2022. Place Branding and Public Diplomacy. https://doi.org/10.1057/s41254-023-00311-8.

Grix, J., Dinsmore, A., & Brannagan, P.M. (2023). Unpacking the politics of 'sportswashing': It takes two to tango. *Politics, 0*(0). https://doi.org/10.1177/02633957231207387

Hussain, U., & Cunningham, G.B. (2024). "The FIFA 2022 Men's World Cup: transformations in Qatar", In Solberg, H., Storm, R.K., & Swart, K. (Eds.), *The Research Handbook on Major Sporting Events.* Cheltenham, UK: Edward Elgar Publishing. https://doi.org/10.4337/9781800885653.00049

Inside FIFA. (2023, January). One Month On: 5 billion engaged with the FIFA World Cup Qatar 2022™. https://inside.fifa.com/tournaments/mens/worldcup/qatar2022/news/one-month-on-5-billion-engaged-with-the-fifa-world-cup-qatar-2022-tm

Jain, S. (2023). Resistance and reform as responses to human rights criticism: Relativism at FIFA World Cup Qatar 2022. *German Law Journal, 24*(9), 1691–1702. www.cambridge.org/core/journals/german-law-journal/article/resistance-and-reform-as-responses-to-human-rights-criticism-relativism-at-fifa-world-cup-qatar-2022/C6D9D4E4C8A80FABBC0EDF6DDF8CC337

Koch, N. (2018). The geopolitics of sport beyond soft power: Event ethnography and the 2016 cycling world championships in Qatar. *Sport in Society, 21*(12), 2010–2031. https://doi.org/10.1080/17430437.2018.1487403

Menon, S. (2019, September 1). Sportswashing, a new word for an old idea. 15 December. Sportstar. https://sportstar.thehindu.com/columns/lastword-suresh-menon/sportswashing-saudi-arabia-manchester-city-united-psg-champions-league-olympics-f1-boxing-athletics-football/article64863590.ece

Millward, P. (2017). World Cup 2022 and Qatar's construction projects: Relational power in networks and relational responsibilities to migrant workers. *Current Sociology, 65*(5), 756–776. https://doi.org/10.1177/0011392116645382

Næss, H.E. (2023). A figurational approach to soft power and sport events. The case of the FIFA World Cup Qatar 2022™. *Frontiers in Sports and Active Living.* www.frontiersin.org/articles/10.3389/fspor.2023.1142878/full

Nye, J.S. (2004). *Soft Power: The Means to Success in World Politics.* New York: Public Affairs.

Nye, J.S. (2021). Soft power: the evolution of a concept. *Journal of Political Power, 14*(1), 196–208. https://doi.org/10.1080/2158379X.2021.1879572

Rosenberg, M. (2022, December 29). Sportswashing is Everywhere, but It's Not New. *Sports Illustrated.* www.si.com/olympics/2022/12/29/sportswashing-olympics-world-cup-daily-cover

Schausteck de Almeida, B., Marchi Júnior, W., & Pike, E. (2014). The 2016 Olympic and Paralympic Games and Brazil's Soft Power. *Contemporary Social Science, 9*(2), 271–83. https://doi.org/10.1080/21582041.2013.838291

Setiawati, S.M., & Roziqin, A. (2023). The relationship between sports, economy, politics, and religion: A case study of the FIFA World Cup in Qatar 2022. *Croatian International Relations Review, 29*(93). https://cirrj.org/menuscript/index.php/cirrj/article/view/808

Skey, M. (2023). Sportswashing: Media headline or analytic concept? *International Review for the Sociology of Sport, 58*(5), 749–764. https://doi.org/10.1177/10126902221136086

Zidan, K. (2022, January 5). Could 2022 be sportswashing's biggest year? *The Guardian.* www.theguardian.com/sport/2022/jan/05/sportswashing-winter-olympics-world-cup

II COMMERCIALISING EVENTS

5 BUYING AND SELLING DAY OF THE DEAD

A history of the holiday's commercialization

Mathew Sandoval

AIM

This chapter aims to explore the historical commercialization of Día de los Muertos, challenging the perception that its commodification is a recent phenomenon. It examines how commercial practices – from church involvement to modern tourism and merchandise – have shaped the holiday's evolution and widespread cultural appeal, both within and beyond Mexico.

LEARNING OBJECTIVES

1. Analyze the historical factors contributing to the commercialization of Día de los Muertos and how these practices evolved over time.
2. Assess the role of various commercial influences, including religious, tourism, and consumer industries, in shaping Día de los Muertos' cultural appeal.
3. Evaluate the impact of commercialization on Día de los Muertos, exploring both the preservation of cultural practices and the transformation of the holiday's meaning and significance across generations and regions.

DOI: 10.4324/9781003490326-8

THEORETICAL FOCUS AND SIGNIFICANCE

The theoretical focus of this chapter lies in examining Día de los Muertos through the lens of commercialization, challenging the notion of its recent commodification by tracing its economic and cultural evolution. It explores how commercial forces – religious, tourism, and consumer industries – have both shaped and preserved the holiday's traditions while transforming its cultural meaning. The chapter further considers the dual impact of commodification: Its role in maintaining cultural continuity and its potential to alter the holiday's authenticity across diverse contexts.

PRACTICAL FOCUS AND SIGNIFICANCE

The practical focus of this chapter is to investigate how commercialization has affected the observance and perception of Día de los Muertos, both within Mexico and internationally. It examines specific commercial practices, such as the sale of themed merchandise, tourism marketing, and religious influences, and their role in shaping public engagement with the holiday. The chapter also addresses practical implications, including how commercialization influences cultural preservation, fosters new generational interest, and potentially risks altering the holiday's original significance.

ARTICLE

There's growing concern among Latinos that Día de los Muertos is becoming commercialized. As a Chicano who holds this holiday sacred, I confess that it's jarring to see how the Day of the Dead is mass-marketed on both sides of the border. For example, the holiday aisles of Target are now crammed with Day of the Dead crafts (Sandoval, 2024). There are Day of the Dead Nike shoes, Day of the Dead Barbie dolls, and Day of the Dead lottery tickets (Sandoval, 2021). The Mexican government paid $US20 million to producers of the James Bond film *Spectre* to positively portray the Day of the Dead in hopes that the blockbuster movie would help generate holiday tourism (Tuckman, 2015). Disney even attempted to trademark 'Día de los Muertos' before the release of their 2017 film *Coco* (Rodriguez, 2013). The examples go on.

Critics lament that such developments have transformed Day of the Dead into 'crass commercialism' (Peltz, 2017). Some blame US marketing and cultural appropriation for the way the Day of the Dead has 'morphed into a commercial machine' (Garcia, 2019). Some blame the North American Free Trade Agreement (Kolhatkar, 2021). Others blame globalization (Colon, 2016). All critics, however, uphold the same narrative – the Day of the Dead's commercialization is a relatively recent phenomenon. I disagree with this narrative, however. In significant ways Día de los Muertos has been commercialized since its inception.

Día de los Muertos, celebrated on and around November 1 and 2, is a seasonal fiesta to honor one's dearly departed. Although it's observed in numerous Latin American countries, it's most associated with Mexico. The Day of the Dead is what anthropologist Hugo Nutini (1988) calls a syncretic holiday, meaning it's a cultural product of two different religious traditions that merged during the European colonization of the Americas. The Day of the Dead contains elements of the annual feasts for the dead celebrated by pre-Hispanic indigenous cultures. During Mexico's colonial era (1521–1821) these indigenous rituals merged with the Spanish Catholic holy days for the dead known as All Saints Day (November 1) and All Souls Day (November 2) to produce the festival now commonly referred to as Día de los Muertos.

The first institution in Mexico to transform the Day of the Dead into a profit-generating enterprise was the Catholic Church. In the 16th and 17th centuries Spanish clergy convinced native peoples that the souls of the dead traveled to 'purgatory', a place where the soul had to be purified before entering heaven. Purification could be achieved through church-sanctioned offerings, which the clergy brokered. Newly converted indigenous peoples, then, had to pay priests for special prayers, special candles, and other religious items during Día de los Muertos, all of which became a great source of revenue for the Church (Lomnitz, 2005, pp. 99–140).

As the popularity of Día de los Muertos grew in Mexico, so too did the amount of commercial activity. In the 1700s the holiday spawned enormous commercial fairs, which enterprising artisans used to make and sell Day of the Dead folk art. According to one historian during this era, merchants stocked their makeshift kiosks with 'thousands' of holiday objects that were sold to 'incredible crowds' of consumers during November 1 and 2 (Ajofrin, 1958, p. 87). These objects included skeleton figurines, toy coffins with miniature cadavers, and candied craniums known as sugar skulls (aka *calaveras* or *alfeñiques*).

During the 1700s and 1800s, Day of the Dead's commercialization was especially egregious in Mexico City. Of all the seasonal fiestas Day of the Dead generated the largest annual market. Merchants, of course, sold items related to the holiday, but they also sold clothing, shoes, furniture, tools, home décor, and many other things. During Day of the Dead the streets and plazas were so overwhelmed with vendors, carts, booths, and makeshift markets that the local government deemed the fiesta a public 'disorder' (Lomnitz, 2005, p. 298). Mexico City's mayor and city council eventually had to control the Day of the Dead's economic frenzy by enacting laws and issuing vendor permits. In other words, the holiday was so commercialized that it required government regulation (Lomnitz, 2005, pp. 292–303).

Día de los Muertos continued to have great economic significance in urban and rural Mexico during the early and mid-20th century. Numerous anthropologists and writers noted that the Day of the Dead generated sizable holiday markets (d'Harnoncourt, 1935; Parsons, 1936; Redfield, 1930; Toor, 1947). Villages were transformed into commercial fairs during the fiesta, and families traveled many miles to celebrate the festival by buying, selling, and trading goods (Fergusson, 1934, pp. 93–96). In Mexico's larger towns and cities the Day of the Dead brought unrestrained commercialization. Plazas, parks, and graveyards were packed with merchants selling all manner of traditional Día de los Muertos items, especially the holiday's instantly recognizable folk art – skeleton toys, sugar skulls, skull masks, papier-mâché figurines, candles, and mortuary dioramas (Brenner, 1929, pp. 23–25). In fact, capitalizing on the Day of the Dead's folk art was a regular cottage industry for Mexican artisans (Pomar, 1995). Holiday crafts weren't trivial commodities, though; they were essential fiesta components. In certain regions of Mexico, it was, and continues to be, a tradition for families to annually replace all elements of an *ofrenda*, the sacred altar decorated with offerings to the dead (Pomar, 1995, p. 24). In that regard, a traditional aspect of the Day of the Dead is consistent consumption of goods; and craftspeople and merchants, of course, worked to fulfill consumer demands.

Day of the Dead tourism has also been a major commercial enterprise. In the early 20th century prominent binational writers featured the Day of the Dead in their popular travel guides. Anita Brenner's *Your Mexican Holiday* (1932) and Frances Toor's *Guide to Mexico* (1936) offered colorful descriptions of the holiday's festivities. Both authors also publicized the Day of the Dead through their popular magazines, which were subsidized by the Mexican government (Lindsay, 2019). Toor's *Mexican Folkways* (1925–1937), featured bilingual articles on holiday-related activities in each autumn issue. Likewise, Anita Brenner's *Mexico This Month* (1955–1972), provided detailed coverage of the fiesta in each October and November publication. These efforts helped promote the Day of the Dead as a cultural attraction for international tourists.

During the mid- and late-20th century the Mexican government also made concerted efforts to sell the Day of the Dead to foreign tourists. They marketed the Day of the Dead as a traditional Mexican cultural experience, which resulted in the fiesta's progressive transformation into a cultural spectacle for tourist consumption. Celebrations in certain regions, like Oaxaca and Michoacán, were strategically marketed as the most 'authentic' for tourists to explore (Norget, 249). As anthropologist Stanley Brandes has shown, the Mexican government 'systematically promoted the touristic development' of Día de los Muertos to 'further its financial and ideological goals' (Brandes, 1988, pp. 88–89). For instance, Día de los Muertos in the village of Tzintzuntzan had long been a minor event celebrated by only a small portion of the community. When the Mexican government intervened in the 1970s to promote the fiesta, they 'embellished the traditional observance beyond recognition' (Brandes, 1988, p. 89). Thousands of tourists began overrunning the village and dozens of tv and film crews flooded the tiny cemetery. Similar developments occurred for the Day of the Dead celebration on the rustic island of Janitzio. Anthropologist Ruth Hellier-Tinoco (2011) has revealed the degree to which the Mexican government 'sold' the island's Day of the Dead as a major cultural attraction. Whereas no outsiders had attended Janitzio's fiesta prior to the late 1920s, by the late 1990s the once-small community ceremony was transformed into a spectacle attended by more than 100,000 tourists each year.

The Day of the Dead's commercialization in the 21st century is merely a continuation of a long-standing tradition. Sure, consumer capitalism and social media have intensified the holiday's commercialization; but they did not initiate it. And while critics bemoan holiday profiteering, the Day of the Dead's commercial appeal produces growing participation, especially among Latinos.

During my recent Día de los Muertos fieldwork in Mexico I spoke with a grandmother building a public altar for her family. For years she tried to persuade her grandchildren to participate, to no avail. It wasn't until they watched Disney's *Coco* and saw sugar skulls at Walmart that they took an interest in the holiday. Now they eagerly help their grandmother build the family altar. Hence, the Day of the Dead's commercialization has ensured its ability to survive to subsequent generations.

QUIZ QUESTIONS

1. What was the first institution to commercialize Día de los Muertos, and how did it profit from the holiday?
2. Which government invested in promoting Día de los Muertos as a tourist attraction, and what were some effects of this promotion?
3. How has modern commercialization affected Día de los Muertos participation among younger generations?

DEBATE QUESTIONS

1. Does the commercialization of Día de los Muertos dilute or strengthen its cultural significance?
2. Should governments actively promote traditional holidays like Día de los Muertos for tourism, or does this compromise their authenticity?
3. Is the influence of US consumer culture responsible for the commercialization of Día de los Muertos, or is commercialization an inevitable part of cultural evolution?

REFERENCES

Ajofrin, F. de. *Diario del Viaje que por Orden de la Sagrada Congregación de Propaganda Fide Hizo a la América Septentrional en el Siglo XVIII,* Real Academia de la Historia, 1958, p. 87.

Brandes, S. *Power and Persuasion: Fiestas and Social Control in Rural Mexico,* University of Pennsylvania Press, 1988, pp. 88–109.

Brenner, A. *Idols Behind Altars*, Payson & Clarke, 1929, pp. 23–25.

Brenner, A. *Your Mexican Holiday*, G. P. Putnam's Sons, 1932.

Colon, V. 'On Día de Muertos, No Elaborate Rituals, Just Honoring My Dad', *NBC News*, November 1 2016, www.nbcnews.com/news/latino/voices-dia-de-muertos-no-elaborate-rituals-just-honoring-my-n675671.

d'Harnoncourt, R. 'The Fiesta as a Work of Art', *Renascent Mexico*, ed. H. Herring & H. Weinstock, Covici Friede Publishers, NY, 1935, pp. 219–232.

Fergusson, E. *Fiesta in Mexico*, Knopf Inc., 1934, pp. 93–96, 200–202.

Garcia, S.E. 'Día de Muertos Barbie: Respectful Tribute, or "Obviously Cultural Appropriation?" ', *New York Times*, September 11 2019, www.nytimes.com/2019/09/11/us/dia-de-muertos-barbie-mattel.html

Hellier-Tinoco, R. *Embodying Mexico: Tourism, Nationalism, and Performance*, Oxford University Press, 2011.

Kolhatkar, S. 'Chicano Artists Resist Commercialization of Día de los Muertos', *YES Magazine*, October 28 2021, www.yesmagazine.org/social-justice/2021/10/28/day-of-the-dead-chicano-artists-los-angeles-commercialization.

Lindsay, C. *Magazines, Tourism, and Nation-Building in Mexico*, Springer International Publishing, 2019.

Lomnitz, C. *Death and the Idea of Mexico*, Princeton University Press, 2005.

Lonely Planet. 10 things to know before going to Oaxaca, one of Mexico's most intriguing destinations, 2025. Available: www.lonelyplanet.com/articles/things-to-know-before-traveling-to-oaxaca

Nutini, H. *Todos Santos in Rural Tlaxcala: A Syncretic, Expressive, and Symbolic Analysis of the Cult of the Dead*, Princeton University Press, 1988.

Parsons, E.C. *Mitla: Town of the Souls*, University of Chicago Press, 1936.

Peltz, J.F. 'Dia de los Muertos gets the American holiday treatment: Commercialization', *New York Times*, October 30 2017, www.latimes.com/business/la-fi-agenda-retail-muertos-20171030-story.html

Pomar, M.T. *El Dia de los Muertos: The Life of the Dead in Mexican Folk Art*, Fort Worth Art Museum, 1995.

Redfield, R. *Tepoztlan, a Mexican Village: A Study in Folk Life*, University of Chicago Press, 1930.

Rodriguez, C.Y. 'Day of the Dead trademark request draws backlash for Disney', *CNN*, May 11 2013, www.cnn.com/2013/05/10/us/disney-trademark-day-dead/index.html

Sandoval, M. 'How commercialization over the centuries transformed the Day of the Dead', *The Conversation*, October 27 2021, https://theconversation.com/how-commercialization-over-the-centuries-transformed-the-day-of-the-dead-170428

Sandoval, M. 'Day of the Dead and Commercialization: A Brief History of a Long Standing Tradition', in José Luis Fitch Jiménez (ed.), *The Art of Luis Fitch*, UNO Publishing, Minneapolis, 2024.

Toor, F. *Guide to Mexico*, Robert M. McBride and Company, 1936.

Toor, F. *A Treasury of Mexican Folkways*, Crown Publishers, 1947.

Tuckman, J. 'Mexico offered James Bond film studios millions to shoot its good side', *The Guardian*, March 12 2015, www.theguardian.com/world/2015/mar/12/mexico-james-bond-film-spectre-tax-incentives

6 FROM REBELLION TO REVENUE
Dance music reckonings

Christopher T. Conner and Danielle Hidalgo

AIM

To shed light on the transformation of EDM culture, from its rebellious beginnings to its current state as a commercialized industry grappling with internal and external tensions.

LEARNING OBJECTIVES

1. Commodification of EDM culture.
2. How subcultural values can change over time.
3. Explore the consequences of commodified culture.

DOI: 10.4324/9781003490326-9

THEORETICAL FOCUS AND SIGNIFICANCE

Theoretically, this chapter focuses on the application of the theory of Horkheimer and Adorno's *Culture Industry Thesis*, and shows the ongoing significance of the culture industry concept, properly reconfigured.

PRACTICAL FOCUS AND SIGNIFICANCE

Practically, this chapter examines the real-world implications of the commodification and cultural evolution within EDM. It shows how the transformation of subcultures into commercialized industries has created tensions on those seeking to preserve the core values, and outsiders who disregard those values.

ARTICLE

Introduction

There's a peculiar relationship between the commodification of a music subculture, and the orientation of the subculture. In this chapter we explore this tension in Electronic Dance Music (EDM) culture. While today large EDM events are massive affairs that attract hundreds of thousands of attendees and generate billions in revenue, behind this massive spectacle is a rich cultural history rooted in egalitarian ideals (Conner & Dickens, 2023a; Hidalgo, 2022). The importance of revisiting this history is that it provides us with insight into how social movements, subcultures, and other cultural movements can become co-opted and diverted from their original orientation.

Major themes in the literature

One of the recurring themes amongst EDM scholars is that there has been a marked shift away from the subcultural values encapsulated as peace, love, unity, and respect (PLUR) (Anderson, 2009). The early EDM scene was anti-capitalist, rejected unjust hierarchies, emphasized charity, and for a time had elements of political action as part of the subculture. Much of this history has been lost, forgotten, or otherwise undocumented here in the United States. From interviews with individuals we spoke to, early EDM gatherings focused on local action, often in the form of mutual aid, donating food to the homeless, raising concern over environmental issues, and organizing anti-war protests. In Europe, however, there exists a more robust, and in some ways overt, record – such as the Love Parade, an EDM event which started as a protest against the Berlin Wall.

Ironically, since 2015 there has also been an emergence of homophobic, transphobic, racist, and sexist tropes existing in a subculture initially created by homosexual men of color. Even within Gay raves, known as circuit parties, this phenomenon of reproducing hierarchies found elsewhere in society are reproduced within the subculture (Schwalbe, 2000; Green, 2008; Conner, 2021; Conner & Dickens, 2023b). This reorganizing of the music subculture, away from core values and towards celebrity culture and consumption, was predicted by the Frankfurt School. Their term for this process was the culture industry, coined as a way to describe how cultural spaces become commodified (Horkheimer & Adorno, 1972 [1944]). We argue that the evolution of EDM illustrates this gradual progression that befalls music subcultures as they move from fringe, countercultural phenomena to being an integrated part of the dominant culture.

Analysis

Early on the EDM subculture was considered a countercultural youth phenomenon. Over time, thanks to sensationalized reporting, a moral panic surrounding the subculture emerged. The pinnacle of this was the introduction of the Reducing American Vulnerability to Ecstasy Act, or RAVE Act, of 2002, proposed by the then senator, Joe Biden. This made it illegal to hold EDM events, reclassified many of the cultural objects as drug paraphernalia, and forced EDM promoters to become licensed businesses. The result has been an increasing shift away from core values of the movement as elements antithetical to collective organizing became more present throughout the culture.

One needs look no further than the reports of 'Nazi Techno' – an idea which would seem unimaginable even in the early 2000s – to understand how much EDM has changed (Sanchez, 2008). While accounts of this have gone largely unreported, other social scientists have written extensively on this within rock, punk, and other spaces. This current phase is best understood as an outright rejection and replacement of egalitarian values, with a full-on embracing of authoritarian and fascist ideology. Two transformations played an important role in this process – the focus on the individual and the spectacle of consumption, in addition to an overall reorienting of countercultural tendencies that support the *status quo*.

Shifting logics

One of the key elements that characterized the early EDM subculture was its emphasis on community. As the EDM subculture has been commodified, there has been an increasing emphasis on hedonism, excess, and prioritizing oneself above the group. Some of this is a by-product, however unintentional, on the part of EDM organizers. As EDM was demonized and moved into licensed, for-profit venues, status in the culture started to shift towards emphasizing the things the early EDM subculture was criticizing (Anderson, 2009). Since 2010 the largest producer of EDM events, Insomniac, has been using the phrase 'you are the experience'. They reinforce this notion by referring to attendees as 'headliners'. They also take pictures of event attendees which appear on their social media page and website. While how these individuals are chosen is unclear, it would appear that those with the most spectacular outfits, those with fit bodies, and those who convey traditional standards of beauty are more likely to appear. This logic stands in stark contrast to the early days of EDM, which stood against sexualized outfits, encouraged equality among participants rather than standing out, and focused on the artistry of EDM (Anderson, 2009).

This shift from the community to the individual can also be seen in the way DJs have become celebrities, often reflected in the branding work that DJs are expected to do (Hidalgo, 2022). In the 1990s, for example, DJs played at parties/raves for the love of the music and scene; the industry had not yet been thoroughly commodified and professionalized (Conner, 2023). Long-time DJ DVS1 has spent years critiquing this shift, highlighting how far the culture has shifted from one of community, particularly local communities, to a global dance music culture industry that emphasizes individualism rather than collective resistance. Reflecting on one of his recent interviews, CCL writes:

> This DVS1 interview has such good insight on what makes US community so special (vs INdustry) and why I don't trust DJs who have never carried a speaker stack/cleaned up event toilet hell (https://twitter.com/ccl_url/status/1730725885702029694?s=46).

Relatedly, this shift is felt on the ground, at the events themselves. For many of the larger events and festivals, those willing to pay extra can avoid long inconvenient lines, are offered more comfortable areas to watch the event, and are even given access to private air-conditioned restrooms (as opposed to overflowing urinals and unsanitary port-a-potties).

Reorienting of countercultural tendencies

The early EDM subculture was anti-capitalist, feminist, anti-racist, and anti-war. As the subculture became more commodified, however, these political positions became less salient. Some DJs and many others in the industry lament this loss today, often stating their disgust at where dance music culture now finds itself.

The ongoing genocide in Gaza is a case in point. While some DJs and other key stakeholders have been extremely vocal about the ongoing genocide, boycotting clubs, events, and promoters that have actively censored Pro-Palestinian DJs, many DJs and clubs are completely unwilling to boycott, support censored DJs, or say anything at all (Ross, 2024). Sites @raversforpalestine and @strikegermany have been actively calling out those unwilling to do anything while also supporting DJs who have been forced to cancel their shows (see: www.instagram.com/p/C4s3_kTsb4I/?igsh=MzRlODBiNWFlZA%3D%3D&img_index=1). Additionally, @raversforpalestine posted a boycott list of five venues, outlining why those venues have been added to the list (see: www.instagram.com/p/C41E_kesiSb/?igsh=MzRlODBiNWFlZA%3D%3D). In their interview with Annabel Ross (2024), Ravers for Palestine emphasize how to approach this reckoning:

> I think it's really important not to necessarily shame artists for doing that … we should be thinking about collective solutions to these structural problems, and I think the structural position of the DJ can be quite a precarious and compromised one due to how the industry works. It's really important to situate that materially and not kind of place it at the feet of the individual, because they're part of this bigger system.

These resistance efforts are all happening at the same time that there is documented evidence of an EDM event blocking humanitarian aid into Gaza, a heinous display of exactly the opposite of PLUR, and one that some scene insiders have been quick to condemn.

For example, in response to this so-called 'rave', WTCHCRFT posted the following:

> insidious co-opting of dance and 'rave' culture for a pro genocide pro ethnic cleansing audience. This is why it was (and still is) important to boycott things like HÖR and going to isr[swearing emoji]el to play shows (https://twitter.com/wtchcrft666/status/1759396475174281471?s=46).

As Hidalgo (forthcoming) shows, the DJs/producers speaking up about the genocide and a number of other problematic trends in EDM (such as sexual assault and harassment, whitewashing dance music's history, etc.) are often already on the margins of dance music culture, a pattern that reflects superstar DJs' (typically white, cishet men) unwillingness to challenge the *status quo*.

Conclusion

We have tried, in the space provided, to produce an overview for how EDM went from being perceived as a deviant, drug-using counterculture into a commodified spectacle of consumption. With profits placed at the center of EDM events and core values pushed to the margins, this has allowed many features of the subculture to be realigned towards values antithetical to the early days of the subculture. The failure of so many folks in the industry today to speak up about genocide, sexual assault and harassment, and a full range of problematic trends while also, in many cases, contributing to these problems, speaks to the ongoing tension we outlined here. As pandemic lockdown restrictions were lifted by Spring 2021, EDM stakeholders openly discussed the ongoing reckonings folks were grappling with in dance music (Hidalgo, forthcoming). Whether or not the subculture takes on those reckonings for the better remains to be seen.

MANAGERIAL IMPLICATIONS

Focus on cultural values rather than profit, and be aware of outside forces seeking to infiltrate the group.

POLICY IMPLICATIONS

They should police hate speech and violence.

RESEARCH IMPLICATIONS

To provide a deep understanding of cultural evolution under commercial pressures, exploring ethical considerations in commodified subcultures, and social and political dimensions.

QUIZ QUESTIONS

1. How has the commodification of EDM culture impacted its original values and orientation?
2. What are some problematic trends that have emerged within the EDM subculture as a result of commercialization?
3. Describe the shift in focus from community-oriented values to individualism and consumerism within the EDM industry.

DEBATE QUESTIONS

1. Should commercialization be seen as a natural evolution or a detrimental influence on subcultural values?
2. Is it the responsibility of event organizers and industry stakeholders to actively preserve the core values of the EDM subculture, or should they prioritize commercial success?
3. To what extent does the emergence of discriminatory behaviors within the EDM community reflect broader societal trends, and how can these issues be addressed?
4. How can subcultural movements like EDM balance individual expression and collective activism in the face of commercialization?

ALIGNMENT TO UNITED NATIONS SUSTAINABLE DEVELOPMENT GOALS

Goal	How
1. No Poverty	
2. Zero Hunger	
3. Good Health and Wellbeing	
4. Quality Education	
5. Gender Equality	While EDM's origins emphasized gender equality, today the scene is hyper masculine, misogynistic, and anti-trans.
6. Clean Water and Sanitation	
7. Affordable and Clean Energy	
8. Decent Work and Economic Growth	
9. Industry, Innovation, and Infrastructure	
10. Reduced Inequalities	The current state of the EDM community is one in which homophobia, transphobia, racism, and sexism thrive.

Goal	How
11. Sustainable Cities and Communities	The commercialization of EDM events raises questions about sustainable urban development. We argue that a balance between commercial success and values that promote community is needed.
12. Responsible Consumption and Production	Encouraging sustainable and ethical approaches within the entertainment industry can minimize negative impacts on society and the environment.
13. Climate Action	
14. Life Below Water	
15. Life on Land	
16. Peace, Justice, and Strong Institutions	The chapter touches upon themes of social activism, ethical considerations, and the role of institutions within the EDM industry.
17. Partnerships for the Goals	

REFERENCES

Anderson, T. 2009. *Rave Culture: The Alteration and Decline of a Philadelphia Music Scene*. Philadelphia, PA: Temple University Press.

Conner, C.T. 2021. "How the gay part scene short-circuited and became a moneymaking bonanza." *The Conversation*. https://theconversation.com/how-the-gay-party-scene-short-circuited-and-became-a-moneymaking-bonanza-153424

Conner, C.T. 2023. 'QAnon, Authoritarianism, and Conspiracy within American Alternative Spiritual Spaces'. *Frontiers in Sociology* 8: 1136333. doi: 10.3389/fsoc.2023.1136333.

Conner, C.T., & Dickens, D.R. 2023a. *Electronic Dance Music: From Deviant Subculture to Culture Industry*. Lanham, MD: Rowman and Littlefield.

Conner, C.T., & Dickens, D.R. 2023b. 'Electric Empires: From Countercultural Movement to Corporate Enterprise'. *Deviant Behavior* 44(7): 1063–1080.

Green, A.I.. 2008. 'The Social Organization of Desire: The Sexual Fields Approach'. *Sociological Theory* 26(1): 25–50. www.jstor.org/stable/20453094.

Hidalgo, D.A. Forthcoming. 'Platformization and Its Ongoing Impact on Dance Music Spaces'. *Dancecult: Journal of Electronic Dance Music Culture, Special Issue: Spaces of Dancing* 16(1).

Hidalgo, D.A. Forthcoming. 'Dance Music Reckonings: Authenticity, Whiteness, and Toxic Masculinity'. In *Handbook of Critical Music Industry Studies*, edited by Arditi, D., & Nolan, R. Switzerland: Springer Nature.

Hidalgo, D.A. 2022. *Dance Music Spaces: Clubs, Clubbers, and DJs Navigating Authenticity, Branding, and Commercialism*. Lanham, MD: Rowman and Littlefield.

Horkheimer, M. & Adorno, T. 1972 [1944]. *Dialectic of The Enlightenment.* Boston, MA: Beacon Press.

Ross, A. 2024. 'Silence is complicity: A conversation with a representative from Ravers for Palestine'. *The Politics of Dancing.* Substack: https://politicsdancingxyz.substack.com/p/silence-is-complicity?r=4uy4t&utm_medium=ios&triedRedirect=true

Sanchez, C. 2008. 'Nazi Techno Fad Hits Dance Floors'. *Southern Poverty Law Center Intelligence Report.* August 29.

Schwalbe, M., Godwin, S., Holden, D., Schrock, D., Thompson S. & Wolkomir, M. 2000. 'Generic Processes in the Reproduction of Inequality: An Interactionist Analysis'. *Social Forces* 79(2): 419–452.

7 EVENTS AND UNHEALTHY SPONSORSHIP
An analysis of Euro 2024

Robin Ireland

AIM

The aim of this chapter is to describe how sporting events are used to promote unhealthy consumption.

LEARNING OBJECTIVES

1. To show how unhealthy brands have been long associated with sport.
2. Event sponsorship forms part of modern brand marketing.
3. Marketing of brands at events is designed to encourage consumption.

DOI: 10.4324/9781003490326-10

THEORETICAL FOCUS AND SIGNIFICANCE

This chapter draws on Bourdieu's sociology of practice in arguing that sport should be studied in the context of consumption practices. Using sporting events to promote unhealthy products to huge television audiences, including significant numbers of children and young people, carries negative major health consequences. The leading risk factors for premature deaths worldwide are poor diets and tobacco consumption.

PRACTICAL FOCUS AND SIGNIFICANCE

Income from the marketing of unhealthy brands and products has become a key part of the staging and delivery of major sporting events. The burden of disease from the consumption of unhealthy food and drink and alcohol remains high globally. The recent introduction of widespread gambling industry sponsorship and marketing has introduced a new and increasing public health harm.

ARTICLE

Transnational corporations have long used mega-events, such as the Olympics and the FIFA World Cup, to enhance exposure of their brands (Madrigal *et al.*, 2005). UEFA has taken the same path with its European Football Championships (Euros) and built an economic model based on revenue from the sale of media rights and sponsorships (Kennedy, 2017; Ludvigsen & Petersen-Wagner, 2022). UEFA's latest tournament – Euro 2024 held in Germany in June and July – was another example of a 'festival of consumption' (Smart, 2018, p. 243). Over 25 years earlier, Bourdieu saw the 1984 World Cup held in France as a 'system of actors competing over commercial stakes' (Bourdieu, 1999).

Modern packages of sponsorships rights were developed for the World Cup by president João Havelange, who was elected in 1974, and whose model for the future of global sporting events was based around funding from transnational corporations and the sale of television rights (Sugden & Tomlinson, 1998). Coca-Cola have been associated with the FIFA World Cup since 1975, and their support was integral to bringing in further funding. The International Olympic Committee (IOC) followed a similar path with global sponsorship developing following the 1984 Olympic Games, which were held in Los Angeles. Thus, from the Olympics to the World Cup and Europe's premier football competitions, major sporting events are run alongside a carnival of corporate advertising often encouraging the consumption of products which are anything but healthy. For many transnational corporations, some heavily criticized by public health campaigners for their high-calorie and unhealthy fast food and drink products, being associated with sport enables them to adopt a 'health halo' whilst marketing direct to young consumers (Harris *et al.,* 2017).

Thus, whilst playing sport may be good for our health and fitness, watching it may be a very different case altogether. Poor diets, smoking, and alcohol are contributors to premature death and health inequalities the world over (World Health Organisation, 2023). And yet UEFA has welcomed sponsors like McDonald's, Coca-Cola, and Carlsberg who produce many products that are considered detrimental to good health (Horne, 2013). Indeed, it has been argued that Big Alcohol and Big Tobacco invented modern sports sponsorship (Crompton, 1993). Transnational corporations from these industries have even avoided national advertising regulations whilst promoting brands. When cigarette advertising had been banned on both British and US television (in 1965 and 1970 respectively), the explosion of sport on our screens following mass popular access to television sets provided a key outlet for companies seeking alternative forms of exposure for their brands. For example, tobacco sponsorship funded the development of limited-over televised cricket in the 1970s and 1980s (Wilson, 1988), whilst the launch of the women's professional tennis circuit in 1971 was bankrolled by Philip Morris (King, 2021). At Euro 2016, Carlsberg found a way to promote its brand despite France's national law prohibiting alcohol marketing in sports events (Purves *et al.*, 2017). Even more blatantly, as FIFA's official sponsor, Budweiser (part of AB InBev) insisted on their beer being available at the 2014 and the 2018 World Cups, overriding Brazilian and Russian national legislation (Ireland, 2023).

Sponsorship is a part of a sophisticated marketing communications mix designed to make a brand stand out (Cornwell, 2020). Whilst Coca-Cola is heavily invested in both the Olympics and the FIFA World Cup, PepsiCo (the owners not only of Pepsi Cola and Gatorade, but also Doritos and Lay's) are strongly associated with American Football's Super Bowl and have been a sponsor of the UEFA Champions League since 2015, as well as being a global sponsor of UEFA Women's Football. Sport's playing fields and pitches have long provided a battleground for sugary drinks companies (McKelvey, 2006) determined to push fans' consumption ever higher at the expense of our oral health, as well as our waistlines.

However, modern sport sponsorship is much more than the advertising that used to be associated with sports events as long ago as 1928, when Coca-Cola took their product to the Olympics (Keys, 2004). Today's sponsorship deals between corporation and club, sport's governing body, and event organizers, are a complex agreement detailing a mix of brand placements, social media presence, and product availability. The agreements are confidential, but occasionally are described, as in the case of Manchester United Football Club's deal with car manufacturer, Chevrolet, in 2012 (Rowe & Zemanek, 2014). Companies use sport because their marketing works, and consumption is directly linked to brand exposure. Whilst corporations and marketing agencies carefully protect their commercial information, we sometimes do hear about the impact of sponsorship. Budweiser's 'Light Up the FIFA World Cup' in 2018 used a global advertising campaign, a commercial showing thousands of drones taking the beer to fans, eight million noise-activated Red Light Cups, digital and social media campaigns, and of course their brand featuring on LED pitch perimeter advertising during the televising of the matches. The marketing ran in 50 countries with a claimed engagement with 3.2 billion fans, contributing to an increase in AB InBev's revenues of 10.1% globally and 16.7% outside of the brand's traditional markets (Arthur, 2018).

In recent times, a few high-profile professional footballers, conscious of their image and their youthful following, have tried to stand up to tournaments' sponsorship agreements, and make it clear they do not support the brand or product being promoted. When Portuguese star, Cristiano Ronaldo, moved Coca-Cola bottles out of the camera frame at a press conference ahead of Portugal's match against Hungary at Euro 2021, he said people should drink water instead (Sweney, 2021). At the 2022 Qatar World Cup, the French footballer Kylian Mbappé, was reportedly hiding Budweiser's logo in his man of the match photographs, because he wanted to avoid promoting the beer brand, being aware that he is a role model for many children (Willcocks, 2022).

The recent explosion of gambling industry marketing in sport has led to further public health concerns about sport sponsorship. The liberalization of laws around the television advertising of gambling brands, together with the development of online gambling, has led to increasing mental health issues around addiction and suicide among those exposed to gambling products (Bunn *et al.*, 2018). At this time, therefore, it is concerning that UEFA have announced Betano, its first-ever betting sponsor, while Betano's parent company, Kaizen Gaming, was the official global sponsor of Euro 2024. UEFA already has Heineken, Lay's/ Walkers (PepsiCo) and Just Eat as Official Global Sponsors of the UEFA Champions' League and UEFA Women's Football. Coca-Cola are Global Sponsors for Euro 2024. Thus, whilst we tune in to watch the athletes on our screen, we'll be encouraged to consume more alcohol and junk food whilst having a bet on the result. Isn't it about time for event organizers to think about our health as well as their wallets?

MANAGERIAL IMPLICATIONS

Event managers should consider social and health factors resulting from unhealthy event sponsorship. This should be an even higher concern if a significant part of their audience is children and young people.

POLICY IMPLICATIONS

Income should not be the sole factor considered in determining appropriate event sponsorship.

RESEARCH IMPLICATIONS

Further research in determining how brand marketing at events encourages consumption is to be encouraged.

QUIZ QUESTIONS

1. Why do corporations want their brands and products to be associated with sport?
2. Is sport sponsorship a recent phenomenon?
3. Are corporations able to use sport to evade advertising restrictions?
4. How may sport sponsorship impact on public health?

DEBATE QUESTIONS

1. Should ethics play a part in determining event sponsorship?
2. Should some types of marketing in sport not be allowed, e.g., front of shirt/uniform sponsorship?
3. Should some industries, e.g., gambling not be permitted to advertise at sporting events?
4. Who should determine what types of sponsorship are permitted?

ALIGNMENT TO UNITED NATIONS SUSTAINABLE DEVELOPMENT GOALS

Goal	How
1. No Poverty	
2. Zero Hunger	
3. Good Health and Wellbeing	Unhealthy sport sponsorship is likely to negatively affect good health and wellbeing.
4. Quality Education	
5. Gender Equality	
6. Clean Water and Sanitation	
7. Affordable and Clean Energy	
8. Decent Work and Economic Growth	
9. Industry, Innovation, and Infrastructure	
10. Reduced Inequalities	Consumption of unhealthy food and drink, tobacco and alcohol is strongly related to socio-economic status. Thus, marketing to encourage such consumption is likely to drive increasing health inequalities.
11. Sustainable Cities and Communities	
12. Responsible Consumption and Production	Marketing is designed to encourage consumption whatever the cost.
13. Climate Action	
14. Life Below Water	
15. Life on Land	
16. Peace, Justice, and Strong Institutions	
17. Partnerships for the Goals	

REFERENCES

Arthur, R. (2018). 'World Cup boost for Budweiser: "Football is a passion point in the new markets we've expanded in"', *Beverage Daily*, 26 July 2018, available: www.beveragedaily.com/Article/2018/07/26/World-Cup-boost-for-Budweiser-and-AB-InBev [accessed 8 July 2022].

Bourdieu, P. (1999). 'The state, economics and sport' in Dauncey, H. & Hare, G., eds., *France and the 1998 World Cup. The National Impact of a World Sporting Event*, London: Frank Cass, 15–21.

Bunn, C., Ireland, R., Minton, J., Holman, D., Philpott, M. & Chambers, S. (2018). 'Shirt sponsorship by gambling companies in the English and Scottish Premier Leagues: global reach and public health concerns', *Soccer and Society*, 20(6), 824–835.

Cornwell, T.B. (2020). *Sponsorship in Marketing. Effective Partnerships in Sports, Arts and Events*, Second ed., London: Routledge.

Crompton, J.L. (1993). 'Sponsorship of sport by tobacco and alcohol companies: a review of the issues', *Journal of Sport & Social Issues*, 73, 148–167.

Harris, J.L., Haraghey, K.S., Lodolce, M. & Semenza, N.L. (2017). 'Teaching children about good health? Halo effects in child-directed advertisements for unhealthy food', *Pediatric Obesity*, 13, 256–264.

Horne, J. (2013). 'Material and representational legacies of sports mega-events: the case of the UEFA EURO™ football championships from 1996 to 2008' in Wolfram Manzenreiter & Georg Spitaler (eds.),*Governance, Citizenship and the New European Football Championships,* London: Routledge, 160–172.

Ireland, R. (2023). *Sport, Sponsorship and Public Health*, London: Routledge.

Kennedy, P. (2017). 'Using Habermas to crack the European football championships', *Sport in Society*, 20(3), 355–368.

Keys, B. (2004). 'Spreading Peace, Democracy, and Coca-Cola®: Sport and American Cultural Expansion in the 1930s', *Diplomatic History*, 28(2), 165–196.

King, B.J. (2021). *All In. An Autobiography*, London: Viking.

Ludvigsen, J.A.L. & Petersen-Wagner, R. (2022). *The UEFA European Football Championships: Politics, Media Spectacle and Social Change*, London: Routledge.

Madrigal, R., Bee, C. & LaBarge, M. (2005). 'Using the Olympics and FIFA World Cup to Enhance Global Brand Equity. A case study of two companies in the payment services category'. in Amis, J. & Cornwell, T. B., eds., *Global Sport Sponsorship*, Oxford: Berg, 179–190.

McKelvey, S.M. (2006). 'Coca-Cola vs. PepsiCo-A "Super" Battleground for the Cola Wars?', *Sport Marketing Quarterly*, 15(2), 114.

Purves, R.I., Critchlow, N., Stead, M., Adams, J. & Brown, K. (2017). 'Alcohol Marketing during the UEFA EURO 2016 Football Tournament: A Frequency Analysis', *International Journal of Environmental Research and Public Health*, 14(704), available: http://dx.doi.org/10.3390/ijerph14070704.

Rowe, W.J. & Zemanek, J.E. (2014). 'Chevrolet and Manchester United: a transformational sponsorship in a traditional industry', *Innovative Marketing*, 10(1), 40–48.

Smart, B. (2018). 'Consuming Olympism: Consumer culture, sport star sponsorship and the commercialisation of the Olympics', *Journal of Consumer Culture*, 18(2), 241–260, available at: http://dx.doi.org/10.1177/1469540517747146.

Sugden, J. & Tomlinson, A. (1998). *FIFA and the Contest for World Football. Who rules the peoples' game?*, Cambridge: Polity Press.

Sweney, M. (2021). 'Coca-Cola's Ronaldo fiasco highlights risk to brands in social media age', *The Guardian*, 18 June 2021, available: www.theguardian.com/media/2021/jun/18/coca-colas-ronaldo-fiasco-highlights-risk-to-brands-in-social-media-age [accessed 17 March 2024].

Willcocks, B. (2022). 'Kylian Mbappe "is deliberately hiding sponsor Budweiser's name in posed photos with his World Cup man of the match awards to avoid promoting alcohol" ... and France are being fined because he refuses to do interviews!', *Mail Online*, available: www.dailymail.co.uk/sport/sportsnews/article-11500205/Kylian-Mbappe-deliberately-hiding-Budweisers-posed-photos-avoid-promoting-alcohol.html [accessed 17 March 2024].

Wilson, N. (1988). *The Sports Business*, London: Piatkus.

World Health Organisation. (2023). *Noncommunicable diseases. Fact sheet*, available at: www.who.int/news-room/fact-sheets/detail/noncommunicable-diseases [accessed 17 March 2024].

III EVENT-LED URBAN TRANSFORMATION

8 NO MORE HUNGER GAMES From Olympic legacy to livability Olympics

Brendan Barratt

AIM

At a time when municipal budgets are tight and/or shrinking almost everywhere, cities are facing an ever more complex array of socio-economic and environmental concerns. In these circumstances, it may be appropriate to focus attention on both the potential benefits and real costs associated with hosting of mega-events such as the Olympic Games.

LEARNING OBJECTIVES

1. Enhance understanding of the challenges facing cities as they seek to maximize the benefits and minimize the costs of hosting the Olympics.
2. Critically evaluate the shift in approach adopted by the International Olympic Committee as it seeks to reframe sustainability and legacy impacts associated with the Games for host cities.
3. Extend and challenge knowledge on the notion of urban livability, particularly focusing on the lived experiences of the residents in Olympic host cities.

DOI: 10.4324/9781003490326-12

THEORETICAL FOCUS AND SIGNIFICANCE

The theoretical focus of this chapter falls under critical urban theory, which calls for forms of urbanization that are more democratic, socially just, and sustainable. It is a critique of how power and interests work to shape cities and how, at times, these powerful forces fail to address concerns around inequality, injustice, and exploitation within cities. The theoretical significance of this chapter relates to on-going debates around how we understand liveability and sustainability in an urban context, and how society utilizes available resources (financial, technical, managerial, etc.) to improve the quality of life of ordinary people in our cities. This contrasts with theories that focus on cities as a world system determined by the need to remain competitive in the global economy. Mega-events such as the Olympics function as part of this 'cities as competitors' worldview, rather than promoting the notion of 'cities as collaborators', which in turn may determine how well we can respond to major problems.

PRACTICAL FOCUS AND SIGNIFICANCE

The practical focus of this chapter is on how our contemporary approach to mega-events like the Olympics needs to substantially change to ensure future viability of the Games. Without this change it may become increasing challenging for cities to continue to host the Olympics in a manner that is affordable, while at the same time bringing real benefits for local communities. The practical significance of this chapter relates to important question of whether the current model for mega-events is sustainable in the longer term, and if we need to begin thinking about alternative models. This may be particularly significant in a world that needs to reach net-zero carbon emissions in the near future.

ARTICLE

Mega sporting events like the Olympics impose significant strain on host cities as they strive to create a legacy that is sustainable and truly beneficial for their local communities. Often, they seem more like corporatized sales events for big companies or a bucket-list experience for privileged globe-trotters. Despite our love for the Olympics and the joy of seeing our teams win, it's imperative to question the value of these games for the cities that host them.

Reflecting on the 2012 London Olympics, also known as the 'Regeneration Games', urban scholar Susan Fainstein observed that 'the huge expenditure involved took away resources from other parts of London and the country more widely without providing them any benefits beyond the glory of hosting the Games] (Fainstein, 2011, p. 132).

A comprehensive review of the London Olympic legacy conducted in 2022 depicted a nuanced picture of mixed outcomes, with limited data on the local benefits realized compared to the original promises and plans (Bernstock *et al.*, 2022). Some even went as far as calling the legacy of the London Olympics a 'massive betrayal' for residents (Wainwright, 2022).

Poverty rates in the Borough of Newham, where the London Olympics were held, remain among the highest in the city (Trust for London, 2021–22). Shockingly, as of September 2022, around 18% of households in London were food insecure (London Assembly, 2023, p. 6). The spectacle of the Olympics may begin to resemble the dystopian future depicted in Suzanne Collins' *Hunger Games* novels, where the poor suffer for the entertainment of the wealthy residents of the 'Capitol'.

STRUGGLING TO MAINTAIN A POSITIVE LEGACY

While the values underlying the Olympic movement are universally recognized, the reality of hosting such mega-events is far from untarnished. In the lead-up to the 2016 Rio Olympics, protesters threw themselves in front of the Olympic torchbearers (Rodrigues & de Freixo, 2016). Large segments of the Brazilian population were concerned that the Olympics brought few benefits for locals and instead enriched the wealthy (Cuadros, 2016). The costs of hosting the Olympics have consistently exceeded US$10 billion, and economic impact studies suggest they are often 'money-losing propositions' for host cities (Baade & Matheson, 2016).

Wouldn't the money be better spent solving problems facing the host city? What if, for example, Rio de Janeiro had used some of the money invested in the Olympics to upgrade the favelas slums? With close to 1.4 million people living in these favelas (around 22% of the Rio population), such an investment would bring about significant enhancements in their quality of life (Miyamoto & Buckman, 2022).

The Tokyo 2020 Olympics, labeled the 'Recovery Olympics', were intended to bring optimism back to Japan after the 2011 Tohoku earthquake and Fukushima nuclear accident (Holthus *et al.*, 2020). However, the advent of COVID-19 led to the event's postponement to 2021, resulting in the first Olympics without spectators. Moreover, calls for cancellation of the games because of the health associated risks were ignored (Shimizu *et al.*, 2021). Consequently, the costs of the Tokyo Olympics doubled compared to initial estimates, leaving the city with several new sporting venues, many of which incurred annual losses (Tsutsui,

2021). This post-Olympic facility maintenance issue is common, with many facilities falling into disrepair (Boscamp, 2013).

While the International Olympic Committee (IOC) emphasizes the need for potential host cities to prioritize sustainability and legacy, the nature of these mega-events may dissuade many cities from bidding in the future due to cost implications, infrastructure challenges, and security concerns (Clift & Manley, 2016).

The Paris 2024 Olympics faced challenges such as the city's transport system not being ready for the games, and significant security concerns around the opening ceremony along the river Seine (Schofield, 2023). In response, Paris organizers highlighted their efforts to align with the IOC's Legacy Strategic Approach adopted in December 2017, which aims to control the discourse around the sustainability and legacy of the Games. The 'legacy approach' was introduced at a time when bidding for the Olympics has dwindled, with only two candidate cities – Paris and Los Angeles – with both bids selected (Gold & Gold, 2021). In this context, the legacy outcomes of the Paris Games may prove influential in determining the future of the Olympics (Schnitzer & Haizinger, 2019).

LIVABILITY OLYMPICS RANKING

As we move forward, there may be calls for alternative models for the Games, including selecting a permanent location, or rotating between a small number of host cities (Baade & Matheson, 2016). It is also crucial to question why so many cities neglect their problems, and invest vast resources in bidding for and hosting mega-sporting events.

We could look more closely at the case of Vienna, which rejected plans to host the Olympics in a March 2013 referendum (Crook, 2013). Perhaps it is no coincidence that Vienna ranked top in 2023 in various quality of life rankings, including the Mercer Quality of Life Ranking, the Economist Intelligence Unit Global Liveability Ranking, and Monocle Magazine's Quality of Life Survey (see Table 8.1).

TABLE 8.1 PERFORMANCE OF VIENNA IN CITY RANKINGS

Mercer Quality of Living City Ranking 2023	EIU Global Liveability Ranking 2023	Monocle Quality of Life Survey 2023
Vienna	Vienna	Vienna
Zurich	Copenhagen	Copenhagen
Auckland	Melbourne	Munich
Copenhagen	Sydney	Zurich

TABLE 8.1 (Continued)

Mercer Quality of Living City Ranking 2023	EIU Global Liveability Ranking 2023	Monocle Quality of Life Survey 2023
Geneva	Vancouver	Stockholm
Frankfurt	Zurich	Tokyo
Munich	Calgary	Helsinki
Vancouver	Geneva	Madrid
Sydney	Toronto	Lisbon
Dusseldorf	Osaka/Auckland	Melbourne

Unfortunately, the Economist Intelligence Unit ranking is not about livability at all; it is designed to help human resource managers for transnational corporations determine compensation for their mobile global talent (Barrett, 2015). Similarly, the Mercer ranking assesses the practicalities of daily life for expatriate employees and their families in 'assignment locations'. Meanwhile, the Monocle ranking commends Vienna for its excellent infrastructure, low crime rates, and a good supply of affordable housing.

Perhaps it would make sense to develop a new city ranking – the Livability Olympics Ranking – focused on the lived experience for people in each city, rather than from the perspective of globally mobile talent or expats. Instead of cities competing to host the Olympics, there could be a global competition between cities, reminiscent of Peter Gabriel's 1979 song, Games without Frontiers (Jeux Sans Frontières). After all, town planning was an Olympic event in the 1928, 1932, 1936, and 1948 games (Elledge, 2016).

How would this work? Instead of traditional Olympic events like volleyball and swimming, cities would compete on measures to tackle hunger, poverty alleviation, unemployment, affordable housing, and more. There could be a situation where a city works on and eventually wins the gold medal for its outstanding efforts to reduce homelessness. This new ranking could measure progress toward resilient, safe, and prosperous living environments, potentially heralding a new era of urban livability Olympics.

MANAGERIAL IMPLICATIONS

City managers involved in bids to host the Olympics and other major sporting events will be increasingly required to examine the costs and benefits for their city, and to ensure that vital resources are not redirected away from addressing major problems that their city faces.

POLICY IMPLICATIONS

Policymakers will need to address the role that major sporting events play in the urban development process, and will need to come up with more sophisticated approaches that ensure these events contribute to, rather than undermine, urban sustainability.

RESEARCH IMPLICATIONS

There has been considerable research undertaken to date on the impacts that major sporting events, such as the Olympics, have on host cities. However, these impacts evolve over time and may only become fully apparent after a couple of decades. As such, longitudinal research is required to monitor the impacts of the Games, and to assess whether the original plans and promises were met. This will require robust methodologies to ensure the accessibility and availability of the relevant data sources.

QUIZ QUESTIONS

1. Which Olympics were named the 'Regeneration Olympics' and why?
2. How did COVID-19 impact the Tokyo 2020 Olympics?
3. How would you define the legacy of the Olympic Games?
4. What kind of environmental impacts might you expect to be associated with the Olympics?
5. What kind of positive impacts does the Olympics have for a host city?

DEBATE QUESTIONS

1. Can you imagine a future without the Olympics? What would be the pros and cons associated with the disappearance of the Games?
2. Why do you think there has been a decline in the number of cities bidding to host the Olympics?
3. What measures can the International Olympic Committee introduce to make it easier for cities to host the Games?
4. Do you think that city rankings have any value? Who uses these city rankings and why?
5. Could you see any merits in your city (where you live now) hosting a mega-event like the Olympics? What kind of problems would you anticipate and how does this influence your thinking?

ALIGNMENT TO UNITED NATIONS SUSTAINABLE DEVELOPMENT GOALS

Goal	How
1. No Poverty	Major sporting events could divert resources that would be better invested in tackling poverty alleviation in the host city.
2. Zero Hunger	Major sporting events could divert resources that would be better invested in tackling hunger in the host city.
3. Good Health and Wellbeing	Major sporting events stimulate interest in exercise, sport, and healthy lifestyles.
4. Quality Education	Sport is an important part of education and should be accessible to all.
5. Gender Equality	Major sporting events like the Olympics play a very significant role in promoting gender equality.
6. Clean Water and Sanitation	Plans to host the Olympics should include measures to ensure that there are limited negative impacts on the water and sanitation system of the host city.
7. Affordable and Clean Energy	Ideally, major sporting events would be powered by clean, affordable energy.
8. Decent Work and Economic Growth	Major sporting events have the potential to create jobs and stimulate economic growth for the local community.
9. Industry, Innovation, and Infrastructure	The Olympics places a massive demand on the infrastructure of the host city.

Goal	How
10. Reduced Inequalities	It is unclear if the Olympics has any impact in terms of reducing inequalities in the host city.
11. Sustainable Cities and Communities	Sustainability issues related to hosting of the Olympics remain a major concern.
12. Responsible Consumption and Production	Major sporting events involve the consumption of goods and services which should be guided by sustainability policies including waste reduction and recycling.
13. Climate Action	Efforts are being made to reduce the carbon footprint of the Olympics and other major sporting events.
14. Life Below Water	Olympics require that marine areas are used for sporting events. Environmental impacts need to be minimized.
15. Life on Land	Olympic facilities have a large land footprint. Where possible existing facilities should be employed, and their post-Olympic use should be carefully considered.
16. Peace, Justice, and Strong Institutions	The Olympics plays an essential role in promoting global peace.
17. Partnerships for the Goals	

REFERENCES

Baade, R.A., & Matheson, V.A. (2016). Going for the gold: The economics of the Olympics. *Journal of Economic Perspectives*, *30*(2), 201–218. https://doi.org/10.1257/jep.30.2.201

Barrett, B. F. D., United Nations University. (2015, June 30). *The world's most liveable cities.* Our World. https://ourworld.unu.edu/en/the-worlds-most-liveable-cities

Bernstock, P., Brownhill, S., Davis, J., Melhuish, C., Minton, A., & Woodcraft, S. (2022, December 12). *State of the legacy: A decade of Olympic 'regeneration'.* UCL. www.ucl.ac.uk/urban-lab/publications/2022/dec/state-legacy-decade-olympic-regeneration

Boscamp, E. (2013, September 14). *Haunting past Olympic venues.* HuffPost. www.huffpost.com/entry/abandoned-olympic-venues_n_3580868

Clift, B. C., & Manley, A. (2016, January 11). *Five reasons why your city won't want to host the Olympic Games.* The Conversation. https://theconversation.com/five-reasons-why-your-city-wont-want-to-host-the-olympic-games-52289

Crook, J. (2013, March 13). *Vienna says no to 2028 Olympic Games bid.* insidethegames.biz – Olympic, Paralympic and Commonwealth Games News. www.insidethegames.biz/articles/1013307/vienna-says-no-to-2028-olympic-games-bid

Cuadros, A. (2016, August 9). *The Rio Olympics are taking from the poor and giving to the rich.* The Atlantic. www.theatlantic.com/international/archive/2016/08/building-barra-rio-olympics-brazil/493697/

Economy Committee. (2023, April 20). *Food Insecurity in London Report.* The London Assembly. www.london.gov.uk/who-we-are/what-london-assembly-does/london-assembly-work/london-assembly-publications/food-insecurity-in-london-report

Elledge, J. (2016, August 9). *Going for the gold: When town planning was an Olympic competition.* Planetizen. www.planetizen.com/node/87885/going-gold-when-town-planning-was-olympic-competition

Fainstein, S.S. (2011). *The just city.* Cornell University Press.

Gold, J.R., & Gold, M.M. (2021). Olympic legacies and the sustainability agenda. *Nature Sustainability, 4*(4), 290–291. https://doi.org/10.1038/s41893-021-00711-9

Holthus, B., Gagné, I., Manzenreiter, W., & Waldenberger, F. (2020). *Japan through the lens of the Tokyo Olympics open access.* Routledge.

Miyamoto, J., & Buckman, S. (2022). Rio de Janeiro's attempt at favela urban upgrading: Analysis of the favela-bairro programme three decades later. *CIDADES, Comunidades e Territórios, 45.* https://doi.org/10.15847/cct.25913

Rodrigues, T., & de Freixo, A. (2016, August 4). *In no mood for games: The pale Olympic flame of Rio 2016.* The Conversation. https://theconversation.com/in-no-mood-for-games-the-pale-olympic-flame-of-rio-2016-63191

Schnitzer, M., & Haizinger, L. (2019). Does the Olympic agenda 2020 have the power to create a new Olympic heritage? An analysis for the 2026 winter Olympic Games bid. *Sustainability, 11*(2), 442. https://doi.org/10.3390/su11020442

Schofield, H. (2023, December 2). *Paris Olympics 2024: Locals ask if they're worth the trouble.* BBC. www.bbc.com/news/world-europe-67564177

Shimizu, K., Sridhar, D., Taniguchi, K., & Shibuya, K. (2021). Reconsider this summer's Olympic and Paralympic Games. *BMJ*, n962. https://doi.org/10.1136/bmj.n962

Trust for London. (2022). *Poverty rates by London Borough.* https://trustforlondon.org.uk/data/poverty-borough/

Tsutsui, K. (2021). The road to the 2020 Tokyo Summer Olympics has been a long and winding one, says Stanford sociologist. Available https://news.stanford.edu/stories/2021/07/long-winding-road-2020-tokyo-games

9 GASTRO-DEVELOPMENT AND GENTRIFICATION

How food promotes urban development and displacement

Pascale Jossart-Marcelli

LEARNING OBJECTIVES

AIM

To show how food is increasingly used to brand and revitalize neighborhoods in ways that often lead to gentrification and displacement of long-term residents.

1. To establish the significance of food as a tool for urban development.
2. To broaden understanding of gentrification dynamics beyond housing.
3. To identify key actors in food-related urban transformations.

DOI: 10.4324/9781003490326-13

THEORETICAL FOCUS AND SIGNIFICANCE

Theoretically, this chapter focuses on the notion of gastrodevelopment – the use of food to promote neighborhood development by drawing desirable and affluent consumers, residents, and investors. This chapter also engages with the concepts of foodscape, gentrification, whiteness, and aesthetics. This is important as scholars grapple with the evolution of gentrification and the various forms it takes in different contexts.

PRACTICAL FOCUS AND SIGNIFICANCE

This chapter practically focuses on the unintended consequences of upper-middle class and primarily white consumers' food practices, including the impact of their quest for unique, authentic, and cosmopolitan food on the historically neglected and segregated places where they search for these exciting food experiences. It is linked to the growing importance of food in urban lifestyles and contemporary cities, and the associated role that local governments, developers, and cultural influencers play in transforming neighborhoods through their material and symbolic investments in food events and spaces.

ARTICLE

Eager to experience exotic and authentic foods and display their cosmopolitan and democratic tastes, foodies (Johnston & Baumann, 2015) are increasingly venturing in unexpected and previously ignored places to discover restaurants, cafés, food trucks, and farmers markets. In the process, working-class, immigrant, and ethnic neighborhoods are being rebranded as 'vibrant and diverse', destinations. While this attention can contribute to neighborhood revitalization, it also leads to tension between long-time residents who often struggle with economic and food insecurity and newcomers who are attracted by the 'authentic' food scene and ready to capitalize on this trend.

San Diego's changing foodscape

My research in San Diego shows how neighborhoods long portrayed as food deserts have become trendy foodie destinations (Joassart-Marcelli, 2021). Ethnic restaurants, street vendors, community gardens, and farmers' markets have been attracting unlikely visitors, including white, affluent, and college-educated people who historically stayed away from such places. Their influx is transforming local foodscapes by prioritizing the desires of newcomers over the needs of long-time residents, producing curated food spaces that both symbolize and fuel gentrification – the process of displacement that occurs when long-term residents of a neighborhood are being pushed out by more affluent newcomers.

For example, City Heights, one of the poorest and most ethnically diverse neighborhoods of San Diego, has become home to *Fair@44* – an outdoor international marketplace where food vendors gather in semi-permanent stalls to sell *pupusas*, *lechon*, single sourced cold brewed coffee and cupcakes to growing crowds of visitors from other parts of the city and tourists. This space was originally launched by a public-private partnership involving several nonprofits to increase 'access to healthy and culturally appropriate food' and serve as 'a business incubator for local micro-entrepreneurs', including the many immigrants and refugees who live in the neighborhood (Joassart-Marcelli, 2021). As the City recently cracked down on sidewalk vending, these types of managed spaces and organized events have facilitated the formalization of informal activity. Meanwhile, vendors who sell fruits, tamales, and ice cream to residents along the neighborhood sidewalks continue to be harassed by the police, often in response to complaints by new middle-class and primarily white residents.

The same social dynamics are unfolding in Los Angeles, Paris, Buenos Aires, and many other cities, where 'ethnic', 'authentic', and 'exotic' foods are seen as cultural assets, and have become magnets for development and drivers of gentrification (Joassart-Marcelli & Bosco, 2023).

Gastrodevelopment and the urban food machine

Attracting the 'creative class', which consists of educated, affluent, and cultured people who will presumably spend their dollars and contribute to economic growth and job creation, has been a popular development strategy in many cities around the world (Florida, 2019). In today's culture, it appears that food has become an ideal tool to lure 'creatives'. In addition to stimulating local economies, street festivals, food district designations, community gardens, and farmers' markets arguably address multiple needs by increasing access to healthy food, creating a sense of community, encouraging multicultural connections, and addressing growing environmental concerns (Joassart-Marcelli & Bosco, 2018). Thus, such projects receive wide support from many stakeholders, especially since they require little public investment, shifting the burden instead onto entrepreneurs and community organizations – a key attribute of neoliberal urbanism (Joassart-Marcelli & Bosco, 2014).

Developers, architects, real estate agents, local media, banks, nonprofits, politicians, and government agencies are now using food to sell homes and new developments and stimulate consumption, changing narratives about historically devalued neighborhoods by portraying them as 'up and coming' foodie destinations.

For example, San Diego Magazine's 'neighborhood guide' highlights City Heights's 'claim to authentic international eats, along with live music venues, craft beer, coffee, and outdoor fun' and recommends several ethnic restaurants, warning readers not to be fooled by appearances. Similarly, San Diego Real Estate Hunter (2024) identifies City Heights as 'a neighborhood filled with potential and endless possibilities' attributed to its 'vibrant tapestry of traditions, languages, and culinary delights'. The tourism industry also relies on food to attract visitors to such locations where 'diversity inspires' and people can enjoy 'some of the best ethnic food in town'. Along with marketing from the food industry itself, affluent consumers reinforce these narratives via social media by posting pictures and reviews of their most recent food 'discoveries' (Joassart-Marcelli, 2021; Joassart-Marcelli & Bosco, 2023).

Together, these actors form what I call the 'urban food machine' – a play on the 'urban growth machine' (Molotch, 1976) which refers to the loose coalition of powerful elites who share a common interest in urban growth. In the current cultural context, food appears to serve that goal; it is used in cities around the world to rebrand and revitalize neighborhoods – a process I describe as 'gastrodevelopment' (Joassart-Marcelli, 2021). Given the popularity of food, this type of development receives very little opposition.

Like investors hoping for a financial windfall from the refashioned food environment, public–private partnerships and nonprofits have joined the urban food machine by supporting food projects that emphasize social and cultural benefits. In City Heights, community gardens, farmers' market, outdoor vending spaces, and street food festivals, such the New Year Lunar Festival, Soul Food Fest, and Brazilian Carnival, are described by their organizers as celebrating cultural diversity, empowering residents, supporting local businesses, and reducing racial disparities in access to food. It is hard to object to these goals that appeal to values of multiculturalism, diversity, and democracy popular among foodies (Johnston & Bauman, 2015).

Gentrification

Low-income residents of neighborhoods where these dynamics are at play have little say in the 'urban food machine'. As a result, their needs are often ignored by new food-driven developments. This is somewhat ironic given the emphasis of such projects on celebrating and uplifting food cultures associated with these long-time residents. The effects of new restaurants and food initiatives on existing ethnic businesses and minoritized residents are rarely given serious consideration, in part because the media coverage of changing foodscapes in low-income neighborhoods like City Heights tend to be overwhelmingly celebratory.

In these newly discovered places, people of color and immigrants have lived, worked, and struggled to feed their families for decades. They have run convenience stores, opened ethnic restaurants, cooked traditional dishes, sold food in parks and alleys, and grown produce to meet community needs, while being ignored by mainstream retailers and receiving minimal support from governments (Joassart-Marcelli, Rossiter & Bosco, 2017).

As I document in *The $16 Taco* (Joassart-Marcelli, 2021), ethnic food businesses often lack access to the financial and social capital needed to compete with new enterprises that feature fresh façades, celebrity chefs, flashy marketing, bogus claims of authenticity, and disproportionate media attention. The arrival of new restaurants, food trucks, farmers markets, and more affluent residents leads to higher rents, making it increasingly difficult for existing businesses and residents to keep up and stay in the neighborhood. The changing foodscape, with its hip décor, 'elevated' cuisine, and matching prices, drives away low-income people who no longer feel that they belong.

Refashioned from 'ethnic' to 'cosmopolitan', the new foodscape both drives and symbolizes gentrification, causing the economic, social, cultural, and emotional displacement of long-time residents whose lived stories are gradually erased and reduced to a selling point – hardly a harbinger of inclusion and empowerment.

MANAGERIAL IMPLICATIONS

Managers of food projects, including restaurants, public markets, farmers' markets, food festivals, etc., should consider the risk that they pose in terms of displacing existing businesses and residents. They should engage with communities to ensure that new projects serve the needs of residents, provide employment opportunities for them, and support rather than compete with existing businesses.

POLICY IMPLICATIONS

Policymakers ought to keep equity in mind when designing and supporting local food projects to ensure that they first meet the needs of those most directly affected by food insecurity, and support small local growers, producers, and retailers.

RESEARCH IMPLICATIONS

Food researchers should consider how seemingly positive food projects might have unintended consequences for the people and communities whom they displace. Urban researchers should broaden their understanding of gentrification to consider the different ways in which it unfolds and displaces people out of their communities symbolically, emotionally, economically, and physically.

QUIZ QUESTIONS

1. What is gastrodevelopment?
2. How does food contribute to gentrification?
3. Why is ethnic food popular among foodies?
4. How do developers and real estate agents use food to sell properties?
5. How do food media change narratives and perceptions about neighborhoods?

DEBATE QUESTIONS

1. Should local governments support the development of food festivals, public markets, and other similar food-based urban projects?
2. Should foodies go out to eat in low-income immigrant communities?
3. Should we regulate street vendors?
4. Is it possible to support neighborhood revitalization without promoting gentrification?

ALIGNMENT TO UNITED NATIONS SUSTAINABLE DEVELOPMENT GOALS

Goal	How
1. No Poverty	
2. Zero Hunger	
3. Good Health and Wellbeing	Looks at the effect of food projects designed to improve access to fresh and healthy food on communities.
4. Quality Education	
5. Gender Equality	
6. Clean Water and Sanitation	
7. Affordable and Clean Energy	
8. Decent Work and Economic Growth	Gastrodevelopment as a new development/growth strategy with unintended consequences.
9. Industry, Innovation, and Infrastructure	
10. Reduced Inequalities	
11. Sustainable Cities and Communities	Looks at local food projects (often aimed at increasing sustainability) and their impacts on communities.
12. Responsible Consumption and Production	Questions the food consumption practices of foodies and their impact on communities (especially as it relates to ethnic food).
13. Climate Action	
14. Life Below Water	
15. Life on Land	
16. Peace, Justice, and Strong Institutions	
17. Partnerships for the Goals	

REFERENCES

Florida, R. (2019). *The rise of the creative class.* Basic books.

Joassart-Marcelli, P. (2021). *The $16 taco: Contested geographies of food, ethnicity, and gentrification.* University of Washington Press.

Joassart-Marcelli, P., & Bosco, F.J. (2023a). 'Best for foodies': Food, digital media and planetary gentrification. *International Journal of Urban and Regional Research*, *48*(1), 74–93.

Joassart-Marcelli, P., & Bosco, F.J. (2023b). Whose sidewalk is it? Street vendors and the battle for the city's foodscape. *Paper presented at the Annual Meetings of the American Association of Geographers*, Denver, CO (March 25).

Joassart-Marcelli, P., & Bosco, F.J. (2020). The Taste of Gentrification: Difference and Exclusion at the Urban Frontier. In Alkon, A.H., Kato, Y., & Sbicca, J. (Eds.), *A Recipe for Gentrification: Food, Power and Resistance in the City* (pp. 31–53). New York University Press.

Joassart-Marcelli, P., Speed Rossiter, J., & Bosco, F.J. (2017). Ethnic markets and community food security in an Urban 'Food Desert'. *Environment and Planning A, 49*(7), 1642–1663.

Joassart-Marcelli, P., & Bosco, F.J. (2018). Food and Gentrification: How Foodies are Transforming Urban Neighborhoods. In Joassart-Marcelli, P., & Bosco, F.J. (Eds.), *Food and place: A critical exploration* (pp. 129–146). Rowman and Littlefield.

Joassart-Marcelli, P., & Bosco, F.J. (2014). Alternative food projects, localization and urban development: Farmers' markets in Southern California. *Métropoles, 15*(1), 2–23.

Johnston, J., & Baumann, S. (2015). *Foodies: Democracy and distinction in the gourmet foodscape.* Routledge.

Molotch, H. (1976). The city as a growth machine: Toward a political economy of place. *American Journal of Sociology, 82*(3), 309–332.

San Diego Real Estate Hunter. (2024). 9 reasons City Heights San Diego is a great place to live in 2024/2025. www.sandiegorealestatehunter.com/blog/6-reasons-why-city-heights-san-diego-great-place-live/.

10 LIVEABLE CITIES AND THE INFRA-ORDINARY VERSUS THE EXTRAORDINARY

Commonwealth Games 2022 and Birmingham's urban transformation

John Bryson

LEARNING OBJECTIVES

AIM

This chapter aims to explore cities as liveable places by highlighting the importance of focusing on the everyday aspects of urban living, rather than unusual or extraordinary events including hosting mega-events.

1. To explore cities as sites for hosting mega-events.
2. To develop a distinction between cities as liveable places that are saturated with the infra-ordinary compared to the extraordinary.

DOI: 10.4324/9781003490326-14

THEORETICAL FOCUS AND SIGNIFICANCE

This chapter engages with on-going debates on ordinary cities, and the distinction made by Perec between the extraordinary versus the infra-ordinary. Too often urban studies place too much emphasis on the extraordinary to the neglect of the infra-ordinary aspects of urban living.

PRACTICAL FOCUS AND SIGNIFICANCE

The chapter's practical focus is to highlight the importance of policy measures that are intended to enhance the quality of everyday urban living, and to balance such investments against those made to support extraordinary events. The chapter's practical significance is about understanding the importance of the interplay of different urban interventions and how these contribute holistically to urban liveability.

ARTICLE

Cities are saturated with activities that Perec defines as the infra-ordinary, or what can be considered as the everyday, mundane, habitual, routine, or taken for granted (Perec, [1973] 1999). The danger is that 'in many cases, we do not see or take notice of, or do not remember, the infra-ordinary' (Bryson *et al.*, 2021a, p. 217). Too often policymakers and academics are distracted by the extraordinary (Bryson *et al.*, 2021b). Birmingham, the UK's second largest city by population, for example, hosted the 2022 Commonwealth Games during the summer of 2022. This was an extraordinary event.

To welcome the athletes and stage this mega-event, the city invested £788 million of public funding, including £594 million from central government. This funding had broad impacts including kickstarting programs to, among other things, get more people taking up physical exercise, starting businesses, and devising tourism experiences. New urban infrastructure was provided, including a new aquatics center, and existing infrastructure was refurbished. The games included the Birmingham 2022 Festival that was a cinematic and poetic celebration of creativity in the West Midlands. A ten-meter high mechanical bull formed the centerpiece of the Games opening ceremony. There is a long association between bulls and Birmingham, for example, the city's Bullring shopping center includes a bronze statue of a running bull that has become a *de facto* city mascot. The mechanical bull was going to be destroyed after the games, but a social media campaign was formed to save it. The outcome was that the bull was relocated to Grand Central, a shopping center located above Birmingham's main railway station (Figure 10.1).

Figure 10.1
Grand Central Birmingham and the Mechanical Bull.

The Games left a permanent legacy in Birmingham. Nevertheless, these infrastructural projects represent a small fraction of the investments that have succeeded in transforming this city over recent decades. Beyond the temporary glow that comes from hosting a mega-event can afford a place, Birmingham is becoming a liveable city (Leach *et al.*, 2019; Andres *et al.*, 2021). Cities are places to live, work, and visit, and they are simultaneously places for local interactions positioned within ever-evolving national and international flows of people, information, money, and products (Radcliffe *et al.*, 2022; Andres *et al.*, 2023).

Like all cities Birmingham is in a continual process of becoming as new investments are layered over preexisting ones. Infrastructure investments also alter a city's connectivity to other places. Deindustrialization from 1966 led the city to experience a long and painful adaptation, as manufacturing companies closed, downsized, or relocated (Bryson *et al.*, 2008). Birmingham's economy diversified from being dominated by manufacturing to one that includes an important business and professional services cluster (Daniels & Bryson, 2005). The city's gradual restructuring of its economy has seen major corporate players consider the city as a suitable business location. In 2015, HSBC chose to build the national headquarters of its UK personal and business bank in Birmingham rather than London. Other major corporate players have followed, including Goldman Sachs, Microland, the Indian IT infrastructure company, and the Advanced Computer Software Group. The city's connectivity to other places, the diversity and strength of its local economy, and the quality of residential living have been important factors in attracting businesses.

Birmingham's recent transformation has roots in Joseph Chamberlain's stewardship of the city in the 1870s. As mayor between 1873 and 1876, Chamberlain developed a tool for local economic development that has become known as tax increment financing (TIF) (Bryson *et al.*, 2017). Conventional wisdom holds that this type of financing was invented in California in 1955. This was, in fact, a Birmingham innovation. Introduced in 1875, this financial innovation was designed to enable the development of 93 acres of Birmingham's city center, which included creating a brand-new street, Corporation Street. This innovative approach to urban development was founded upon the local authority releasing development sites on relatively short, 75-year leaseholds to the private sector, but retaining the freeholds. This was an extremely clever move. As Chamberlain himself noted at the time, his approach was based on 'sagacious audacity' and he argued that 'The next generation will have cause to bless the Town Council', and this 'blessing' still holds true today (Bryson *et al.*, 2017, p. 460).

Birmingham City Council still retains the freeholds for most of the land in the city center. One consequence is that the Council has been able to directly shape what is built and where in the city center, and this has included the ability to focus on enhancing the quality of the built environment. Thus, Birmingham's old Central Library, built in 1971, was demolished in 2016. This resulted in the release of a 6.8-hectare (17-acre) site at the center of the city, which has become the on-going

Paradise redevelopment. The city council was behind this £500 million, 1.8 million square foot office-led mixed commercial scheme and stands to benefit from additional business rates and ground rents (Bryson *et al.*, 2017). Most importantly, this project is creating a landmark office, retail and leisure development that is attracting major companies to relocate to Birmingham.

Connectivity is central to city living and to unlocking land values. Birmingham's economic development strategy includes a major focus on improving local transportation. Extensions to the city's metro, as well as railway, network are underway, including the introduction of new stations and major extensions to existing stations. These interventions include the £705 million redevelopment of New Street railway station, completed in 2015. In April 2022, the UK government allocated £1.05 billion from its City-Region Sustainable Transport Settlements initiative to the West Midlands region. Further funding from the West Midland Combined Authority and Birmingham City Council will top this up to £1.3 billion. Investing in this way in local infrastructure will only make Birmingham a more attractive place to live and work. Public transport is set to increasingly displace the use of private cars, thereby reducing air pollution and traffic noise (Liu *et al.*, 2023).

Birmingham increasingly provides the kind of urban lifestyle that attracts highly skilled workers and their employers. It provides more affordable housing than London. It has excellent dining and retail amenities, as well as cultural and leisure attractions that arguably rival the best in London and elsewhere, from Birmingham Royal Ballet to the City of Birmingham Symphony Orchestra (Bryson, 2007). In 2016, concert hall acoustics expert Leo Beranek ranked the city's Symphony Hall as having the finest acoustics in the UK and the seventh best in the world.

In 2021, the city council launched a consultation, dubbed Our Future City Plan, on how to transform Birmingham into a 'city of proximities' (Andres *et al.*, 2021). Based on the 15-minute city approach in which access to essential services – including schools, shops, green spaces, and public transport – would be within a 15-minute walk or cycle ride, thereby prioritizing residents' health and wellbeing.

Birmingham's hosting of the Commonwealth Games is an example of a city hosting an extraordinary mega-event. Nevertheless, this role should not distract from the city's innovative and experimental approach to creating healthier neighborhoods and an urban environment that supports the everyday world of the infra-ordinary. Local planning and policy interventions are focused on making Birmingham one of the UK's most liveable cities, with the emphasis being on creating sustainable urban environments that support everyday urban living.

MANAGERIAL IMPLICATIONS

There are two managerial implications. First, for urban managers the implication is about the importance of planning interventions to support the creation of liveable cities. Second, for private sector managers the implication focuses on the importance of urban liveability in attracting and retaining skilled employees.

POLICY IMPLICATIONS

Policymakers involved with planning and managing cities should appreciate the importance of planning to support the infra-ordinary and the everyday rather than overfocusing on planning to support extraordinary events.

RESEARCH IMPLICATIONS

Urban research tends to celebrate the exceptional or the extraordinary, and more attention must be given to understanding everyday living and the infra-ordinary.

QUIZ QUESTIONS

1. What characterizes the world of the infra-ordinary?
2. How do investments designed to support the hosting of urban mega-events contribute to liveability and the everyday world of the infra-ordinary.
3. What tensions exist between the extraordinary and the infra-ordinary in planning and managing cities?

DEBATE QUESTIONS

1. How should a city maximize the infra-ordinary benefits that come from hosting a mega-event?
2. What defines a liveable city?
3. One person's liveable city is to some other people experienced as a hostile and unwelcoming or unsupportive urban environment. Discuss.

ALIGNMENT TO UNITED NATIONS SUSTAINABLE DEVELOPMENT GOALS

Goal	How
1. No Poverty	
2. Zero Hunger	
3. Good Health and Wellbeing	
4. Quality Education	
5. Gender Equality	
6. Clean Water and Sanitation	
7. Affordable and Clean Energy	
8. Decent Work and Economic Growth	
9. Industry, Innovation, and Infrastructure	
10. Reduced Inequalities	
11. Sustainable Cities and Communities	To create urban environments that support liveability with a focus on health and wellbeing.
12. Responsible Consumption and Production	
13. Climate Action	
14. Life Below Water	
15. Life on Land	
16. Peace, Justice, and Strong Institutions	
17. Partnerships for the Goals	

REFERENCES

Andres, L., Bryson, J.R., & Moawad, P. (2021). Temporary Urbanisms as Policy Alternatives to Enhance Health and Well-Being in the Post-Pandemic City. *Current Environmental Health Report,* 8, 167–176. https://doi.org/10.1007/s40572-021-00314-8

Andres, L., Bryson, J.R., Graves, W., & Warf, B. (2023). Urban Value Chains and Re-Framing Agglomeration-Centric Conceptions of Urban Theory. *Urban Geography*, 44(8), 1701–1722. https://doi.org/10.1080/02723638.2022.2125665

Bryson, J.R. (2007). Arts, Dance, Cultural Infrastructure, and City Regeneration: Knowledge, Audience Development, Networks, and Conventions, and the Relocation of a Royal Ballet Company from London to Birmingham. *Norsk Geografisk Tidsskrif*, 61(3), 98–110. https://doi.org/10.1080/00291950701553848

Bryson, J.R., Kalafsky, R.V., & Vanchan, V. (2021a). Reframing Urban Theory: Smaller Towns and Cities, Forms of Life, Embeddedplasticity and Variegated Urbanism. In J.R. Bryson, R. Kalafsky, & V. Vanchan (Eds), *Ordinary Cities, Extraordinary Geographies: People, Place and Space* (pp. 212–235). Edward Elgar.

Bryson, J.R., Kalafsky, R.V., & Vanchan, V. (2021b). Ordinary Cities, Extraordinary Geographies: Parallax Dimensions, Interpolations and the Scale Question. In J.R. Bryson, R. Kalafsky, & V. Vanchan (Eds), *Ordinary Cities, Extraordinary Geographies: People, Place and Space* (pp. 1–22). Edward Elgar.

Bryson, J.R., Mulhall, R.A., & Song, M. (2017). Urban Assets and the Financialisation Fix: Land Tenure, Renewal and Path Dependency in the city of Birmingham. *Cambridge Journal of Regions, Economy and Society*, 10(3), 455–469. https://doi.org/10.1093/cjres/rsx013

Bryson, J.R., Taylor, M., & Cooper, R. (2008). Competing by Design, Specialization and Customization: Manufacturing Locks in the West Midlands (UK). *Geografiska Annaler: Series B, Human Geography*, 90(2), 173–186.

Daniels, P.W., & Bryson, J.R. (2005). Sustaining Business and Professional Services in a Second City Region: The Case of Birmingham, UK. *The Service Industries Journal*, 25(4), 505–524.

Leach, J.M., Mulhall, R.A., Rogers, C.D.F., & Bryson, J.R. (2019). Reading Cities: Developing an Urban Diagnostics Approach for Identifying Integrated Urban Problems with Application to the City of Birmingham, UK. *Cities*, 86, 136–144. https://doi.org/10.1016/j.cities.2018.09.012,

Liu, B., Bryson, J.R., Sevinc, D., Cole, M, Eliott, R.J.R., Bartington, S., Bloss, W.J., & Shi, Z. (2023). Assessing the Impacts of Birmingham's Clean Air Zone on Air Quality: Estimates from a Machine Learning and Synthetic Control Approach. *Environmental and Resource Economics*, 86, 203–231. https://doi.org/10.1007/s10640-023-00794-2

Perec, G. ([1973] 1999). Approaches to What? In G. Perec (Ed), *Species of Spaces and Other Places* (pp. 209–212). Penguin.

Radcliffe, J., Bryson, J.R., Cox, E., Leach, J., Luiu, C., & Reardon, L. (2022). A Regional Approach to Covid-19 Recovery. *Town Planning Review*, 93(1), 7–14. https://doi.org/10.3828/tpr.2021.40

11 HOW DO FESTIVALS CATALYSE GROWTH IN BANYUWANGI, INDONESIA?

Thor Kerr and Irfan Wahyudi

LEARNING OBJECTIVES

AIM

The aim of this chapter to describe how robust development of an annual festival program in Banyuwangi, Indonesia, has been transformational because of its orientation around local places, cultures, and infrastructure.

1. To provide an accessible case study on festival development and urban transformation in Java.
2. To present a study of transformation around festivals before and after the COVID-19 pandemic.
3. To further understanding of the relationship between events, heritage, places, and identity.

DOI: 10.4324/9781003490326-15

THEORETICAL FOCUS AND SIGNIFICANCE

Theoretically, this chapter focuses on the relationship between urban transformation and government-supported events that provide space for expression, particularly social imagining of local histories and heritage. The significance of this relates to the chapter's demonstration of a positive relationship between local festival development, economic growth, and transformation before and after pandemic.

PRACTICAL FOCUS AND SIGNIFICANCE

Practically, this chapter outlines the development of Banyuwangi's festival program in the early 21st century within a context that includes heritage around international communications infrastructure from the late 19th century. The significance of this is to further understand Banyuwangi's context and festival economy ahead of redevelopment of its colonial telegraph complex as a hotel and museum facing its downtown festival square.

ARTICLE

On the eastern tip of Java, Banyuwangi Regency is a transformational case study on how local government can support growth through festival events. This chapter outlines the successes of Banyuwangi's strategic agenda prior to the COVID-19 pandemic, and how its festival program and tourism industry have recovered since the removal of public activity and mobility restrictions in 2022. The speed and consistency of this recovery indicates not only the transformational potential of festival events in Banyuwangi, but also their capacity for revival after crisis.

Building local economy on festival events

Prior to the COVID-19 pandemic, Banyuwangi was named the most promising regency for strategic development in East Java, thanks to its growing festival program and associated five-fold leap in tourist visits. Up from 802,475 in 2011 to 5,039,132 in 2018 (Sodiqin, 2019). Flourishing tourism enabled Banyuwangi to become the fastest growing economy in the easternmost horseshoe region of Java. This was celebrated because Banyuwangi's growing tourist numbers were seen as potentially stabilising the rapid decline in Java's international tourism arrivals while easing tourism development pressure on Bali (Wahyudi & Kerr, 2020), only 5 kilometres away by ferry (Figure 11.1). Inventing and hosting festivals for dance, music, sport, and other events had enabled a mode of development in Banyuwangi that avoided the tensions that may emerge from overtourism

Figure 11.1
View to Bali from Banyuwangi. Photograph by Kerr on 7 December 2019.

Figure 11.2
Kuwung Festival in Banyuwangi Square. Photograph by Kerr on 7 December 2019.

(Duignan, Everett & McCabe, 2022) and mega-resort development (Kerr & Wardana, 2020).

Banyuwangi's development successes were supported by its reputation as a safe space for creative expression – particularly for dancers from diverse Indigenous cultures – after the Regency Government engaged progressive religious leaders to deal with conservative harassment. The cultural events (Figure 11.2) and corresponding economic revival of Banyuwangi were nurtured

Figure 11.3
Asrama Inggrisan. Photograph by Kerr on 6 December 2019.

by Regent Abdullah Azwar Anas. As elected regent from 2010 to 2021, Anas positioned himself as an innovative technocrat (Hatherell, 2019) who rallied his electorate successfully around the promise of economic growth from creative, digital, and heritage projects (Anas, 2019).

Banyuwangi's annual calendar of arts and multicultural festivals flourished prior to the pandemic with mostly domestic, but also some international, participation. The annual event calendar grew from 12 events in 2012 to 99 in 2019 (Wahyudi & Kerr, 2020). In 2019, Banyuwangi Festival won 45th place for public service innovation from over 3,000 submissions to Indonesia's Ministry of Administrative and Bureaucratic Reform. Amid these successes, Regent Anas (2019) laid out an agenda for further transformation of Banyuwangi as a hub for multicultural entertainment and digital industries. These plans included restoring and redeveloping *Asrama Inggrisan* (British Hostel), a 19th-century complex (Figure 11.3) adjacent to the city square, that had housed telegraph station employees when Banyuwangi was an important node within the first worldwide telecommunications network.

RECOVERING FROM COVID-19: FESTIVAL EVENTS AND TOURISM

However, there was no sign of redevelopment at the *Asrama Inggrisan* complex on the author's most recent visit to Banyuwangi in January 2024 (Figure 11.4). This lack of redevelopment appeared emblematic of the devastation to festival events wrought by the COVID-19 pandemic, and by mobility restrictions that

Figure 11.4
Asrama Inggrisan gate. Photograph by Kerr on 16 January 2024.

limited public gatherings and travel from April 2020. Yet, as Indonesia's restrictions were removed in stages between January and May 2022, different sectors of the economy recovered at different speeds (Ramayandi & Negara, 2022). The staging of festival events and tourist visits had recovered in Banyuwangi, but there was an apparent lack of major building works downtown since our last visit in December 2019.

Banyuwangi's festival calendar has increased from 55 events in 2023 to 79 for 2024 (Ikhwan, 2023). Festival promotion and tourism bounced back in 2022, when almost three million tourist visits were recorded. Rapid growth has continued, with data showing international tourist visits climbing from 29,020 in 2022 to 36,829 in just the first eight months of 2023 (Antara, 2023).

AS FESTIVALS RECOVER, CONSTRUCTION FOLLOWS

As festival events and tourism visits recover, renewed confidence has extended to other parts of the economy. In late 2023, local government announced that long-anticipated site works at *Asrama Inggrisan* would commence in 2024 (Fauziyah & Afifa, 2023). To attract history tourists, the heritage façade would be retained at this former colonial complex facing the festival square (Figure 11.5) in the heart of Banyuwangi. This priority redevelopment would include a museum,

Figure 11.5
Festival stage with Asrama Inggrisan in background. Photograph by Kerr 15 January 2024.

hotel, and meeting point, according to Indonesia's Director of Strategic Infrastructure in the Ministry of Public Works and Public Housing, Essy Asiah. Meanwhile, current Regent Ipuk Fiestiandani has envisaged increased tourism and economic growth from the redevelopment.

The Regent can be confident about growing Banyuwangi's economy through strategic investment in the festival events calendar. The strategy engages Banyuwangi's Blambangese (*Osing*) Indigenous culture, its location, its coastal and mountain environments, and its rail, ferry, and airport infrastructure. From this position of strength, the Regency can enable local reimagining of the role Banyuwangi played in developing the first telecommunications network to span the globe in the late 19th century (Kerr & Wahyudi, 2021) when a multicultural workforce connected East Java to Jakarta and Singapore, then to Darwin and Broome through undersea telegraph cables.

While preparing to visit Banyuwangi in 2019 to investigate contemporary representations of the subsea cable network, we were invited by Broome's Shinju Matsuri festival to help create an interactive screen installation reconnecting Broome and Banyuwangi for its 50th iteration in 2020. With partners, we conceived a production to enable Indigenous artists in Banyuwangi and Broome to share stories and visualizations of their heritage as nodes in the first worldwide telecommunications network. The work would further inter-cultural understandings and artist networks, while enabling Banyuwangi and Broome to benefit from mutual publicity. Sadly, the project was halted when festivals were disrupted by the Pandemic in 2020.

FESTIVALS CAN BE TRANSFORMATIONAL AND RESILIENT

From observations over five years, the Banyuwangi case suggests that robust development of festivals in a small city can transform the city if supported by government in alignment with the city's cultures, places, and infrastructure. A successful festival calendar enables creative production, tourism, and construction. Also, we now know, festivals can rebound from crisis ahead of other economic sectors.

MANAGERIAL IMPLICATIONS

Managers should take seriously the importance of engaging local communities, heritage, environment, and infrastructure in events production, and seeing the economic and transformational potential of events.

POLICY IMPLICATIONS

Policymakers must think about the need to engage local community leaders in making events safe spaces for creative expression, and aligning event development with available heritage, histories, places, and infrastructure.

RESEARCH IMPLICATIONS

Researchers should consider the applicability of longitudinal research using, for example, fieldwork observations and textual analysis in investigating the relationship between events and transformation.

QUIZ QUESTIONS

1. Where is Banyuwangi?
2. Which Regent initiated the rapid development of cultural events in Banyuwangi?
3. How many events were listed in Banyuwangi's event calendar in 2012 and in 2019?
4. What name is given to the 19th century complex facing Banyuwangi's main festival square?
5. What is the relationship between Banyuwangi and Broome?

DEBATE QUESTIONS

1. How important has location been in the development of events and stimulation of tourism in Banyuwangi?
2. What role should local government play in developing an annual events program?
3. What role does heritage play in the development of events and transformation of a city?
4. Does heritage matter more for some types of events than others, for example a music festival versus a triathlon?

ALIGNMENT TO UNITED NATIONS SUSTAINABLE DEVELOPMENT GOALS

Goal	How
1. No Poverty	By arguing the importance of local government making space safe for diverse creative expression.
2. Zero Hunger	By arguing the importance of local government making spaces safe for diverse creative expression.
3. Good Health and Wellbeing	By arguing the importance of local government making space safe for diverse creative expression.
4. Quality Education	By providing a case study on successful innovations by a region that may be largely unknown outside of Indonesia.
5. Gender Equality	By arguing the importance of local government making spaces safe for diverse creative expression.
6. Clean Water and Sanitation	
7. Affordable and Clean Energy	
8. Decent Work and Economic Growth	By arguing for local determination in economic growth and for safe spaces of creative expression.

Goal	How
9. Industry, Innovation, and Infrastructure	By describing events innovations and their impact on local economy. Also by describing the importance of local heritage context and infrastructure in creative industry innovation.
10. Reduced Inequalities	By arguing the importance of local government making spaces safe for diverse creative expression.
11. Sustainable Cities and Communities	By demonstrating how a regional community can innovate through events production to transform their economy as well as their heritage and identity.
12. Responsible Consumption and Production	By indicating the importance of domestic over international tourism for a regional economy.
13. Climate Action	
14. Life Below Water	By arguing the importance of diverse heritage for coastal communities.
15. Life on Land	By arguing the importance of enabling heritage.
16. Peace, Justice, and Strong Institutions	By arguing the importance of making a safe space for diverse creative expressions and for engagement of community in the social re-imagining of heritage.
17. Partnerships for the Goals	By promoting the sharing of localised expressions of heritage between communities.

REFERENCES

Anas, A.A. (2019). *Anti-mainstream Marketing: 20 Ways Changing Banyuwangi.* Jakarta: Gramedia.

Antara. (2023, December 30). Kunjungan wisatawan ke Banyuwangi saat Libur Natal 2023 miningkat. https://mataram.antaranews.com/berita/314892/kunjungan-wisatawan-ke-banyuwangi-saat-libur-natal-2023-meningkat

Duignan, M.B., Everett, S. & McCabe, S. (2022). Events as catalysts for communal resistance to overtourism, *Annals of Tourism Research* 96, 1–15. https://doi.org/10.1016/j.annals.2022.103438.

Fauziyah, N.N. & Afifa, L. (2023, November 3). Inggrisan Dormitory to become heritage tourism in Banyuwangi. *Tempo.* https://en.tempo.co/read/1792141/inggrisan-dormitory-to-become-heritage-tourism-in-banyuwangi

Hatherell, M. (2019). *Political Representation in Indonesia: The Emergence of the Innovative Technocrats.* Routledge. https://doi.org/10.4324/9781351063227

Ikhwan. (2023, December 19). Lama hiatus, Banyuwangi Fest 2024 munculkan kembali ITDBI dan Kuwung. *Suara Jatim Post.* https://suarajatimpost.com/lama-hiatus-banyuwangi-fest-2024-munculkan-kembali-itdbi-dan-kuwung

Kerr, T. & Wahyudi, I. (2021). Social imaginaries of subsea cables: Recovering connections between Broome and Banyuwangi, *Media International Australia* 181(1), 32–43. https://doi.org/10.1177/1329878X20985961

Kerr, T. & Wardana, A. (2020). Utopian resort living: Islands of reclamation and environmental resistance in Bali and Western Australia, *Journal of Tourism and Cultural Change* 18(6), 629–642. https://doi.org/10.1080/14766825.2019.1694534

Ramayandi, A. & Negara, S. D. (2022, July 28–29). *Indonesia's Covid-19 mobility restrictions: Rationales and consequences* [Paper presentation]. ISEAS-Yusof Ishak Institute Conference: Covid-19 in Southeast Asia, 2020–2022: Restriction, relief, recovery. www.iseas.edu.sg/wp-content/uploads/2022/07/ISEAS-Conference_Covid-19-in-SEA_Indonesia_Mobility-restrictions.pdf

Sodiqin, A. (2019, October 19). Kunjungan wisatawan dongkrak pajak pariwisata Banyuwangi. *Radar Banyuwangi.* https://radarbanyuwangi.jawapos.com/travelling/75881981/kunjungan-wisatawan-dongkrak-pajak-pariwisata-banyuwangi

Wahyudi, I. & Kerr, T. (2020, February 1). How Banyuwangi grows an economy through creative engagement. *The Conversation.* https://theconversation.com/how-banyuwangi-grows-an-economy-through-creative-engagement-129143

12 AUSTRALIA AND THE OLYMPIC GAMES

An outline of participation and Games hosting

Richard Baka and Tracy Taylor

AIM

The aim of this chapter is to highlight some impacts and considerations associated with Australia's involvement in hosting and participating in the Olympic Games.

LEARNING OBJECTIVES

1. Describe Australia's level of involvement in Summer and Winter IOC Olympic and Paralympic events.
2. Consider the implications of the growth in number and scale of Olympic related events.
3. Discuss the place of the Games as socio-cultural assets and in relation to sustainability goals.

DOI: 10.4324/9781003490326-16

PRACTICAL FOCUS AND SIGNIFICANCE

Practically, this chapter highlights Australia's involvement in the Olympic and Paralympic Games. This chapter outlines some of the positive contributions associated with Australia, through both participation and as a host country. The significance of this is to provide information for readers to analyse when reflecting on the societal contributions and implications associated with major IOC events.

ARTICLE

Australia has a long and proud history of involvement in the Olympic and Paralympic Games. Australia made its Olympic debut at the 1896 Athens Sumer Olympics, among 14 nations, with one athlete taking home three medals (Baka, 2010). Since that time Australia has participated in every Summer Games, with its team size growing to 486 in 2020 Tokyo, where it won 46 medals. Overall, Australia has achieved 566 Summer Games medals, positioning the country with a world ranking of 14th.

Its first involvement in the Paralympic Games was at the 1960 Rome Paralympics, where Australia finished in 7th place with 10 medals. Australian athletes have gone on to attain great success, and ranks 6th in the world for the Summer Paralympics with 1,240 medals, and 20th for Winter Paralympic with 35 medals.

Australia was not represented at the inaugural 1924 Winter Olympics. In 1936, it participated at its first Winter Olympics in Garmisch-Partenkirchen, Germany, with just one competitor, speed skater Kenneth Kennedy, and won its first winter medal in 1994. Since then, Australia has won medals at every Games and its world rank has risen to 25th with an overall medal count of 19 after the Beijing 2022 Winter Olympics, where a record four medals were won (Baka, 2024).

The Youth Olympic Games (YOGS), summer and winter, for athletes aged from 15 to 18 years, were added to the Olympic schedule starting in 2010. Australia participated in the inaugural games in Singapore with 100 athletes, and has been an active participant in subsequent summer and winter editions of the Youth Games (Baka, 2024). Of note is the fact that before the instigation of the YOGs, the Australian Olympic Committee hosted six Australian Youth Olympic Festivals (2001, 2003, 2005, 2007, 2009, and 2013), with these Festivals being international multi-sport events for athletes between 13 and 19 years. These Festivals were largely superseded with the advent of the YOG (see AOC Annual Reports, 2010 to 2023).

The fourth Youth Winter Olympics were held in Gangwon, South Korea, from January 19 to February 1, 2024. With over 70 nations, 81 events, and 1,900 athletes participating, this youth-based event continues to grow in stature and popularity. In 2024, Australia had its largest representation ever, with a record 47 athletes competing in eight disciplines, including the first all-Australian ice hockey team. At the previous three Youth Games, Australia won seven medals. In South Korea three more medals were added to this tally.

WINTER GAMES

Since it began in 1924, the Olympic Winter Games has gradually grown in popularity. While the first were held in both Mont Blanc in Chamonix, and Haute-Savoie, France, and were originally part of an International Winter Sports Week, the IOC retrospectively designated the Games as the first Olympic Winter Games. Their growth is attributed to factors such as: The addition of many new sports and events; a response to added competition from the X Games, given the latter's appeal to a youth audience; the addition of sports that are television-friendly and (more recently) that grab social media attention; the promotion of gender parity; increased corporate and sponsorship funding; and, starting in 1994, putting the Winter Games on a new cycle of even years between the Summer Games (Barjolin-Smith, 2020; Dichter & Teetzel, 2020; Essex & De Groot, 2016; Markula, 2017). At the 2022 Beijing Games, the numbers expanded to 2,092 athletes, seven sports, 15 disciplines, 109 events and 91 nations, including those with little or no history in winter sports.

Australia's Winter Olympics journey

Australia's most famous winter medallist is arguably Steven Bradbury, who won a bronze medal in team speed skating in 1994, achieving the country's first ever gold medal in the same sport at the 2002 Salt Lake City Games. The spectacle of his win, coming from the back of the pack to win after all the leaders collided and fell, made for great television and thus garnered massive media coverage. His triumph, dubbed the 'accidental gold', became legendary and part of Olympic lore. It also entered the vernacular, as now to 'do a Bradbury' means to win in an unusual and unexpected circumstance. Bradbury's achievements have been recognized, with an ice rink named after him at the O'Brien Icehouse in Melbourne (Baka, 2012).

Australia recognized that it needed to better support its winter athletes and consequently established the Olympic Winter Institute of Australia in 1998, funded by the Australian Olympic Committee and the Australian Sports Commission. It has been a major reason for increased Olympic success. The purpose of this investment is to develop talent and increase the nation's ability to compete in the Winter Olympics (Baka, 2012).

Success brings attention, and Australia has (as of 2024) won 19 Winter Olympic medals, and the media, the corporate sector, and the public are now much more aware of the Winter Olympics. The next Games in Milan and Cortina d'Ampezzo in 2026 represent a good chance for a best-ever medal result.

AUSTRALIA AS A GAMES HOST

Australia was the host nation for the Summer Games in 1956, making Melbourne the first city to hold the Olympics in the Southern Hemisphere, and earning itself the affectionate title of 'The Friendly Games'. With many notable performances, Australia won 13 gold medals and finished third overall behind the USA and the USSR. Despite the fact that equestrian-related events had to be held in Stockholm, the staging of the Games at the Melbourne Cricket Ground ensured the venue's long-lasting legacy as a sporting venue (Baka, 2018).

The 2000 Sydney Games included both Olympic and Paralympic events, and were so successful that they were labelled The Best Games Ever by then IOC President Juan Samaranch. Indigenous Australian culture was showcased at the opening ceremony with a symbolic Torch Relay ending with Cathy Freeman lighting the cauldron. The redevelopment of an industrial waste site into Sydney Olympic Park was met with accolades for the transformation of the area into a sporting, business, and housing precinct, but also with notable criticism related to its under-utilization, creating what was metaphorically termed a 'white elephant'. The Sydney Paralympics achieved record participation with over 3,800 athletes from 123 countries, creating increased awareness and accessibility design considerations for people with disabilities in infrastructure planning. The high levels of volunteerism and community engagement during these Games has been noted as a major cultural and social legacy. However, as Simon Darcy noted, 'From a planning perspective whether it was venues, common domain, customer service, or transport it has been shown what people with disabilities should expect every day of our lives, and not just when the world was watching. Yet for many people with disabilities in NSW the Games has had no material impact on their lives, they live in a continued state of unmet needs and will continue to do so long after the Games are just a memory' (Darcy, 2003, p. 754).

2032 Brisbane Summer Olympic Games

With the growing reluctance of countries to take on the huge financial burden of hosting events like the Olympics (Chappelet, 2021), the IOC took the unprecedented step of concurrently awarding Los Angeles and Paris the 2024 and 2028 Games in 2017. Faced with a dwindling number of potential host cities, the IOC changed its bidding rules and in 2020 Brisbane became the first city selected through the new process.

Hosting a global sporting event such as the Olympics is a massive logistical exercise, and the Brisbane Organising Committee for the 2032 Olympic and Paralympic Games (BNEOCOG) was established early in the planning process through the Brisbane Olympic and Paralympic Games Arrangements Act 2021. These games were won on the premise that they would not 'break the bank' with expensive facilities, staying within budget, and also delivering key legacy goals that include the promise of the first climate positive Games (Forth *et al.*, 2022; Tham, 2023).

However, some recent disagreement within the infrastructure planning process has led the Queensland state government to instigate a review of the master plan and what it says are the 'over the top costs'. These are estimated at $2.7 billion to refurbish the Gabba as the main Olympic stadium, and a new $2.5 billion Brisbane Arena. As of early 2024, there has been a furore related to Brisbane cancelling the proposed new buildings, and instead upgrading smaller facilities, namely Lang Park, for opening and closing ceremonies, and QE 2 for track and field (Lockstone-Binney *et al.*, 2024). Notably, the IOC and the AOC do not support expensive new facilities and welcomed the changes, hoping to avoid the cost and legacy issues of Rio and Athens, and even Montreal (IOC Agenda 2020 + 5). The IOC and nations such as Australia are increasingly cognizant of United Nations Sustainable Development Goals. The Brisbane decision complements the 2032 Games Vision which was noted for being mindful of host community interests (Weaver *et al.*, 2024). This is at a time when the halo effect attributed to the Olympics is countered by a well-documented tendency to exaggerate the benefits and underestimate the costs of holding the Games in the *ex ante* versus the *ex post* studies (Scandizzo & Pierleoni, 2018).

THE FUTURE OF THE OLYMPICS

In many ways, Australia has been a stellar contributor to the Olympic and Paralympic movement. For a country its size it has 'punched above its weight' in winning medals (Weissensteiner, 2023), is ranked in the top 20 countries for its achievements, and in 2032 is on track to host for the third occasion. Additionally,

Australians (e.g., John Coates, Kevin Gosper) have held senior influential IOC leadership positions (Shilbury *et al.*, 2023).

However, as the direct and indirect costs of hosting these mega events, and of sending progressively larger teams of athletes escalate, governments and the general public are questioning what is being spent on elite sport, and its carbon footprint contribution. The challenge for Australia, and indeed other nations, how to manage the tensions associated with delivering on Agenda 2020+5, while contributing to contemporary issues, such as achieving sustainability and climate change goals.

MANAGERIAL IMPLICATIONS

The key implications relate to how to create a sustainable Olympics – financially, environmentally, and responsibly. This could be through considerations of these concerns for a host nation and/or for the Olympic movement more holistically.

POLICY IMPLICATIONS

Policies of event host nations should outline the process of Olympic legacy development, resource-allocation, and key performance indicators, and ensure sufficient funding for transparent outcome evaluation.

RESEARCH IMPLICATIONS

Further research on sport policy development and implementation is needed, in terms of its causality and measurability; for both hosting events, and preparation of athletes to participate in the various Olympic events.

QUIZ QUESTIONS

1. What was the year and location of the first Olympic Games that Australia sent athletes to?
2. Who is Australia's most well-known winter medallist – and why is he famous?
3. What are some notable 'legacies' of the Melbourne and Sydney Games?
4. What are some of the challenges facing the Brisbane Games Organising Committee.

DEBATE QUESTIONS

1. Does hosting the Olympic Games bring a sustainable legacy or expensive extravagance?
2. The Olympic Games have helped position Australia on the world stage.
3. The Olympic Games stimulate grass roots sport participation.

REFERENCES

Australian Olympic Committee Annual Reports, 2010–2023.

Barjolin-Smith, A. (2020). Snowboarding youth culture and the Winter Olympics: Co-evolution in an American-driven show. *International Journal of the History of Sport, 37*(13), 1322–1347.

Baka, R. (2010). Olympic Glory: An Analysis of Australia's Success at the Summer Olympics. *Journal of Olympic History, 18*(3), 6–16.

Baka, R. (2012). Australia at the Olympic Winter Games: A Late Bloomer. *Journal of Olympic History, 29*(3), 38–47.

Baka, R. (2018). Melbourne's status as an Olympic city: Past, present, and future perspectives. *International Journal of the History of Sport, 35*(9), 874–897.

Baka, R. (2024). 2024 is a huge year for the Olympics – and its not just about the Paris Games, *The Conversation*, January 25, 2024.

Chappelet, J.L. (2021). Winter Olympic referendums: Reasons for opposition to the Games. *International Journal of the History of Sport, 38*(13–14), 1369–1384.

Darcy, S. (2003). The politics of disability and access: The Sydney 2000 Games experience. *Disability & Society, 18*(6), 737–757.

Dichter, H.L., & Teetzel, S. (2020). The Winter Olympics: A century of games on ice and snow. *International Journal of the History of Sport, 37*(13), 1215–1235.

Essex, S.J., & De Groot, J. (2016). The winter Olympics: Driving urban change, 1924–2022. In J. Gold & M. Gold (Eds), *Olympic Cities* (pp. 84–109). Routledge.

Foth, M., Kamols, N., Turner, T., Kovachevich, A., & Hearn, G. (2022). Brisbane 2032: The promise of the first climate-positive Olympics for regenerative cities. In R. Roggema (Ed), *Design for Regenerative Cities and Landscapes: Rebalancing Human Impact and Natural Environment* (pp. 227–248). Springer International Publishing.

Lockstone-Binney, L., Mair, J., Holmes, K., & Burton., P. (2024). Recovering after a false start? What's the state of play for Brisbane's 2032 Olympic and Paralympic planning? *The Conversation*, March 21, 2024.

Markula, P. (2017). Twenty-two Olympic Winters: The media and the (non-) making of the Games. In L.A. Wenner & A.C. Billings (Eds), *Sport, Media and Mega-events* (pp. 69–84). Routledge.

Scandizzo, P.L., & Pierleoni, M.R. (2018). Assessing the Olympic Games: The economic impact and beyond. *Journal of Economic Surveys, 32*(3), 649–682.

Shilbury, D., Phillips, P., Karg, A., Rowe, K., & Fujak, H. (2023) The Olympic and Commonwealth Games Movements. In D. Shilbury, P. Phillips, A. Karg, K. Rowe, & H. Fujak (Eds), *Sport Management in Australia* (pp. 44–66). Routledge.

Tham, A. (2023). Getting a head start: The 2032 Olympic Movement through the preferred candidature bid involving Brisbane, Australia. *Sport in Society, 26*(3), 536–552.

Weaver, D., McLennan, C.L., Moyle, B., & Casali, G.L. (2024). Early community recommendations for sustainable mega-events: evidence from the 2032 Brisbane Olympic Games. *Journal of Sustainable Tourism, 32*(2), 364–384.

Weissensteiner, J.R. (2023). The global evolution of talent promotion within Olympic sports: A focus on the national systems and contribution of the former German Democratic Republic, Australia, and the United Kingdom. *Frontiers in Sports and Active Living, 4*, 1124234.

IV EVENT BIDDING AND BUSINESS MODELS

13 LEANER, COST-EFFECTIVE, PRACTICAL

How the 2032 Brisbane Games could revolutionise the Olympics

Kirsten Holmes, Judith Mair, and Leonie Lockstone-Binney

AIM

To examine the changes to Olympic and Paralympic hosting and legacy as a result of the introduction by the International Olympic Committee of the 'New Norm'.

LEARNING OBJECTIVES

1. Comprehend the positive and negative impacts of hosting the Olympic and Paralympic Games for the host city.
2. Understand the International Olympic Committee's 'New Norm' approach.
3. Evaluate the potential changes to Olympic and Paralympic hosting as a result of the introduction of the 'New Norm'.

DOI: 10.4324/9781003490326-18

THEORETICAL FOCUS AND SIGNIFICANCE

The focus of this chapter is the impacts and legacies of hosting the Olympic and Paralympic Games, particularly in light of the IOC's New Norm. This chapter is theoretically significant because it interrogates the impacts and legacies of Olympic hosting in a time of change for the Olympic movement.

PRACTICAL FOCUS AND SIGNIFICANCE

The practical focus of the chapter is to identify some of the ways in which the IOC's New Norm may affect planning for the 2032 Olympic and Paralympic Games in Brisbane, and its legacy. This is significant because successful legacy planning must be conducted well in advance of the staging of the event (ideally during the host city's candidature process). For Brisbane, there is ample time to consider how to plan for and deliver a positive legacy.

ARTICLE

Brisbane, Australia, has been awarded the hosting of the 2032 Summer Olympic and Paralympic Games. This is potentially a great opportunity to showcase Brisbane, Queensland, and Australia to the world. It is also anticipated to accelerate the long-term planning agendas for South-East Queensland (SEQ), one of the fastest growing regions in Australia.

In the past, Olympic Games have resulted in soaring costs and budget overruns, leaving infrastructure largely unused at the end of the 16-day event. For example, the final cost of the Tokyo Olympics was $12.9 billion, 20% more than initial estimates, and with an additional $9.8 billion spent on other Games-related projects (Sankar, 2022). This has led to justified criticism that the Olympics are not the jewel in the crown they were once considered (Flyvbjerg, 2020). Indeed, for many past host cities, the Games have not been a boon, but a drag. The Greeks, for instance, have questioned how their country benefited from hosting the 2004 Summer Olympics, which left Greece in crippling debt and with many venues abandoned and in disrepair (Bloor, 2014; Malkoutzis, 2012).

So, what will make Brisbane 2032 different?

Temporary venues and a more dispersed Games

The International Olympic Committee (IOC) has introduced a new approach to hosting the Games: The 'New Norm' (International Olympic Committee, 2018). The New Norm aims to facilitate a more sustainable Games, with a reduction in the new infrastructure that is required to host the mega-event. This should result in fewer new venues, and a smaller athletes' village. The New Norm also allows for temporary, flexible venues, which can be shared among multiple sports. Athletes will also fly in just for their competitions and leave when they are over. This new approach has resulted in a lower cost, more affordable, bid for Brisbane. Given the excessive costs and budget overruns of previous Olympic Games, the operating cost for the Brisbane Olympic and Paralympic Games is projected to be a modest A$7 billion (US$4.6 billion), significantly less than the final budget for Tokyo (CNBC, 2023). In contrast, the London 2012 Games cost US$15 billion (Flyvbjerg, Budzier & Lunn, 2021) and the Rio 2016 Games cost US$13.2 billion (Reuters, 2017). There is still controversy over whether a refurbished or new stadium offers the best return for Brisbane's investment in the Games (McKenna & Riga, 2024).

Next, the plans for the Brisbane Olympics and Paralympics are strongly aligned with the city's current development plans (KPMG, 2021). In contrast with past Olympic regeneration projects, these Olympics will be the catalyst for accelerating already planned new infrastructure and urban development. This includes bringing forward around $400 million in road network improvements and $23 million in transport upgrades (KPMG, 2021). This approach to urban development reflects the frequently cited 'Barcelona model', whereby the Spanish city used the 1992 Olympics as the catalyst to implement a long-term, city-wide 'event-themed' regeneration blueprint (Smith, 2012). The 'Barcelona model' is frequently used as an exemplar in legacy teaching and research (Holmes *et al.*, 2015).

Finally, the 2032 Games will be the first to distribute Olympic events, athletes' villages and other event infrastructure across the SEQ region. This hub-and-spoke model aims to disperse the benefits of hosting beyond the city of Brisbane, with permanent and temporary venues planned across the SEQ region, including the two main regional zones: Gold Coast and Sunshine Coast (respectively 79 km and 106 km to Brisbane city). A smaller number of venues will be distributed across Redland Bay (40 km), Ipswich (39 km), and the Scenic Rim (96 km). The model also includes three regionally distributed Olympic villages to provide easy access for athletes and officials to these venues (Cassidy, 2021). This regional event distribution is a key part of the event's legacy plans.

A significant challenge for both the Olympic organising committee and governments at all levels (Federal, State, and local) will be delivering on expensive new transport plans. This is a key component of the regional distribution model, linking the event sites and enabling visitors, athletes, and their support crews, and the media to travel quickly between venues. The hub-and-spoke model was proposed to create a 45-minute travel region, radiating out from Brisbane (Council of Mayors SEQ, 2019). Most recent estimates suggest that the completion of a direct rail line to the Sunshine Coast will cost $12 billion, but this will only be partially completed by 2032 (Queensland Government, 2023a). Currently better serviced by rail, upgrades to the Gold Coast-Brisbane line are estimated to cost $5.75 billion (Queensland Government, 2023b).

Long-term social and environmental planning

The environmental and social aspects of hosting the Olympics are at the core of the Brisbane bid. Preliminary research projects an AU$17.61 billion economic and social benefit for Australia overall with AU$8.1 billion for Queensland (KPMG, 2021).

'Social benefits' of mega-events of these type can be measured in several ways (Mair *et al.*, 2023). The prestige of hosting the Games and resulting civic pride should lead to enhanced community spirit amongst locals. The Olympics can also potentially promote health and wellbeing outcomes and behaviours by encouraging increased participation in physical activity (Thomson *et al.*, 2019).

Finally, a much-touted social benefit of hosting mega-events relates to the participation of volunteers needed to support such events., These benefits, for both volunteers themselves and the wider community, are well-documented (Holmes, Davies & Lockstone-Binney, 2018). Volunteer numbers in Australia have been in long-term decline (Davis *et al.*, 2021). The visibility of Olympic volunteering could be a great way to catalyse a new drive to encourage people to volunteer, although there are questions about whether volunteer participation in such mega-events translates to less glamorous forms of community volunteering (Lockstone-Binney, 2012).

Noting that mega-event hosting significantly impacts the environment, the Olympics are often associated with a large carbon footprint. Brisbane's bid document, however, highlights amelioration strategies to reduce waste and pollution. As a result of the 'New Norm', Brisbane's contract for the 2032 Olympics requires the host to deliver a 'climate positive' event, by both minimising emissions and implementing a long-term, net-zero carbon reduction plan for the destination (Heynen & Ambeth, 2023). Such measures will be widespread, and include Queensland's plastic pollution reduction plan (Queensland Government, n.d.) and the expanded use of public transport to reduce traffic congestion and emissions. These efforts need to be weighed against the anticipated carbon footprint of international visitors, athletes, support staff, and media travelling to reach Brisbane as a long-haul destination. It seems likely that the Brisbane 2032 Organising Committee will need to use carbon off-sets to achieve their climate positive Olympics (Heynen & Ambeth, 2023), which queries whether the New Norm is achievable for a long-haul destination.

WHY LEGACY PLANNING MATTERS

Intangible legacy benefits, such as promoting sporting and volunteering participation, requires directed planning and resourcing to be realised. This effort should start right after hosting rights are awarded. This will ensure that legacy planning is not overshadowed by the pressing work of event planning and delivery (Lockstone-Binney *et al.*, 2016). Additionally, this is needed so that legacy work and the associated budget continue long after the Olympics leave town, as Olympic organising committees usually disband shortly after the Games, with the staff moving on to other (often international) events.

Yet host cities have not yet adopted such a strategic legacy model. London 2012, while widely acknowledged as the first Olympic Games of the so-called 'legacy era' still received criticism for leaving its legacy planning to the last minute, limiting its effectiveness. The 2032 Brisbane Games can showcase a new and improved model of Olympic hosting. This 'Brisbane model' could be one that the IOC and future host cities seek to praise and emulate.

MANAGERIAL IMPLICATIONS

The 2032 organising committee have the extended timeline and opportunity to fully adopt the New Norm in delivering a leaner, more cost-effective Games that creates planned and appropriately resourced legacies for the host city.

POLICY IMPLICATIONS

Policymakers should be mindful that legacy generation requires a dedicated governance structure, ongoing funding (in the lead up to and after the Games), and long-term planning, ideally aligned to the existing plans of the host city.

RESEARCH IMPLICATIONS

More research is needed on legacy at all stages, from planning, through to execution and evaluation. This is particularly important in light of the introduction of the New Norm, as this should lead to differences in how legacies are conceptualised and measured in the future.

QUIZ QUESTIONS

1. What are the key principles of the IOC's 'New Norm'?
2. How do these differ from previous IOC approaches?
3. Identify some of the positive and negative economic impacts of hosting an Olympic Games.
4. Identify some of the positive and negative social impacts of hosting an Olympic Games.
5. Identify the factors required for successful legacy generation.

DEBATE QUESTIONS

1. Discuss the impacts of the introduction of the IOC New Norm for Olympic and Paralympic Games candidacy and hosting.
2. Consider whether the Olympics should continue in its current form, weighing up the pros and cons of hosting such a mega event.
3. Debate what an 'ideal' Olympics legacy should look like.
4. Debate the extent to which host cities should focus on event delivery versus legacy generation.
5. Debate the extent to which host cities should focus on creating tangible (event infrastructure, transport) versus intangible legacies (sports participation, volunteering). Is there an ideal mix?

ALIGNMENT TO UNITED NATIONS SUSTAINABLE DEVELOPMENT GOALS

Goal	How
1. No Poverty	
2. Zero Hunger	
3. Good Health and Wellbeing	Sports mega-event legacy plans often seek to promote sports participation leading to improved health.
4. Quality Education	
5. Gender Equality	
6. Clean Water and Sanitation	

Goal	How
7. Affordable and Clean Energy	The New Norm requires future Olympic and Paralympic Games to be climate-positive, using renewable energy.
8. Decent Work and Economic Growth	Mega-events can bring many opportunities for economic growth to a host city. However, often the employment opportunities associated with mega-events are limited, temporary, or low-skill positions.
9. Industry, Innovation, and Infrastructure	Mega-events often create new infrastructure – any new infrastructure creates needs to have a clear post-event use and funding model to ensure its sustainability.
10. Reduced Inequalities	
11. Sustainable Cities and Communities	Mega-events have the potential to transform cities, but this should only happen where it will benefit the local communities and residents in the long term.
12. Responsible Consumption and Production	
13. Climate Action	The New Norm requires future Olympic and Paralympic Games to be climate positive, creating long-term, zero-carbon initiatives for the host city.
14. Life Below Water	
15. Life on Land	
16. Peace, Justice, and Strong Institutions	
17. Partnerships for the Goals	

REFERENCES

Bloor, S. (2014). Abandoned Athens Olympic 2004 venues, 10 years on – in pictures. *The Guardian*. Available here: www.theguardian.com/sport/gallery/2014/aug/13/abandoned-athens-olympic-2004-venues-10-years-on-in-pictures.

Cassidy, T. (2021). Robina 'ideal location' for Brisbane 2032 Olympics athletes' village if designed for future property market. *ABC News*. Available here: www.abc.net.au/news/2021-06-14/brisbane-olympics-village-proposed-for-robina/100211106.

CNBC. (2023). *Australia to spend $5 billion on Brisbane Olympics venues*. Available here: www.cnbc.com/2023/02/17/australia-to-spend-5-billion-on-brisbane-olympics-venues.html#:~:text=An%20aerial%20view%20of%20Brisbane,2032%20Olympics%20will%20be%20held.&text=The%20Australian%20federal%20government%20and,the%202032%20Olympics%20in%20Brisbane.

Council of Mayors SEQ. (2019). *South East Queensland Olympic and Paralympic Games feasibility study*. Available here: https://firebasestorage.googleapis.com/v0/b/council-of-mayors.appspot.com/o/publications%2Fsp4dv2zdezomPjqhx WEm?alt=media&token=aade24fd-27fc-43be-9f79-0b472d44000b.

Davis, A., Holmes, K., & Lockstone-Binney, L. (2021). Loss of two-thirds of volunteers delivers another COVID blow to communities. *The Conversation*. Available here: https://theconversation.com/loss-of-two-thirds-of-volunteers-delivers-another-covid-blow-to-communities-159327.

Flyvbjerg, B. (2020). *Time to scrap the Olympics?* University of Oxford. Available here: www.sbs.ox.ac.uk/oxford-answers/time-scrap-olympics.

Flyvbjerg, B., Budzier, A., & Lunn, D. (2021). Regression to the tail: Why the Olympics blow up. *Environment and Planning A, 53*(2). https://doi.org/10.1177/0308518X20958724.

Heynen, A., & Ambeth, P. (2023). Sustainable legacies of a climate positive Olympic Games: An assessment of carbon off-sets and renewable energy for Brisbane 2032. *Sustainability, 15*(2), 1207.

Holmes, K., Davies, A., & Lockstone-Binney, L. (2018). *The social and economic sustainability of WA's volunteer workforce*. BCEC: Perth. Available here: https://bcec.edu.au/publications/the-social-and-economic-sustainability-of-was-rural-volunteer-workforce/.

Holmes, K., Hughes, M., Mair, J., & Carlsen, J. (2015). *Events and sustainability*. London: Routledge.

International Olympic Committee. (2018). *The New Norm: It's a Games changer*. Available here: https://olympics.com/ioc/news/the-new-norm-it-s-a-games-changer.

KPMG. (2021). *Brisbane 2032 Olympic and Paralympic Games preliminary economic, social and environmental analysis summary report*. Available here: https://stillmed.olympics.com/media/Documents/International-Olympic-Committee/Commissions/Future-host-commission/The-Games-of-The-Olympiad/2032-Games-Economic-Analysis-Summary-Report.pdf?_ga=2.137907831.672462490.1623341765-1084266659.1621838810.

Lockstone-Binney, L. (2012). Volunteering at The Olympics is a thrill, but will it last? The Conversation. Available at: https://theconversation.com/volunteering-at-the-olympics-is-a-thrill-but-will-it-last-8335.

Lockstone-Binney, L., Holmes, K., Shipway, R., & Smith, K.A. (2016). Evaluating the volunteering infrastructure legacy of the Olympic Games: Sydney 2000 and London 2012. Lausanne: International Olympic Committee. Available here: https://library.olympics.com/Default/doc/SYRACUSE/165803/evaluating-the-volunteering-infrastructure-legacy-of-the-olympic-games-sydney-2000-and-london-2012-l?_lg=fr-FR

Mair, J., Chien, P.M., Kelly, S.J., & Derrington, S. (2023). Social impacts of mega-events: A systematic narrative review and research agenda. *Journal of Sustainable Tourism*, *31*(2), 538–560. https://doi.org/10.1080/09669582.2020.1870989

Malkoutzis, N. (2012). How the 2004 Olympics triggered Greece's decline. *Bloomberg*. Available here: www.bloomberg.com/news/articles/2012-08-02/how-the-2004-olympics-triggered-greeces-decline

McKenna, K., & Riga, R. (2024). Queensland Government rejects Victoria Park Olympic stadium proposal and will instead upgrade Lang Park. *ABC News*. Available: www.abc.net.au/news/2024-03-18/graham-quirk-olympic-stadium-review-gabba-2032-games/103599506

Queensland Government. (n.d.). Tackling plastic waste: Queensland's plastic pollution reduction plan. Available here: www.qld.gov.au/__data/assets/pdf_file/0022/113368/plastic-pollution-reduction-plan.pdf

Queensland Government. (2023a). *Direct Sunshine Coast rail line business case summary released*. Available here: https://statements.qld.gov.au/statements/99856#:~:text=Stage%201%20works%20are%20expected,for%20their%20review%20and%20assessment.

Queensland Government. (2023b). *Logan and Gold Coast faster rail*. Available here: www.tmr.qld.gov.au/projects/programs/logan-and-gold-coast-faster-rail

Reuters. (2017). *Rio 2016 price tag rises to $13.2 billion*. Available here: www.reuters.com/article/us-olympics-brazil-cost-idUSKBN19539C/

Sankar, V. (2022). Hosting Tokyo 2020 cost $12.9 billion, 20 per cent more than initial calculations. *Inside the Games*. Available here: www.insidethegames.biz/articles/1131922/tokyo-costs

Smith, A. (2012). *Events and urban regeneration: The strategic use of events to revitalise cities*. London: Routledge.

Thomson, A., Cuskelly, G., Toohey, K., Kennelly, M., Burton, P., & Fredline, L. (2019). A sport event legacy: A systematic quantitative review of literature. *Sport Management Review*, *22*(3), 295–321.

14 CRISIS OR TRANSITION

Understanding the wave of Australian music festival cancellations

Sam Whiting and Ben Green

AIM

The aim of this chapter is to discuss the multiple factors afflicting the Australian music festival market, explain their various causes, and provide recommendations towards addressing the current crisis in the sector.

LEARNING OBJECTIVES

1. Explain how issues relevant to supply and demand are adding to the current series of cancellations of long-standing and established Australian music festivals.
2. Discuss how changing consumption habits and audience behaviors, mediated by algorithmically driven recommendation systems and new technologies of taste, may be exacerbating these issues further.
3. Provide recommendations to industry, policymakers, and government as to how to address the current crisis and support the Australian festival sector.

DOI: 10.4324/9781003490326-19

THEORETICAL FOCUS AND SIGNIFICANCE

The theoretical focus of this chapter is a political economy approach to the live music sector within the specific context of the Australian festival market. It will discuss how factors of supply and demand relevant to Australian festivals are being affected by national and transnational economic fluctuations, how uncertainty has crept into the Australian events space following the COVID-19 pandemic; affecting demand, and how changing audience behaviors and music consumption habits mediated by new technologies are reducing the popularity of multi-genre, multi-stage outdoor music festivals, all of which are contributing to a crisis in the sector. This chapter is significant as the Australian festival market is experiencing an unprecedented series of compounding crises and the cancellation of long-standing annual events. Understanding how these crises are intersecting and reinforcing each other, their underlying cause, and potential solutions is integral to the wellbeing of the sector if it is to recover.

PRACTICAL FOCUS AND SIGNIFICANCE

So severe is this crisis that the Australian federal government have just announced a parliamentary inquiry into the live music sector, with findings and insights from this chapter to be provided to this inquiry as a parliamentary submission. This chapter will therefore inform policy, and *vice versa*.

ARTICLE

Introduction

The Australian music festival market has faced a significant crisis in the years following the COVID-19 pandemic. As a result of compounding issues, multiple longstanding music festivals announced cancellations throughout 2023 and 2024. This chapter will unpack the cause and effect of these cancellations and consider the future of the Australian music festival market.

Context: Signs of crisis

Throughout the early months of 2024, a series of Australian music festival promoters cancelled their upcoming events. The highest-profile cancellations were Groovin' the Moo (GTM), a nationally touring festival with six regional locations, and the 22nd annual edition of Splendour in the Grass (SITG), Australia's self-proclaimed 'biggest' music festival with capacity for 50,000 patrons in north coast New South Wales. Both events were cancelled within their first eight days of sales. These followed smaller festival cancellations across several states, including 5,000-capacity Coastal Jam festival (Mornington Peninsula, Victoria) only three days before the event, and two-day, 50,000-capacity South Australian festival Vintage Vibes, less than three weeks out.

Promoters and commentators blamed economic pressures, citing low sales during a 'cost of living crisis' (Mascarenas, 2024; Newstead, 2024; Taylor, 2024). The decisive question of financial viability is the result of a range of issues facing Australian music festivals. In the following sections, we address five major challenges for festivals in Australia, with relevance internationally.

Current challenges

1. Higher overheads

Research by national arts body Creative Australia (2024) found the most significant concern of festival organisers to be rising operational costs, with 35% of festivals reporting a deficit in 2022–23. The director of the Australian Festival Association observed that costs are 'up 30 to 40 per cent across the board' (Grounds & Medhora, 2024), including the cost of international performers, compounded by a weak Australian dollar and increased travel expenses. Such factors exacerbate the perennial issue of competition to secure a compelling lineup. Currency fluctuations, travel costs, and crowded markets are issues for festival lineups internationally.

Another increased overhead for live events in Australia has been the cost of public liability insurance. Following the COVID-19 pandemic, rapidly increasing public liability insurance costs, for both venues and festivals alike (Opray, 2024), have substantially affected the viability of live music events and venues. This problem began with the COVID pandemic, but extreme weather exacerbated by climate change has compounded the cost of insurance, affecting the viability of outdoor music festivals.

2. Extreme weather

In March 2024, a heatwave over south-east Australia saw festivals cancelled, and in one case evacuated (Pitch Music & Arts), adding to the sense of accumulating crises. Extreme weather is a growing threat to Australian festivals, with more than 40 events cancelled between 2013 and 2023 due to heat, fires, rain, and floods, including more than 20 in 2022 alone (Green & Strong, 2023). That year, SITG's return to the festival circuit (after two years lost to COVID-19) faced heavy rain, causing the cancellation of the first day's performances, flooded grounds, and traffic chaos, prompting a $100,000 penalty (White & Herbert, 2022).

Climate change means that Australia will experience more frequent and severe weather events, including more extreme heat and concentrated rainfall, yet the festival sector and governments have been slow to respond (Green & Strong, 2023). Both the risks of inaction and the costs of adapting are challenges for promoters and further contribute to consumer uncertainty.

3. Slower sales

While event attendance remains a priority expense for many Australians, there is a significant trend towards delayed 'commitment-to-buy', with a third of consumers buying their tickets later (Bolster & Tixel, 2023). This conflicts with promoters' reliance on strong opening sales, explaining the cancellations of GTM and SITG only days after going on sale. Conventional industry wisdom asserts that an event won't recover from a failed or delayed ticket launch, and the material reality is that capital is needed for early outlays, with costs and risks accumulating as an event approaches. Eventgoers desire for flexibility is informed by the post-COVID attitude that 'anything could happen' (ibid), in conjunction with the difficulties that young people now face in synchronising leisure time with friends (Woodman, 2021). Late commitment-to-buy is also further enabled by the rise of second-hand ticket platforms like Tixel and Viagogo, which offer last-minute and, in some cases, cheaper tickets.

4. Youth avoidance

Young people are a core audience for music festivals. Arts participation surveys confirm that Australians aged 15–34 are most likely to attend live events and festivals, with attendance decreasing by age (Creative Australia, 2023). However, industry observers have noted a drop in youth attendance, especially at the younger end. Victorian research found that people aged 16–18 were the least likely among under-35s to have attended a festival in the past year, with figures around 20% below historical expectations (Music Victoria, 2024). Patrons in their mid-to-late 20s have overtaken 18–24 year-olds as the dominant ticket purchasers (Creative Australia, 2024). This is a concern for contemporary music festivals that target younger markets.

A significant factor is the contemporary impact of the 'cost-of-living crisis' on young people. The 2022–24 financial period saw considerable inflation within the Australian economy, and financial reasons are the most reported barrier to attendance at cultural events, with this having the most pronounced impact on young people, affecting a majority of under-35s (Patternmakers, 2023).

5. Changing tastes

While large festivals with diverse, multi-genre lineups – such as Falls Festival and Groovin' the Moo – are clearly struggling, more targeted festivals and major artist tours are performing well. These include hard rock and metal festivals such as Knotfest and Good Things, and recent stadium tours by Blink-182, Pink, and, of course, Taylor Swift. This might be related to the increasing siloing and consolidation of music taste within niches, encouraged by the digitalisation of media via highly curated streaming platforms and algorithmically driven recommendation systems.

The struggles of festivals historically backed by national youth broadcaster Triple J may also reveal the station's loosening grip on relevance, and its inability to appeal to a broad audience, in an increasingly curated media environment dominated by digital platforms which feed consumers what algorithms have already discerned they want to hear. That these 'variety' music festivals – which usually host a diversity of styles and genres across their programming – have seen the greatest increase in cancellations may reflect changing consumption habits amongst music audiences generally.

Where to go from here

Music festivals are one of the main ways that Australians engage with the arts, and they provide significant social and economic benefits (Creative Australia, 2024). Festivals have become a focal point for broader societal challenges, from economic to environmental crises. These challenges must be confronted to develop and sustain a vibrant, diverse, and accessible festival sector. For Australia's festival landscape to survive, it will require new ways of navigating uncertainty – such as financial buffers, government-backed insurance schemes, tariffs on major international tours, big ticket levies, and climate action. In March 2024, the Australian federal government launched a parliamentary inquiry into the live music industry. Recommendations from this inquiry will be integral to understanding the problems and potential solutions available to the sector.

MANAGERIAL IMPLICATIONS

Festival promoters should consider the highly curated and personalised way in which music consumers increasingly discover new music via digitally mediated, algorithmically driven recommendation systems, and adjust their programming to suit these new consumption habits, so that festival programming reflects emerging taste profiles.

POLICY IMPLICATIONS

Policymakers should consider legislating caps on insurance premiums, as well as subsidies for specific overhead costs relevant to music festivals, such as production costs that build skills and develop new employment pathways (i.e., audio-visual technicians, sound engineers, environmentally-sound event managers, and producers, etc.)

RESEARCH IMPLICATIONS

More research is needed to uncover the significant crisis facing the Australian music festival sector, methods for mitigating its effects, and sustainable solutions that will return confidence to the sector.

DEBATE QUESTIONS

1. Should state and/or federal governments intervene to support Australian music festivals? Why?
2. Should festival promoters adapt their business models to changing consumer/audience behaviours? Why?
3. What are the economic, social and cultural value of music festivals?

QUIZ QUESTIONS

1. What are the leading causes behind the cancellation of Australian music festivals?
2. Which Australian music festivals have been cancelled?
3. What policy solutions exist to tackle this crisis?

ALIGNMENT TO UNITED NATIONS SUSTAINABLE DEVELOPMENT GOALS

Goal	How
1. No Poverty	
2. Zero Hunger	
3. Good Health and Wellbeing	Participation in arts and cultural events contributes to overall health and wellbeing.
4. Quality Education	
5. Gender Equality	
6. Clean Water and Sanitation	
7. Affordable and Clean Energy	
8. Decent Work and Economic Growth	Public subsidy and intervention from government is needed to ensure work in the events sector is equitable and decent. Such intervention will also bolster certainty and promote economic growth.
9. Industry, Innovation, and Infrastructure	As the festival market continues to face disruption, new solutions are needed for new and old problems.
10. Reduced Inequalities	
11. Sustainable Cities and Communities	
12. Responsible Consumption and Production	A better understanding of how to make music festivals more environmentally sustainable is integral to their prosperity.
13. Climate Action	
14. Life Below Water	
15. Life on Land	
16. Peace, Justice, and Strong Institutions	
17. Partnerships for the Goals	

REFERENCES

Bolster & Tixel (2023). *All Options Open 2022: Ticketing State of Play* (report). https://tixel.com/blog/ticketing-state-of-play

Creative Australia (2023). *Creating Value: Results of the National Arts Participation Survey* (report). https://creative.gov.au/advocacy-and-research/creating-value/

Creative Australia (2024). *Soundcheck: Insights into Australia's Music Festival Sector* (report). https://creative.gov.au/advocacy-and-research/soundcheck-insights-into-australias-music-festival-sector/

Green, B. & Strong, C. (2023). 'What if it rains? What if there are bushfires?': Extreme weather, climate change and music festivals in Australia. *Media International Australia* (OnlineFirst), https://doi.org/10.1177/1329878X231184913

Grounds, E. & Medhora, S. (2024). Splendour in the Grass is the latest festival to call it quits for 2024, sparking concern about the future of the live music industry. *ABC News*, 27 March. www.abc.net.au/news/2024-03-27/splendour-in-the-grass-cancelled-triple-j-hack-music-festivals/103641604

Mascarenas, C. (2024). 'Ruin everything': Coastal Jam Festival scrapped days before it was to start. *News.com.au*, 10 January. www.news.com.au/entertainment/music/music-festivals/ruin-everything-coastal-jam-festival-scrapped-days-before-it-was-to-start/news-story/266f8eb315aa9b62544e483583582d3c

Music Victoria (2024). *Perceptions of Live Music: Insights from Young Victorians* (report). www.musicvictoria.com.au/resource/report-perceptions-of-live-music-insights-from-young-victorians/

Newstead, A. (2024). Groovin the Moo cancellation signals 'feast or famine' Australian festival crisis. *ABC News*, 21 February. www.abc.net.au/news/2024-02-21/groovin-the-moo-cancellation-australian-music-festival-crisis/103483890

Opray, M. (2024). Costs killing music festivals. *The Saturday Paper,* 10 April. www.thesaturdaypaper.com.au/post/max-opray/2024/04/10/over-third-australian-music-festivals-are-losing-money

Patternmakers (2023). *City Lights to Red Dirt: Connecting With Audiences Across Australia* (report). Creative Australia. https://creative.gov.au/advocacy-and-research/audience-outlook-monitor/

Taylor, H. (2024). South Australian festival Vintage Vibes with Groove Armada, Rudimental, postponed. *7News*, 11 January. https://7news.com.au/news/south-australian-festival-vintage-vibes-with-groove-armada-rudimental-postponed-c-13184043

White, L. & Herbert, B. (2022). Byron Bay's Splendour in the Grass festival forced to pay $100,000 to schools for traffic chaos. *ABC News*, 20 December. www.abc.net.au/news/2022-12-20/splendour-in-the-grass-fine-festival-traffic-chaos-pay-schools/101793530

Woodman, D. (2021). Making time for the tribes: The work of synchronisation in the making of youth collectivities in the age of digital media. In Schiermer, B. Gook, & V Cuzzocrea (eds) *Youth Collectivities: Cultures and Objects.* Routledge.

15 MEDIA EVENTS 2.0

How social media developments impact event narratives

Katerina Girginova

AIM

The aim of this chapter is to illustrate the concept of media events practically and theoretically, through the example of the Olympic Games (the world's biggest and oldest event). In addition, this chapter discusses how social media developments impact event narratives.

LEARNING OBJECTIVES

1. To become familiar with the concept of media events in practice and in theory.
2. To develop a literacy around the roles of audiences in co-creating media content and event narratives.

DOI: 10.4324/9781003490326-20

THEORETICAL FOCUS AND SIGNIFICANCE

This chapter draws from communication, sociology, and media studies literature to explore the concepts of media events, active audiences, and new media technologies. The theoretical scaffolding presented in this chapter helps readers to understand the important and often under-studied communicative side of events like the Olympic Games.

PRACTICAL FOCUS AND SIGNIFICANCE

The chapter's practical focus is on the world's largest and oldest media event, the Olympic Games, which reaches an unparalleled global audience of 3–4 billion, and a similar number on social media. Nonetheless, lessons from the Olympics may be extrapolated to other global events. The 2024 Olympic Games are just over and there are Olympics (summer/winter) every two years. Furthermore, understanding how 'the media' works is key to engaging effectively and critically with any modern event.

ARTICLE

As I write this chapter, we are 100 days away from the world's oldest and biggest event: The 2024 Paris Olympic and Paralympic Games (see Figure 15.1). The origin of the Games dates back 3,000 years to Ancient Greece, and the modern Olympics regularly draws an unrivalled 3–4 billion broadcast viewers globally; that is about half the world's population (International Olympic Committee, 2024). Given their magnitude, the Olympic Games become a stage for many performances beyond sport, including, most often, politics, and they serve as a rich case study for numerous event-related topics including environmental, financial, and social issues. This chapter, however, makes the case that the modern Olympic Games (or any large-scale contemporary event) would not be possible without the media, and it uses the Olympics to illustrate the popular communication and sociology studies concept of *media events*. Furthermore, given the proliferation of social media platforms and voices around large-scale events, this chapter engages with the question of *who* exactly constitutes 'the media', and *how* a proliferation of voices impacts the overall event narrative?

According to one official definition from the International Olympic Committee (IOC), success is measured by media audience engagement (International Olympic Committee, 2016). The more of it, the better. This helps to explain why the Rio Organizing Committee for the 2016 Olympic and Paralympic Games declared that Games Time would begin after the inauguration of the Main Press

Figure 15.1
Paris Olympics. Photo Credit: Nicolas Michaud 2017, Flickr, Creative Commons.

Center – even though actual sporting competition would not start until a month later (Rio Strategic Communication Plan, 2012).

This explicit focus on mediation fits with early articulations of the media event concept as an extraordinary happening organized with and for the media (which, at the time this concept was initially articulated, largely meant television). The concept bridged between ideas from anthropology, sociology, linguistics, and mass media to contrast media events with regular media consumption (Dayan & Katz, 1992). Importantly, media events, which included royal weddings and the Olympics, were described as unifying experiences for audiences, whose role was to be relatively passive viewers. Yet, this understanding has evolved in practice and is evolving in theory, too.

Take, for example, another notable comment and first for the Olympic movement: The 2016 Games organizers stated that the success of the Olympics would be defined by citizens on social media (Rio Strategic Communication Plan, 2012). Certainly, the growth of social media during the past decade has been staggering: London's 2012 Summer Olympic Games had a following of 4.7 million users across official IOC accounts on Facebook and X (the platform formerly known as Twitter) Almost ten years later, at Tokyo's 2020 Games (which were postponed to 2021 due the global COVID-19 pandemic), there were a reported 3.7 billion user engagements across the official Olympic accounts on TikTok, Instagram, Weibo, Facebook, and X (Olympic Blog, 2021). This engagement figure on social media now mirrors the Olympics' television broadcast reach. However, what is social media's potential impact on the Games beyond the official channels? Can citizen social media content really define their success, and where does this leave media events in theory?

We need to be skeptical about statements that exaggerate the role of social media, as research has shown that any substantial social change rests on elaborate human connections (Gladwell, 2010). Nonetheless, social media can facilitate alternate types of storytelling (Shirky, 2010). For instance, social media served as an important, albeit peripheral, channel for remediating NBC's coverage of the 2014 Sochi Olympic Games (Girginova, 2016). A group of global users rallied around the #NBCFail hashtag to caricature the network's gaffes and, importantly, to analyze and expose the parts of the event that were omitted from NBC's coverage. These included the removal of a Soviet era act from the opening ceremony, and the editing out of Thomas Bach, IOC President's speech, during which he spoke about human rights.

Social media users created their own politicized version of the Olympics, which often read like a critique against NBC's momentously paid broadcast rights to set the official storyline in the US. Since then, #NBCFail has continued to present what is often a counternarrative to mainstream media which, during competition time, tend to focus on medal counts and athletes' stories. While these are not the first instances of a hashtag being used to expose what was not shown on television, they do highlight the potential for active spectatorship to result in alternate, citizen-led storytelling on social media.

Ironically though, these counter-narratives on social media frequently reinforce the central role of broadcasters like NBC, even if through their critique. Furthermore, these alternative narratives compete against a torrent of sponsored media including from the likes of Coca-Cola and now, AirBnB; key players in the Olympics' TOP sponsorship program. According to Graeme Menzies, who was the communication director for the Vancouver Olympics, the 2010 Games were the first and last people's social media Games (Graeme Menzies, Personal Communication, February 18, 2016). Soon thereafter, the IOC began to exert more control over the social media space, partnering with a range of channels like YouTube and Facebook to create official Olympic content. This trend of content institutionalization has continued to evolve and today we see cases like Great Britain's Olympic 'Team GB', who themselves have signed deals with TikTok to train their athletes on creating social media posts.

The IOC also developed explicit sets of guidelines for how athletes and Olympic personnel should use social media. These strict guidelines have been somewhat relaxed for the 2024 Paris Olympics, permitting athletes to post up to two minutes of video content, including from the opening and closing ceremonies, though footage from competitions and the use of AI are strictly banned.

So, where do these complex dynamics leave media events in theory? The public has grown progressively suspicious of grand, uniting narratives like those presented by NBC and the IOC (Rivenburgh, 2002); a breakdown in shared beliefs that some argue showcases the conditions of modernity (Alexander, 2005). At the same time, we see media event audiences, like those for the Olympics, continue to grow. In turn, we can understand media events as temporally and spatially connected hubs or thickenings (Couldry, Hepp & Krotz, 2009) of thematic communication across a plethora of media platforms. Furthermore, 'media events lend themselves to a rich grammar of appropriations', (Dayan, 2009, p. 30), which leaves some room for the likes of citizens and brands on social media to connect to a range of Olympic themes.

Most people who engage with the Paris 2024 Olympics will not be physically present, and will do so via some form of media. Subsequently, despite being harder to capture and measure than 'hard legacy' like urban infrastructure, this soft 'communication legacy' is immensely important for understanding media events today. It also emerges as one of *the* main legacies of such events, with the potential to touch the most people worldwide. In turn, the power of the citizens' social media content lies in its ability to showcase something different from the large media corporations or event sponsors. If it is possible for that to occur (which requires some media literacy, activism, and digging on behalf of audiences), we can still expect a multiplicity of event narratives. Furthermore, as we await the unveiling of the extensive use of AI, spatial media, and biometrics in future Olympic Games, we must now prepare for the next task of understanding the construction media events 3.0.

MANAGERIAL IMPLICATIONS

Managers of events, and event-related organizations should carefully consider the communicative legacy they wish to create, and the ways in which to most effectively and ethically do so.

POLICY IMPLICATIONS

This chapter is not particularly focused on policy, however, I could offer two connected thoughts:

Policymakers are advised to consider what could be done to ensure that there remains a safe space for citizen social media content creation that does not get drowned out by big corporations.

Furthermore, policymakers need to consider how media literacy can be introduced as an important aspect of the public unveiling of future technologies.

RESEARCH IMPLICATIONS

Researchers may wish to address how the core ideas of the Olympic Games or other events get appropriated by users globally and to what avail? Furthermore, what will the future of media events 3.0 look like with the extensive use of AI, spatial computing, and biometrics?

QUIZ QUESTIONS

1. Why are the Olympic Games a media event?
2. How has the theoretical understanding of media events evolved since the concept was initially articulated?
3. Can you give one example of social media serving as a counter-narrative to broadcast media during the Olympic Games and one example of the limitations of social media's counter narratives?

DEBATE QUESTIONS

1. Can there be an event in today's day and age without media?
2. How much agency do audiences have in shaping event narratives and is anyone left out?
3. Given the proliferation of media, devices, and narratives, can we still claim that we are all witnessing the same event?
4. How do you imagine that extensive AI, spatial computing, and biometrics will impact the future of events?

ALIGNMENT TO UNITED NATIONS SUSTAINABLE DEVELOPMENT GOALS

Goal	How
1. No Poverty	
2. Zero Hunger	
3. Good Health and Wellbeing	
4. Quality Education	Potentially, through media literacy.
5. Gender Equality	
6. Clean Water and Sanitation	
7. Affordable and Clean Energy	
8. Decent Work and Economic Growth	
9. Industry, Innovation, and Infrastructure	Potentially, through media literacy.
10. Reduced Inequalities	
11. Sustainable Cities and Communities	
12. Responsible Consumption and Production	
13. Climate Action	
14. Life Below Water	
15. Life on Land	
16. Peace, Justice, and Strong Institutions	
17. Partnerships for the Goals	

REFERENCES

Alexander, J.C. (2005). 'Globalization' as collective representation: the new dream of a cosmopolitan civil sphere. *International Journal of Politics, Culture, and Society*, *19*(1–2), 81–90.

Couldry, N., Hepp, A., & Krotz, F. (Eds.). (2009). *Media events in a global age*. London, UK: Routledge.

Dayan, D. (2009). Disenchantment, derailment, disruption. In N. Couldry, A. Hepp & F. Krotz (Eds.), *Media events in a global age*. London, UK: Routledge.

Dayan, D., & Katz, E. (1992). *Media events: the live broadcasting of history*. Cambridge, MA: Harvard University Press.

Girginova, K. (2016). New media, creativity, and the Olympics: a case study into the use of# NBCFail during the Sochi Winter Games. *Communication & Sport*, *4*(3), 243–260.

Gladwell, M. (September 27, 2010). Small change. *The New Yorker*. www.newyorker.com/magazine/2010/10/04/small-change-malcolm-gladwell

International Olympic Committee (2016). *Marketing Report 2016*. IOC. https://stillmed.olympics.com/media/Document%20Library/OlympicOrg/Games/Summer-Games/Games-Rio-2016-Olympic-Games/Media-Guide-for-Rio-2016/IOC-Marketing-Report-Rio-2016.pdf

International Olympic Committee (2024, February). *Olympic Marketing Fact File*. IOC. https://stillmed.olympics.com/media/Documents/International-Olympic-Committee/IOC-Marketing-And-Broadcasting/IOC-Marketing-Fact-File.pdf

Olympic Blog (2021, July 31). *IOC.com*. Retrieved May 1, 2024, from https://urldefense.com/v3/__https://olympics.com/ioc/news/more-fans-than-ever-connected-to-the-olympic-games__;!!IBzWLUs!XymcOOEQ6_qdS0y4siiIPYOmq_FCsbm__kpf-8zBNknp92EvMT3Sc8FHR8VZ-NPrIDrTdkdniONqgY6f0x8WvsCST-05y-PwMsK2FJI$

Rio Strategic Communication Plan (2012, May). *Organizing committee for the Olympic and Paralympic Games (ROCOG)*. Retrieved May 11, 2014, from http://doc.rero.ch/record/255030

Rivenburgh, N.K. (2002). The Olympic Games: twenty-first century challenges as a global media event. *Sport in Society*, 5(3), 32–50.

Shirky, C. (December 20, 2010). The political power of social media. *Foreign Affairs*. www.foreignaffairs.com/political-power-social-media

16 AUSTRALIAN MUSIC FESTIVALS

Is the current crisis a perfect storm or passing shower?

John Weldon

AIM

The aim of this chapter is to highlight the factors impacting negatively on the Australian music festival industry, and the uncertainty this is causing.

LEARNING OBJECTIVES

1. Articulate the factors currently impacting negatively on the Australian music festival industry.
2. Discuss the ways in which these factors interconnect and compound to create a crisis.
3. Appreciate the difficulty involved in looking for solutions to an evolving and unstable set of interrelated problems.

DOI: 10.4324/9781003490326-21

THEORETICAL FOCUS AND SIGNIFICANCE

Theoretically, this chapter seeks to understand that, like many other contemporary industries, the Australian music festival sector is, and will continue to be, impacted by a combination of factors for which there is no easy or immediate solution. This leaves the industry on a knife edge: Try to wait out the storm, or adapt radically to what may or may not be a new normal? Try to understand that the factors impacting Australian music festivals, particularly those associated with climate change, are global issues that the industry as a world-wide whole must confront, if large outdoor festivals and events are to continue to remain viable.

PRACTICAL FOCUS AND SIGNIFICANCE

Practically, this chapter seeks to highlight the urgency of the situation confronting the Australian music festival industry, and the difficulty inherent in trying to understand and address these. The problems facing the Australian music festival industry may prove fatal to existing business and operational models if they are not addressed as a priority by relevant government and industry bodies.

ARTICLE

A decade ago, concerns were raised that the Australian festival scene was over-saturated (Jenke, 2024; Potter, 2024; Weldon, 2015). And indeed, there was a seeming readjustment, around that time, with major music festivals such as Homebake, Soundwave, Stereosonic, and perhaps most notably the Big Day Out (Jenke, 2024) ceasing to operate by 2016, for various reasons tied to the 'uncertainty … inherent in the music business' (Whiting & Green, 2024).

In early 2024, the sudden cancellation of long-running music festival, Splendour in the Grass (Fry, 2024; Potter, 2024; Quinn, 2024a; Whiting & Green, 2024) due to 'unexpected events' (Geraets & Galvin, 2024), and on the back of a 30% decline in ticket sales in 2023 (Herbert & Farrow-Smith, 2023), sent 'shockwaves through the Australian music industry' (Quinn, 2024a). The cancellation of Groovin the Moo, just a month prior and the cancellations of Pandemonium, Dark Mofo, and The Sunshine Coast Music Festival soon after, meant that upwards of 20 Australian music festivals had been cancelled or postponed since 2020. These shockwaves generated national media coverage, drawing attention to the crisis the Australian festival industry in general, and music festivals in particular, currently finds itself in (Green & Strong, 2023; Manibog, 2024; Pitt, 2024; Quinn, 2024a).

This chapter will explore this moment of crisis for the industry and the conundrum that confronts it: The need for immediate answers to issues, problems, and 'unexpected events' (Geraets & Galvin, 2024) that may take years to investigate, let alone be understood or addressed.

Three main factors, among a host of others, emerged in media discussion of this crisis: The lingering effects of COVID-19 on ticket buying behavior, and the place of music festivals in the cultural landscape of young Australians, in particular; cost of living pressures and rising costs for festival promoters and attendees, and climate change and its effect on outdoor festivals in remote places.

The cancellation of more than 20 festivals in recent years is largely attributed to a combination of extreme weather and rolling COVID-19-shutdowns (Quinn, 2024a). This had an understandably devasting effect on the industry at the time, and has affected festival attendance in ways perhaps unexpected since.

As a consequence of these ongoing cancellations, festival goers became wary of purchasing tickets to events that might not go ahead. Ticket buying patterns changed; people became more inclined to wait until the last minute to commit. This continues to have major viability impacts on an industry that needs to 'shift at least half of its tickets within the first 24 hours' to cover risk (Quinn, 2024a).

This change in buying patterns is most clearly seen in 18–24-year-olds. This has traditionally been the biggest ticket buying group, but there has been a massive decline in their doing so since 2020 (Bolster & Tixel, 2023; Creative Australia, 2024; Quinn, 2024b). Some researchers suggest this change is attributed to their having missed out on attending festivals during COVID-19-shutdowns, meaning they did not grow up with music festivals as either a rite of passage and/or a part of their cultural landscape (Green & Bennett, 2020; Whiting & Green, 2024). The pipeline effect of this may be felt for years to come, and it remains to be seen whether the next generation of 18–24-year-olds will revert to pre-COVID-19 ways of attending and buying, or whether this is a new state for that age-group.

Cost of living pressures compound this change in buying behavior (Bolster & Tixel, 2023; Creative Australia, 2024; Geraets & Galvin, 2024). Australia has experienced high inflation, interest rates, and rental costs for a number of years, and this has had an impact on the willingness of people to spend money on festivals. Added to this, more than half of Australia's 535 music festivals take place in rural or remote places, meaning that attendees must factor in accommodation, travel, and food and beverage costs on top of ticket prices, thereby increasing their level of investment in what is proving to be an increasingly risky purchase for buyers (Creative Australia, 2024).

Climate change plays a massive role in the viability or otherwise of festivals held in rural or remote Australian locations. This has long been a point of discussion for the industry (Arthurs, 2013), especially in more recent times, due to the significant number of festivals cancelled due to extreme weather events since 2020 (Geraets, 2024: Green & Strong, 2023; Strong & Green, 2023). However, the Australian Government seems to be dragging its feet in this regard; the effects of climate change remain unmentioned in *REVIVE*, the national Cultural Policy for the period 2023–2028 (Australian Government, 2023). Even if there is no further increase in extreme weather events, this kind of climate volatility makes the staging of events in remote or rural areas, where emergency access and egress may be an issue, and limited Wi-Fi, making communication to and with attendees even riskier, more complicated, and costly.

The volatility of the Australian weather, in the age of climate change, leads to increased costs for festival promoters too, in terms of insurance, health and safety, and policing costs. These in turn lead to increased ticket prices, and a reduced purse when it comes to paying for overseas acts. This situation is made even worse in light of the ongoing weakness of the Australian dollar.

This crisis is ongoing, amorphic, and evolving; there are no swift or easy solutions. It is compounded by other issues such as audience fragmentation, complex and inconsistent regulatory provisions across the nation, and the consolidation of the festival industry into the ownership of a few, mainly overseas-based players, such as Live Nation, AEG Worldwide, and TEG. Industry bodies and concerned politicians are calling for government intervention and support (Geraets & Galvin, 2024; Manibog, 2024), but the answer will not lie in simply throwing tax-payer money at this problem.

It may be the case that buying patterns will return to normal as COVID-19 becomes a memory and cost of living pressures eventually ease, but this is not guaranteed. Regardless, it is likely that some revision of the Australian music festival business model will be needed. Is it still viable to stage large festivals in remote locations given the increasing frequency of extreme weather events in Australia? Does the industry need to consider making festivals smaller, bringing them closer to major cities, and/or holding them indoors? Is it possible to make ticket buying less risky for attendees through buy-now-pay-later or other such schemes, which limit their exposure to loss?

The biggest question is: Is this crisis the new normal for the Australian music festival industry, or is it just a perfect storm of factors, some of which will dissipate over time? The industry needs answers to this question now, but may not get them for years to come. Therein lies the conundrum.

MANAGERIAL IMPLICATIONS

The managerial implications are business model related. Are current strategic and operational approaches to the staging of outdoor music festivals in Australia still viable?

POLICY IMPLICATIONS

The policy implications are complicated. Yes, governments and regulators need to support the industry, but throwing money at a business model that may no longer be viable is not the answer. Research into short-, medium-, and long-term approaches to the staging of music festivals must take place before significant investment of tax-payer monies are made.

RESEARCH IMPLICATIONS

The research implications are broad and compelling. Is the new normal for Australian music festivals a state of increasing uncertainty and risk? How do we effectively research a set of circumstances that are interwoven and evolving?

QUIZ QUESTIONS

1. What are the key factors impacting negatively on the Australian music festival scene?
2. Does the Australian government include a focus on climate change in its cultural policy?
3. What ongoing effects have COVID-19-shutdowns had on the ticket buying behavior of 18–24-year-old Australians?

DEBATE QUESTIONS

1. How might traditional music festival business models be adapted or changed to lessen risk?
2. Could climate change mitigation, e.g., the lessening of festival carbon footprints, have a short-term positive effect on festival sustainability, or is it just a waste of time and resources that could be better spent elsewhere?
3. Are large outdoor festivals doomed in the face of climate change?

4. Will the next generation of 18–24-year-olds get back into festivals, or has COVID-19 erased the cultural place of festivals in the life of young Australians forever?
5. Who should bear the biggest level of financial risk in regard to festivals being cancelled: Promoters, artists, or festival attendees?

ALIGNMENT TO UNITED NATIONS SUSTAINABLE DEVELOPMENT GOALS

Goal	How
1. No Poverty	
2. Zero Hunger	
3. Good Health and Wellbeing	
4. Quality Education	
5. Gender Equality	
6. Clean Water and Sanitation	
7. Affordable and Clean Energy	
8. Decent Work and Economic Growth	How does the Australian music festival industry maintain an equitable, and sustainable workplace in the face of ongoing instability and increasing financial risk?
9. Industry, Innovation, and Infrastructure	
10. Reduced Inequalities	
11. Sustainable Cities and Communities	Music festivals play important cultural and economic roles in communities and cities – how does the industry adapt and how should it be supported such that it can continue to contribute?
12. Responsible Consumption and Production	

Goal	How
13. Climate Action	Some music festivals are employing climate change mitigation in their staging, by attempting to reduce their carbon footprint. How can they be supported in this work, by governments and communities? Does increasing climate change and instability mean that current business models for the staging of large outdoor music festivals in remote areas of Australis is unsustainable? If festivals manage to successfully adapt their business models in the face of this, there could be lessons to be learned by the wider, global community.
14. Life Below Water	
15. Life on Land	
16. Peace, Justice, and Strong Institutions	
17. Partnerships for the Goals	

REFERENCES

Arthurs, A. (2013, December 12). Music festivals are in trouble but the shows must go on. *The Conversation.* https://theconversation.com/music-festivals-are-in-trouble-but-the-shows-must-go-on-21035

Australian Government. (2023). *REVIVE: Australia's Cultural Policy for the next five years.* www.arts.gov.au/sites/default/files/documents/national-culturalpolicy-8february2023.pdf

Bolster & Tixel. (2023). *Big Ticket Items: Ticketing State of Play.* https://tixel.com/blog/ticketing-state-of-play

Creative Australia. (2024). *Soundcheck: Insights into Australia's music festival sector.* https://creative.gov.au/advocacy-and-research/soundcheck-insights-into-australias-music-festival-sector/

Fry, C. (2024, March 27). Splendour In The Grass has been cancelled for 2024. *The ABC.* www.abc.net.au/triplej/news/splendour-in-the-grass-2024-cancelled/103639330

Geraets, N. (2024, March 15). Extreme weather is wreaking havoc on Australian music festivals. Can they survive? *The Sydney Morning Herald.* www.smh.com.au/culture/music/extreme-weather-is-wreaking-havoc-on-australian-music-festivals-can-they-survive-20240313-p5fc2d.html

Geraets, N., & Galvin, N. (2024, March 27). Splendour organisers confirm cancellation due to 'unexpected events'. *The Sydney morning Herald.* www.smh.com.au/culture/music/iconic-outdoor-music-festival-splendour-in-the-grass-cancelled-20240327-p5ffng.html

Green, B., & Bennett, A. (2020, September 7). No festivals, no schoolies: young people are missing out on vital rites of passage during COVID. https://theconversation.com/no-festivals-no-schoolies-young-people-are-missing-out-on-vital-rites-of-passage-during-covid-145097

Green, B., & Strong, C. (2023). 'What if it rains? What if there are bushfires?' Extreme weather, climate change and music festivals in Australia. *Media International Australia.* 1–17. DOI: 10.1177/1329878X231184913.

Herbert, B., & Farrow-Smith, E. (2023, July 19). Ticket sales down by 30 per cent for Australian mega music festival Splendour in the Grass. *The ABC.* www.abc.net.au/news/2023-07-19/splendour-in-the-grass-ticket-sales-down-by-30-per-cent/102620896

Jenke, T. (2024, February 2). 'The Ultimate Gig': Reflecting on big day out 10 years after the last iteration of the festival. *theMUSIC.* https://themusic.com.au/features/the-ultimate-gig-reflecting-on-big-day-out-10-years-after-the-last-iteration-of-the-festival/xLR61tnY29o/02-02-24

Manibog, R. (2024, March 27). Splendour in the grass cancellation prompts greens senator to call for more music & arts funding. *Pedestrian TV.* www.pedestrian.tv/news/splendour-in-the-grass-senator-sarah-hanson-young-calls-for-funding/

Pitt. (2024, March 22). 'What's going on?': Punters left hanging over controversial rock festival. *The Sydney Morning Herald.* www.smh.com.au/culture/music/what-s-going-on-punters-left-hanging-over-controversial-rock-festival-20240322-p5fehb.html

Potter, B. (2024, March 31). From Splendour to surrender: Why music festivals are out in the cold. *Fry, The Age.* www.theage.com.au/culture/music/from-splendour-to-surrender-why-music-festivals-are-out-in-the-cold-20240328-p5ffxb.html

Quinn, K. (2024a, March 28). Splendour's cancellation will send shockwaves through Australia's music industry. *The Sydney Morning Herald.* www.smh.com.au/culture/music/splendour-s-cancellation-will-send-shockwaves-through-australia-s-music-industry-20240327-p5ffqr.html

Quinn, K. (2024b, April 9). Festivals 'in the thick of a real crisis', says Music Australia chief. *The Age.* www.theage.com.au/culture/music/collapse-in-number-of-young-australians-going-to-festivals-amid-rising-costs-20240409-p5ficr.html

Strong, C., & Green, B. (2023, February 1). Climate change is transforming Australia's cultural life – so why isn't it mentioned in the new national cultural policy? *The Conversation.* https://theconversation.com/climate-change-is-transforming-australias-cultural-life-so-why-isnt-it-mentioned-in-the-new-national-cultural-policy-198881

Weldon, J. (2015, November 24). Crowded house: how to keep festivals relevant in an over-saturated market. *The Conversation.* https://theconversation.com/crowded-house-how-to-keep-festivals-relevant-in-an-oversaturated-market-50760

Whiting, S., & Green, B. (2024, March 27). Why are so many Australian music festivals being cancelled? *The Conversation.* https://theconversation.com/why-are-so-many-australian-music-festivals-being-cancelled-223559

17 ESPORTS AND THE OLYMPIC GAMES

Hopeless marriage or obvious pairing?

Thomas Burelli, Marie Dykukha, and Haoran Liu

AIM

This chapter mainly focuses on the potential inclusion of esports within the Olympic Games, while providing an overview of the challenges and benefits of such a convergence.

LEARNING OBJECTIVES

1. To better understand the modern landscape of esports, which are characterized by a rapid growth in popularity and by their potential to rival traditional sports.
2. To understand some of the various challenges of integrating esports within the Olympic Games.
3. To explore potential opportunities of merging traditional sports with esports

DOI: 10.4324/9781003490326-22

THEORETICAL FOCUS AND SIGNIFICANCE

This chapter briefly explains the different types of esports and compares them to traditional sports, prior to elaborating on how challenging it could be to seamlessly integrate esports into the Olympic games. Esports' popularity is growing, while traditional sports viewership seems to be falling. Therefore, discussing the implications of merging the two disciplines together under the Olympic umbrella provides insights into how the Olympic games might potentially evolve.

PRACTICAL FOCUS AND SIGNIFICANCE

Despite the difficulties which can occur when there is a convergence between traditional sports and esports, this chapter presents multiple examples of Olympic sanctioned competitions which included esports to illustrate the gradual evolution of such an integration. Prior to looking for solutions to the many challenges which can arise from blending esports and the Olympic games, it is crucial to understand how the Olympic Committee integrated esports in the past to come up with the best possible scenario.

ARTICLE

The rise of esports

Esports (Electronic sports) are a recent occurrence that emerged in the 1990s and which has grown rapidly over the last 15 years. Over time, esports became a global phenomenon that now captivates millions of viewers, and whose market has been estimated at more than US$1.38 billion in 2022.[1] So, it comes as no real surprise that esports are now whetting the appetites of various players, such as the International Olympic Committee (IOC), which view esports as an excellent way of connecting with new audiences and rejuvenating their image.

But first, what are we talking about when discussing esports? Are we talking about the virtual practice of traditional sports such as basketball or soccer? Or are we referring to video games in general, such as strategy games (e.g., League of Legends) or first-person shooters (e.g., CS-GO)? Esports can be simply described as video games played in a competitive environment.[2] This practice therefore includes a wide variety of games, i.e., all those that can give rise to confrontations between players. There are, for example, MOBA games (multiplayer online battle arena) such as League of Legends, in which two teams of five players face off against one another. Another example would be first-person shooters such as Valorant, CSGO, Overwatch, and Fortnite. But esports also include the virtual practice of traditional sports such as basketball, hockey, and soccer, with games like the FIFA franchise published by Electronic Art. There is thus a huge variety of disciplines in the field of esports (probably more than the number of sports that are part of the Olympic Games program today), and it, therefore, becomes difficult to determine precisely how many games are played competitively today.[3]

Today, esports have their own national and international competitions, such as the *Worlds*, the annual world championship for League of Legends organized by Riot Games. These competitions tend to attract an ever-growing audience[4] consisting predominantly of individuals between the ages of 16 and 35.[5] In view of the popularity of esports, and the revenues generated in this field, the question of convergence with traditional sports has been increasingly raised, and organizations such as the IOC are showing a growing interest in esports.

Against this backdrop, we might ask to what extent video games and traditional sports could coexist under the same roof, particularly under that of the Olympic Games? And more specifically, what challenges does such integration pose?

Esports and traditional sports: The same battle?

At first glance, one might think that esports and traditional sports are complete opposites. Some have even gone so far as to provocatively assert that esports should not be called *sports*.[6] Indeed, esports are not activities based on the expression of physical qualities and skills in the same way as traditional sports.[7] However, in our opinion, the comparison between traditional sports and esports in terms of physical commitment deployed by athletes is irrelevant for several reasons. In fact, not all sports among those recognized by the IOC require a high level of physical commitment. Shooting is a good example of this. Not to mention the fact that the IOC also recognizes other activities (although they are not included in the official program) which do not require an important physical interaction, such as chess[8] or, more surprisingly, bridge.[9]

Moreover, the practice of esports does in fact involve a certain degree of physical commitment: You need to be well prepared and physically fit to be able to compete for hours on end, while also being able to demonstrate qualities such as strategy and dexterity.[10] Today, both a professional athlete and a professional esports player devote countless hours to training or strategizing, with the aim of mastering their games to perfection. Thus, we can conclude that the gap between these two sectors isn't as wide as it might appear at first sight.

Beyond these debates, for the IOC, there is no doubt that esports are activities worthy of interest. Indeed, the IOC has been gradually integrating esports into its competitive ecosystem for several years now. It is, however, important to emphasize that the IOC's motivations are not only linked to the nature of esports, but also to the commercial prospects they offer.

Convergence has already begun and is set to accelerate

The IOC's interest in esports and their gradual integration into various IOC-organized or IOC-sanctioned competitions is a recent but rich story.[11] Yet, due to differences between the showcased esports, it becomes quite a challenge to determine games to put forth in a particular competition, as these games' content must be carefully assessed to ensure their compatibility with Olympic values. Besides choosing a game, the rights to use these video games can make it difficult to seamlessly integrate them into an IOC-sanctioned event.

Esports first entered the scene through the back door, with demonstrations such as the one organized by the International eGames Committee in the British team pavilion at the 2016 Rio Olympics.[12] However, it wasn't until the 2018 Winter Olympics in PyeongChang that the first event to feature the Olympic emblem was organized: The Intel Esports Masters. During this event, players competed against each other within the Starcraft II game,[13] and not within traditional sports simulations. That same year, at the 7th Olympic Summit, the IOC expressed its interest in integrating esports into the Olympic Games, but rather than putting forth the most popular esports, the IOC's event featured virtual versions of the sports included in the Olympic Games program.[14] The IOC reiterated this interest at its summits in 2019 and 2020.[15] Therefore, as a first step towards a harmonious integration, it seems appropriate and desirable for the IOC to include sports simulations in its program, rather than only the most popular competitive video games.

Reassuringly, popular games nonetheless continue to appear in regional competitions officially sanctioned by the IOC, such as at the 2019 Southeast Asian Games. During this competition, athletes competed on six games: Dota II, Starcraft II, Hearthstone, Tekken 7, Arena of Valor, and Mobile Legends: Bang Bang.

The IOC broke new ground in 2021 with the creation of the Olympic Virtual Series. This competition featured simulations of sports included in the Olympic Games program, and did not include popular titles such as League of Legends and Counter Strike, which has led many to criticize the IOC's strategy.[16] The games were chosen on the basis of their compatibility with Olympic values. After all, the IOC has repeatedly stated that violent games are incompatible with Olympic values.[17] It is worth noting that Fortnite made its appearance on the Olympic Virtual Series program in 2023, despite being a shooting game in which the objective is to eliminate all opposing players.

At the 2023 Asian Games in Hangzhou (China), seven esports titles received official medals. These included some very popular games like League of Legends.[18] It's hardly surprising to see a greater openness to the most popular competitive video games in Asian competitions, as these games are extremely popular in these regions.

Finally, at the 141st IOC Session, IOC President Thomas Bach stressed the importance of esports as part of the IOC's strategy to attract a new audience.[19] He also asked the IOC Esports Commission to study the possibility of creating a new category of event: The Olympic Esports Games.[20]

As we can see, the integration of esports into IOC-organized or IOC-sanctioned competitions is already well underway. However, there is still a great deal of hesitation and fluctuation as regards the titles selected. While the most popular competitive video games have made their appearance in IOC-sanctioned regional competitions (particularly in Asia), IOC-organized competitions such as the Olympic Virtual Series are still limited to traditional sports simulations. This can be explained by certain legal issues, in particular the compatibility of video games with the Olympic Charter, and the rights to use games protected by intellectual property rights.

A convergence that poses legal and practical challenges

While the integration of esports into the environment of traditional sports, and in particular within the Olympic Games, is now underway and is set to become even more prevalent, this integration is not without its share of challenges.

Games and disciplines controlled by private entities rather than by federations

The first major obstacle to the integration of esports is access to, and control of, video games that are being considered for inclusion in the Olympic Games program. According to the Olympic Charter, to be recognized by the IOC, a sport must be administered by an international federation.[21]

Unlike traditional sports, which belong to noone, video games are the property of the companies that own the intellectual property rights. As such, these companies have the right to control the ways in which their games are used. In particular, they can control the competitive scene. For example, a company like Riot Games is heavily involved in managing the various competitions and championships organized around the world. Conversely, a company like Nintendo has opposed the organization of a major international competition for its Super Mario SmashBros game.[22] Companies are therefore key players when it comes to managing their games (until the games fall into the public domain several decades from now).

A few federations have emerged in recent years in the field of esports.[23] However, these federations are far from integrating and representing all video games played competitively. Further, none of these federations has yet been recognized by the IOC.[24] It is also possible to anticipate that game publishers will not necessarily be open to allowing one or more international federations to administer their games.[25] In any case, because of their rights over the games, game publishers will always remain key players with whom the IOC will have to negotiate[26] alongside any emerging international federations.

Technical and complex games to master

Unlike many traditional sports, where the rules and basic skills required to play are generally intuitive and accessible to a wide audience, video games that are part of the esports scene can include numerous and complex game mechanics to master, and can involve considerable strategic depth. So, for most esports (especially games that are not simulations of traditional sports) the learning curve for the public to understand and enjoy a competition can be particularly steep. Despite this, just as in traditional sports, there are many high-quality professional commentators in esports who can make the viewing experience easier. The fact remains, however, that the technical nature of certain commentaries can be an obstacle to attracting a new audience.

These games are also subject to regular updates and metagame changes that can have a significant impact not only on athletes, but also on spectators. While there is also a learning curve in traditional sports for spectators, the regular update of games represents an additional barrier to accessibility for spectators and new players interested in esports.

In this respect, chess has been recognized in the IOC sphere for some time, even though its rules and players' strategies are also very complex for neophytes or occasional spectators.

A multitude of games to consider

The abundance of games available in the world of esports also presents a challenge for their integration into the Olympic Games fold. Unlike traditional sports, which are based on a relatively small set of disciplines, esports encompass a multitude of titles from different genres and platforms. Hence, this diversity and quantity of available games make it difficult to select specific games that could be added to the Olympic Games program, as each game has its own community of players, and its own competitive ecosystem.

Additionally, the popularity and lifespan of video games can vary. Some games may disappear from the competitive scene due to mismanagement on the part of publishers, or because of competition from other games.[27] For example, the 2018 Asian Games included six video games as part of the competition, but only two of the six games were retained for the 2022 Asian Games, to which five new games were added. So, from the get-go, the games to be considered for IOC-affiliated competitions have not been stable and perennial. This is not a major problem in itself, as the same applies to certain sports that are represented at certain Olympiads, but which are not included as permanent sports disciplines.[28]

A more serious challenge relates to the content of certain games whose violent content would be incompatible with Olympic values. This is particularly true of first-person shooter games. In 2018, IOC President Thomas Bach declared that 'so called killer games which promote violence or discrimination cannot be brought into accordance with the Olympic values and therefore should not be recognized by the Olympics'.[29] It is therefore highly likely that certain games will find it difficult to integrate into the Olympic program. We're thinking in particular of CS GO. However, the IOC's assessment is questionable, since in a game like League of Legends, despite not being as graphic as first-person shooters, the aim of the game remains to kill your opponent. Not to mention the fact that some of the sports currently on the Olympic program are violent, particularly boxing.[30]

Already a busy schedule for esports

The convergence of esports and traditional sports competitions also raises questions of scheduling and calendar management. Like soccer or hockey, esports have their own regional leagues and regular tournaments organized throughout the year. These tournaments are promotional tools, and sources of revenue (direct or indirect) for game publishers and their partners. These competitions, and their potential overlap with the Olympic Games program, can make it difficult, if not impossible, to attract the best players to take part in competitions organized by the IOC. Nevertheless, this challenge does not appear insurmountable, as there are already programming mechanisms integrated into the organization of the Olympic Games.[31] For example, the League of Legends competition organized in 2023 was held without any major problems, and included the participation of the best players in the world before the World Championships in Korea.

All of this will also involve the IOC having to decide which competitions will include esports. Will they be included in the Winter and Summer Olympic Games, or within dedicated esports competitions as at present? The inclusion of new disciplines in the Summer and Winter Olympics represents a major challenge, given the already busy schedule of these competitions, and the additional infrastructure required to accommodate esports.

CONCLUSION

The inclusion of esports as part of the Olympic Games presents significant opportunities for both the Olympic movement and the esports industry. It would modernize the Olympic Games and make them more relevant to a new generation of spectators and participants, who are already familiar with video games. With the inclusion of esports, the Olympic Games could attract a wider and more diverse audience, reinforcing their status as the world's most important sporting event.

For the esports industry, this inclusion could stimulate investment from new sponsors, and offer new competitive opportunities for professional players and teams.[32] In addition, presenting esports as a globally recognized and respected form of entertainment would have an invaluable effect on destigmatizing video games, and would further contribute to the growth of the industry. Some major video game developers have already begun discussions with the IOC with a view to forging a closer relationship.[33] It is therefore highly likely that esports will be increasingly present in competitions organized or sanctioned by the IOC in the years to come.

As such, the marriage between esports and the Olympic Games already appears to be well underway. This union is an opportunity that could benefit both the IOC and game publishers. As we have seen, this convergence is not without its challenges, but none of them seem insurmountable. Esports at the Olympic Games therefore have a bright future ahead of them. A fine revenge for a practice that has not always received a good press.

MANAGERIAL IMPLICATIONS

Managers, especially those in the field of esports, can assess the gap between the current requirements in esports and in traditional sport events to determine how to reduce it.

POLICY IMPLICATIONS

With this chapter, policymakers are given a map of challenges to consider and to address, in order to ensure a better convergence between esports and traditional sport events.

RESEARCH IMPLICATIONS

This chapter draws a map of the main challenges related to the inclusion of esports as part of the Olympic Games. Each of these challenges is an area of interest for research. The future of esports, and its inclusion into traditional sport events, is also a fast-evolving topic which deserves more attention from researchers.

QUIZ QUESTIONS

1. What are the main challenges of integrating esports into the Olympic Games?
2. What was the criteria used to determine which game would be represented in the Olympic Virtual Series?
3. Name two fundamental differences between traditional sports and esports.
4. Name two similarities between traditional sports and esports.
5. Could the virtual practice of traditional sports be considered as esports?

DEBATE QUESTIONS

1. Will the inclusion of esports in the Olympics dilute the essence of traditional sports, or will it enrich the Games by attracting a new and younger audience?
2. Are there ethical concerns with promoting esports considering issues such as gaming addiction, or the promotion of violent content? How should these concerns be addressed?
3. How important is physical exertion in defining what constitutes a sport? Can mental and strategic skills alone justify the inclusion of esports in the Olympics?
4. What steps should be taken to ensure the health and wellbeing of esports athletes, considering the long hours of practice and the length of a competition?
5. Can the technical complexity of many esports hinder their acceptance by a broader Olympic audience? How can this barrier be overcome?

ALIGNMENT TO UNITED NATIONS SUSTAINABLE DEVELOPMENT GOALS

Goal	How
1. No Poverty	
2. Zero Hunger	
3. Good Health and Wellbeing	Esports can be a competitive activity bringing fulfillment to its participants.
4. Quality Education	
5. Gender Equality	Esports are available to both women and men. Teams can be composed of men and women.
6. Clean Water and Sanitation	
7. Affordable and Clean Energy	
8. Decent Work and Economic Growth	
9. Industry, Innovation, and Infrastructure	
10. Reduced Inequalities	
11. Sustainable Cities and Communities	
12. Responsible Consumption and Production	
13. Climate Action	
14. Life Below Water	
15. Life on Land	
16. Peace, Justice, and Strong Institutions	
17. Partnerships for the Goals	

NOTES

1 Newzoo. 'eSports market revenue worldwide from 2020 to 2025 (in million US dollars)'. Chart. April 19, 2022. Statista. Accessed May 07, 2024. www.statista.com/statistics/490522/global-esports-market-revenue/.
2 Daniel C. Funk, Anthony D. Pizzo, & Bradley J. Baker, 'eSport management: Embracing eSport education and research opportunities', (2018) 21 Sport Management Review, pp. 7–13; Seth E. Jenny, R. Douglas Manning, Margaret C. Keiper, & Tracy W. Olrich, 'Virtual(ly) athletes: Where eSports fit within the definition of "sport"' (2017) 69 Quest, pp. 1–18.
3 Quinn A. Stigers 'Legal and Practical Barriers to the Viability of Traditional Esports Titles as Olympic Medaling Sports' (2021) 32:1 Marquette Sports Law Review 333, pp. 335–336.
4 Statista 'eSports audience size worldwide from 2020 to 2025, by type of viewers', www.statista.com/statistics/490480/global-esports-audience-size-viewer-type/
5 Francesco Alivia 'Opportunities for Brands and Rights Holders from a Growing E-sports Audience' (2021) Infront Sports, www.infront.sport/blog/sports-sponsorship/esports-audience-growth#:~:text=More%20than%20six%20in%20every,female%20audiences%20are%20growing%20too.
6 Jim Parry 'E-sports are not sports' (2019) 13 Sport, Ethics and Philosophy 3, p. 4. Parry does, however, offer an interesting critique of the (lacking) institutionalization of esports.
7 Jim Parry 'E-sports are not sports', p. 4.
8 The World Chess Federation is currently recognized by the IOC: https://olympics.com/ioc/recognised-international-federations.
9 World Bridge Federation 'What is Bridge?', www.worldbridge.org/what-is-bridge/. The World Bridge Federation is currently recognized by the IOC: https://olympics.com/ioc/recognised-international-federations. This card game has been included in IOC sanctioned events such as the Asian Games in 2018: https://olympics.com/en/news/bridge-at-the-2018-asian-games-a-sport-or-not-a-sport.
10 Michael L. Naraine 'Actually, Esports Is Sport: A Response to Parry's (2019) Misguided View' (2021) 2 *Sports Innovation Journal* 33, pp. 39–40.
11 Andy Miah & Alex Fenton, 'Esports in the Olympic and Paralympic Games. The business case for integration' in Dikaia Chatziefstathiou, Borja García, Benoit Séguin, *Routledge Handbook of the Olympic and Paralympic Games*, Routledge International Handbook, 2020, pp. 165–166; Cem Abanazir, 'The Olympic Movement and esports governance', in Anne Tjønndal, (ed), *Social issues in esports*. Routledge, 2020, pp. 149–150.
12 Miah and Fenton, *supra* note 10, p. 160.
13 https://olympics.com/ioc/news/intel-brings-esports-to-pyeongchang-ahead-of-the-olympic-winter-games; Miah, and Fenton, *supra* note 10, p. 160.
14 'The Summit encourages the IFs to explore the potential benefits and applications of the electronic and virtual versions of their sports'. International Olympic Committee. (2018). *Communique of the 7th Olympic Summit*, www.olympic.org/news/communique-of-the-7th-olympic-summit.
15 Abanazir, *supra* note 10, p. 149.
16 Keza MacDonald 'Pushing Buttons: Is the Olympics getting video games all wrong?' (2023), *The Guardian*, www.theguardian.com/games/2023/mar/08/pushing-buttons-olympic-games-esports-competition
17 See the opinion of Thomas Bach cited in Stigers, *supra* note 3, p. 343.
18 Z.K. Goh 'Esports make historic medal debut at 19th Asian Games in Hangzhou' (2023), https://olympics.com/en/news/esports-historic-medal-debut-19th-asian-games-hangzhou-schedule-live / and www.wada-ama.org/en/2023-asian-games-hangzhou

19 International Olympic Committee, Opening Ceremony of the 141st IOC Session, Mumbai, 2023, p. 6
20 International Olympic Committee, p. 7.
21 International Olympic Committee 'What are the conditions required for a sport to be recognised by the IOC?', https://olympics.com/ioc/faq/sports-programme-and-results/what-are-the-conditions-required-for-a-sport-to-be-recognised-by-the-ioc
22 Medium 'Smash World Tour Official Statement' (2022), https://medium.com/@smashworldtour/smash-world-tour-official-statement-f568a3d135c8
23 See, for example, the international Esports Federation: https://iesf.org/; Stigers, *supra* note 3, p. 341.
24 Stigers, *supra* note 3, p. 342
25 Stigers, *supra* note 3, pp. 342–343
26 Stigers, *supra* note 3, p. 344.
27 Stigers, *supra* note 3, p. 346.
28 This is the case of breakdance as part of the 2024 Olympic Games in Paris.
29 Thomas Bach cited in Stigers, supra note 3, p. 343.
30 Joanne Orlando & Keith Parry 'The IOC thinks eSports are too violent for the Olympics, but traditional sports are violent too' (2018), *The Conversation*, https://theconversation.com/the-ioc-thinks-esports-are-too-violent-for-the-olympics-but-traditional-sports-are-violent-too-96346
31 International Olympic Committee 'How are competition schedules changed during the Olympic Games?' (2021), https://olympics.com/ioc/news/how-are-competition-schedules-changed-during-the-olympic-games
32 Challenges could nevertheless arise in this area if the traditional sponsors of eesports are not the same as those of the Olympic Games. Stigers, 'Legal and Practical Barriers to the Viability of Traditional Esports Titles as Olympic Medaling Sports' (2021) 32:1 Marq Sports L Rev 333, p. 345.
33 Dexerto 'Riot in talks with Olympic leadership about League of Legends esports future' (2021), www.dexerto.com/league-of-legends/riot-in-talks-with-olympic-leadership-about-league-of-legends-esports-future-1692722/

REFERENCES

Abanazir, C. 'The Olympic Movement and esports governance', in Tjønndal, A. (ed), *Social issues in esports*. Routledge, 2020, pp. 149–150.

Alivia, F. 'Opportunities for Brands and Rights Holders from a Growing E-sports Audience' (2021), Infront Sports, www.infront.sport/blog/sports-sponsorship/esports-audience-growth#:~:text=More%20than%20six%20in%20every,female%20audiences%20are%20growing%20too

Dexerto 'Riot in talks with Olympic leadership about League of Legends esports future' (2021), www.dexerto.com/league-of-legends/riot-in-talks-with-olympic-leadership-about-league-of-legends-esports-future-1692722/

Encabo, L. 'Bridge at the 2018 Asian Games: A sport, or not a sport?' (2018), https://olympics.com/en/news/bridge-at-the-2018-asian-games-a-sport-or-not-a-sport.

Funk, D.C., Pizzo, A.D. & Baker, B.J. 'eSport management: Embracing eSport education and research opportunities', (2018) 21 *Sport Management Review*, pp. 7–13.

Goh, Z. "Esports make historic medal debut at 19th Asian Games in Hangzhou" (2023), https://olympics.com/en/news/esports-historic-medal-debut-19th-asian-games-hangzhou-schedule-live / and www.wada-ama.org/en/2023-asian-games-hangzhou

International Esports Federation. About us https://iesf.org/

International Olympic Committee. 'Communique of the 7th Olympic Summit' (2018), www.olympic.org/news/communique-of-the-7th-olympic-summit.

International Olympic Committee. 'How are competition schedules changed during the Olympic Games?' (2021), https://olympics.com/ioc/news/how-are-competition-schedules-changed-during-the-olympic-games

International Olympic Committee. 'Intel brings esports to PyeongChang ahead of the Olympic Winter Games' (2017), https://olympics.com/ioc/news/intel-brings-esports-to-pyeongchang-ahead-of-the-olympic-winter-games

International Olympic Committee. 'Opening Ceremony of the 141st IOC Session, Mumbai' (2023), p. 6

International Olympic Committee. 'Recognized Federations', https://olympics.com/ioc/recognised-international-federations

International Olympic Committee. "'What are the conditions required for a sport to be recognised by the IOC?', https://olympics.com/ioc/faq/sports-programme-and-results/what-are-the-conditions-required-for-a-sport-to-be-recognised-by-the-ioc

MacDonald, K. 'Pushing Buttons: Is the Olympics getting video games all wrong?' (2023), www.theguardian.com/games/2023/mar/08/pushing-buttons-olympic-games-esports-competition

Medium 'Smash World Tour Official Statement' (2022), https://medium.com/@smashworldtour/smash-world-tour-official-statement-f568a3d135c8

Miah, A., & Fenton, A. 'Esports in the Olympic and Paralympic Games. The business case for integration' in Chatziefstathiou, D., García, B., & Séguin B. (eds), *Routledge Handbook of the Olympic and Paralympic Games* Routledge International Handbook, 2020, pp. 165–166.

Naraine, M.L. 'Actually, Esports is Sport: A Response to Parry's (2019) Misguided View' (2021) 2 *Sports Innovation Journal* 33, pp. 39–40.

Newzoo. 'eSports market revenue worldwide from 2020 to 2025 (in million U.S. dollars)'. Chart. (April 19, 2022). Statista. www.statista.com/statistics/490522/global-esports-market-revenue/. Accessed May 07, 2024.

Orlando, J., & Parry, K. 'The IOC thinks eSports are too violent for the Olympics, but traditional sports are violent too' (2018), *The Conversation*, https://theconversation.com/the-ioc-thinks-esports-are-too-violent-for-the-olympics-but-traditional-sports-are-violent-too-96346

Parry, J. 'E-sports are not sports' (2019) 13 *Sport, Ethics and Philosophy* 3, p. 4.

Seth, E., Jenny, R., Manning D., Keoper, M.C., & Olrich, T.W. 'Virtual(ly) athletes: Where eSports fit within the definition of "sport"' (2017) 69 *Quest*, pp. 1–18.

Statista. 'eSports audience size worldwide from 2020 to 2025, by type of viewers', www.statista.com/statistics/490480/global-esports-audience-size-viewer-type/

Stigers, Q.A. 'Legal and Practical Barriers to the Viability of Traditional Esports Titles as Olympic Medaling Sports' (2021) 32:1 *Marquette Sports Law Review* 333, p. 345.

Stigers, Q.A. 'Legal and Practical Barriers to the Viability of Traditional Esports Titles as Olympic Medaling Sports' (2021) 32:1 *Marquette Sports Law Review* 333, pp. 335–336.

IOC [Online]. Recognised International Federations. Available: https://olympics.com/ioc/recognised-international-federations

World Bridge Federation 'What is Bridge?' www.worldbridge.org/what-is-bridge/

18 ARE MAJOR SPORTS EVENTS WORTH HOSTING?

A closer look

John Varano

AIM

This chapter delves into the complex dynamics surrounding major sports events, examining why western economies have become more hesitant to bid, the financial implications involved, and contrasting this with the enthusiasm displayed by emerging economies.

LEARNING OBJECTIVES

1. To demonstrate that major sports events incur significant cost overruns due to the problematic nature and flaws of hosting.
2. To illustrate that the allure of hosting major sports events for western economies has faded and is not economically viable.
3. To highlight that emerging economies are eager to host major sports events to transform their country's profile, despite the high costs of hosting.

DOI: 10.4324/9781003490326-23

THEORETICAL FOCUS AND SIGNIFICANCE

To synthesise the empirical evidence and literature currently available to demonstrate the economic, political, and social implications of hosting major sports events for western and emerging economies. To highlight the causality of the economic, political, and social implications of hosting major sports events. To prompt debate and discussion on the consequences of cost overruns, budgetary mismanagement, and optimism bias of risk management during the delivery cycle of a major sports event.

PRACTICAL FOCUS AND SIGNIFICANCE

1. The prevalent cost overruns attributed to facilitating a major sports event, such as the Olympic Games, FIFA World Cup, and the Commonwealth Games.
2. The declining allure of hosting a major sports event due to its significant costs and obligations, particularly for western economies.
3. Major sports events, specifically the Olympic Games and FIFA World Cup, are the largest, most high profiled and expensive megaprojects in the world. The economic, political, and social impacts of these events are immensely significant to the viability of nation-states.
4. There is a historical trend that host cities of major sports events mismanage time, budget, and risk dimensions of hosting the event.

ARTICLE

Introduction

In recent years, the allure of hosting major sports events like the Olympics, FIFA World Cup, and Commonwealth Games has dimmed for many western economies. Once seen as prestigious opportunities to showcase national prowess and stimulate economic growth, these events now prompt careful consideration, due to their hefty financial commitments and associated risks.

Conversely, emerging economies are increasingly eager to seize the chance to host such events, viewing them as catalysts for infrastructural development and international recognition.

This chapter delves into the complex dynamics surrounding major sports events, examining why western economies have become more hesitant to bid, the financial implications involved, and contrasting this with the enthusiasm displayed by emerging economies.

It only took one black swan for Tokyo: COVID-19

Hosting major sports events often requires significant initial public investment in infrastructure. The justification for these expenditures is typically based on expected long-term benefits, such as improved infrastructure, increased tourism, and enhanced global image (McBride & Manno, 2021). The financial commitments for hosting can be enormous, often leading to cost overruns.

Faced with high costs and public scepticism, Japan's management of the Olympics demonstrated the challenges of balancing public health with the economic and reputational benefits of hosting. Initially projected as a showcase of Japan's recovery from the 2011 tsunami and nuclear disaster, the Tokyo Olympics were instead marred by delays and public health concerns due to COVID-19.

The financial outlays ballooned because of health and safety measures and postponements, with the final cost reaching US$13 billion (Wade, 2022). The public opposition was significant, with many questioning the prioritisation of the games over public health. Despite efforts to mitigate risks, including strict health protocols and spectator limitations, the event incurred vast financial losses and logistical hurdles, underscoring the unpredictable nature of hosting major sports events in a volatile global landscape.

Away from the Olympics, Melbourne decided to cancel its 2026 Commonwealth Games in July 2023, after the State Government's inquiry indicated that the expected cost of US$1.7 billion blew out to US$4.5 billion (Associated Press, 2024). Weeks after, Alberta followed and withdrew its bid to host the 2030 Commonwealth Games due to projected cost overruns (*The Guardian*, 2023).

Faded allure as the economics do not add up

With the decline of many western economies bidding for major sports events, both the Olympic Games and FIFA World Cup are no longer attracting the high number of bids that were formerly experienced. The vast overspend incurred by its hosts is proving to be an unappealing disincentive, notwithstanding the prestige it brings.

Both the 2024 and 2028 Summer Olympics were awarded to Paris and Los Angeles to host unanimously as Budapest, Hamburg, and Rome withdrew during the candidature stage. For 2032, Brisbane was the only city to nominate. For 2036, only emerging economies nominated, including Indonesia, Turkey, and India. Given these trends, the International Olympic Committee (IOC) instituted the Olympic Agenda 2020 reforms, where it made concessions, adjusted its competitive process to allow cities greater preparation time, funding, and allowances to provide cost-saving measures and reducing the complexity of the bidding process (IOC, 2020).

Comparatively, FIFA selected Saudi Arabia to host the 2034 World Cup. Both the 2026 and 2030 World Cups see a shift to three host countries joined together to share responsibilities. Previously, developing economies were awarded the last four World Cups (South Africa, Brazil, Russia, and Qatar). The 2018 and 2022 World Cup bids encountered issues of bribery and corruption, which potentially prevented western economies from being successful at the time.

The question remains, does hosting such major sporting events stack up? A study led by the University of Oxford on the Olympics Games observed that in real terms the average cost overrun for all Olympic Games is 172% (see Table 18.1) (Flyvbjerg, Budzier & Lunn, 2021). While it is not unexpected, the high cost overrun for the Olympics is primarily attributed to the fixed deadline set for project completion. Given the immense pressure faced by host organisers, it is common practice for them to throw money into resolving any issues that surface, as shown by the cost overruns of the Olympic Games (Varano, 2017).

The findings of this research confirmed that the 2014 Sochi Winter Games was the most expensive Olympics to date, at US$22 billion. The 1976 Montreal Summer Games illustrated the highest cost overrun at 720%. Further to that, 15 of 19 Olympic Games have cost overruns above 50%. The 1984 Los Angeles Summer Games are the only ones to date that have profited. Table 18.2 highlights that nearly all the Olympic Games from 1960 to 2016 faced significant cost overruns.

TABLE 18.1 THE OLYMPICS COST OVERRUN COMPARED TO OTHER TYPES OF LARGE-SCALE PROJECTS

	Roads	Bridges, Tunnels	Energy	Rail	Dams	IT	Olympics
Cost overrun	20%	34%	36%	45%	90%	107%	172%
Frequency of cost overrun	9 of 10	9 of 10	6 of 10	9 of 10	7 of 10	5 of 10	10 of 10
Schedule overrun	38%	23%	38%	45%	44%	37%	0%
Schedule length, years	5.5	8.0	5.3	7.8	8.2	3.3	7.0

Sources: Flyvbjerg et al., 2002; Ansar et al., 2017; Budzier & Flyvbjerg, 2011; Flyvbjerg, Budzier & Lunn, 2021.

TABLE 18.2 THE COST OVERRUNS FOR THE OLYMPICS IN REAL TERMS AND CALCULATED IN LOCAL CURRENCIES

Games	Country	Type	Cost overrun %
Montreal 1976	Canada	Summer	720
Barcelona 1992	Spain	Summer	266
Atlanta 1996	United States	Summer	151
Sydney 2000	Australia	Summer	90
Athens 2004	Greece	Summer	49
Beijing 2008	China	Summer	2
London 2012	United Kingdom	Summer	76
Rio 2016	Brazil	Summer	352
Grenoble 1968	France	Winter	181
Lake Placid 1980	United States	Winter	324
Sarajevo 1984	Yugoslavia	Winter	118
Calgary 1988	Canada	Winter	65
Albertville 1992	France	Winter	137
Lillehammer 1994	Norway	Winter	277
Nagano 1998	Japan	Winter	56
Salt Lake City 2002	United States	Winter	24
Torino 2006	Italy	Winter	80
Vancouver 2010	Canada	Winter	13
Sochi 2014	Russia	Winter	289

Source: Flyvbjerg, Budzier & Lunn, 2021.

Emerging powers seeing the value instead

In contrast to western economies, emerging economies view hosting major sports events as opportunities for economic growth and global recognition. It can project an image of growth and modernisation, potentially attracting foreign investment and enhancing diplomatic stature.

Countries like Saudi Arabia and Qatar view these events as a platform to transition from oil-based economies to diversified, service-oriented ones. Despite criticisms and challenges, the strategic value aligned with national goals often outweighs the apparent economic costs.

Notwithstanding the financial risks, emerging economies are keen to host these events to boost their international image and stimulate local economic development. These countries may see short-term boosts in employment and tourism, although these benefits are not always sustained long-term. The example of Qatar hosting the 2022 World Cup highlights both the potential for increased global visibility, the challenges related to costs, and international criticism regarding issues such as labour rights.

Conclusion

Major sports events continue to captivate nations worldwide, offering unparalleled opportunities for economic growth, cultural exchange, and global recognition. However, the decision to bid for and host such events entails careful consideration of the financial commitments, risks, and long-term implications involved.

While western economies have become more cautious in their approach, due to mounting concerns over costs and social impacts, emerging economies increasingly view hosting major sports events as strategic investments that can propel national development agendas, and elevate their international standing.

Overall, while hosting major sports events can elevate a country's global profile and spur temporary economic activity, the financial risks and long-term burdens often make it an economically unviable endeavour for many countries. Emerging economies continue to bid for these events in hopes of transforming their global image and catalysing development, albeit with mixed outcomes.

While the allure of hosting major sports events continues, especially among emerging economies aiming for transformative economic and global image changes, the financial realities and socio-political implications often paint a more complex and cautionary tale. The data and case studies suggest a critical need for potential hosts to weigh the long-term economic burdens against the short-lived glamour of hosting such global spectacles.

MANAGERIAL IMPLICATIONS

1. Understand the true risks of hosting major sports events.
2. Comprehend the need for larger budgets and additional cost contingencies that are realistic.

POLICY IMPLICATIONS

1. Consider reducing the long multiyear delivery cycle of major sports events to minimise risks.
2. Utilise semi-permanent host locations to re-use infrastructure facilities.

RESEARCH IMPLICATIONS

1. Greater empirical evidence of cost overruns across various major sports events, such as the FIFA World Cup and Commonwealth Games, is an opportunity for exploration.
2. Researching the political, economic, and social impacts of hosting major sports events in emerging economies post the event.

QUIZ QUESTIONS

1. Why are western economies disinclined to host major sports events?
2. What were the economic and social impacts for Japan hosting the 2020 Summer Olympics?
3. What is the average cost overrun of the Olympics to date?
4. Is there an Olympic Games that generated a profit for its host city?
5. What are the geopolitical benefits for an emerging economy to host a major sports event?

DEBATE QUESTIONS

1. Is it a worthwhile endeavour for a country to host a major sports event?
2. What are some proposed strategies to reduce the costs of hosting a major sports event?
3. Should an international sporting body allow a country with questionable human rights and labour practices to host a major sports event?

ALIGNMENT TO UNITED NATIONS SUSTAINABLE DEVELOPMENT GOALS

Goal	How
1. No Poverty	N/A
2. Zero Hunger	N/A
3. Good Health and Wellbeing	
4. Quality Education	The findings and research presented reveals the spiralling cost overruns associated with hosting major sports events. In addition, it demonstrates the benefits and challenges of major sports events for both western and emerging economies.
5. Gender Equality	N/A
6. Clean Water and Sanitation	N/A
7. Affordable and Clean Energy	N/A
8. Decent Work and Economic Growth	The arguments and empirical evidence put forward highlights the importance of policy areas needed to be improved and refined for infrastructure, economic, political, and social policies.
9. Industry, Innovation, and Infrastructure	As outlined in goal 8.
10. Reduced Inequalities	N/A
11. Sustainable Cities and Communities	As outlined in goal 8.
12. Responsible Consumption and Production	As outlined in goal 8.
13. Climate Action	N/A
14. Life Below Water	N/A
15. Life on Land	N/A
16. Peace, Justice, and Strong Institutions	N/A
17. Partnerships for the Goals	N/A

REFERENCES

Ansar, A., Flyvbjerg, B., Budzier, A., & Lunn, D. (2017). Big is fragile: an attempt at theorizing scale. In Flyvbjerg, B. (Ed.), *The Oxford handbook of megaproject management* (pp. 60–95). Oxford University Press. https://papers.ssrn.com/sol3/papers.cfm?abstract_id=2741198

Associated Press (AP). (2024, March 20). Decision to cancel 2026 Commonwealth Games in Australia based on 'overstated' cost estimates. *Associated Press (AP).* https://apnews.com/article/2026-commonwealth-games-cancellation-melbourne-49139ec906f5cfd06d4a6beaab669ea1

Flyvbjerg, B., & Budzier, A. (2011). Why your IT project may be riskier than you think. *Harvard Business Review,* 89, 23–25. https://hbr.org/2011/09/why-your-it-project-may-be-riskier-than-you-think

Flyvbjerg, B., Budzier, A., & Lunn, D. (2021). Regression to the tail: why the Olympics blow up. *Environment and Planning A: Economy and Space*, 53(2), 233–260. https://doi.org/10.1177/0308518X20958724

Flyvbjerg, B., Holm, M.S. & Buhl, S. (2002). Underestimating costs in public works projects: *error or lie? Journal of the American Planning Association*, 68(3), 279–295. https://doi.org/10.1080/01944360208976273

International Olympics Committee (IOC). (2020). *Olympic agenda 2020 closing report.* https://olympics.com/ioc/olympic-agenda-2020

McBride, J., & Manno, M. (2021, December 14). The economics of hosting the Olympic Games. *Council on Foreign Relations (CFR).* www.cfr.org/backgrounder/economics-hosting-olympic-games

The Guardian. (2023, August 4). Alberta withdraws support for 2030 Commonwealth Games bid due to cost. *The Guardian.* www.theguardian.com/sport/2023/aug/04/commonwealth-games-2030-alberta-cancels-bid-victoria

Varano, J. (2017, August 9). Major sports events: are they worth it? *The Conversation.* https://theconversation.com/major-sports-events-are-they-worth-it-80691

Wade, S. (2022, June 22). Tokyo closes books on delayed Games; $13 billion price tag. *Associated Press (AP).* https://apnews.com/article/winter-olympics-politics-sports-japanese-yen-d4c65d8e702c455ed54fa1e9a667891b

19 THE RUGBY WORLD CUP

A major event in an odd-shaped world

John Harris

AIM

To consider the place of the Rugby World Cup (RWC) as a major sporting event.

LEARNING OBJECTIVES

1. Critically assess the position of the Rugby World Cup in contemporary society.
2. Reflect upon the significant developments in world rugby since the 2015 Rugby World Cup.
3. Consider the growth of rugby union as an international game.

DOI: 10.4324/9781003490326-24

THEORETICAL FOCUS AND SIGNIFICANCE

This overview is informed by work on globalization and labor migration. It also considers some of the power relations shaping international rugby governance. Despite continued attempts to further develop the sport across different parts of the world, there is still a very narrow core group of nations that dominate the sport.

PRACTICAL FOCUS AND SIGNIFICANCE

The practical focus of this chapter is to demonstrate where international rugby union is developing the reach of the Rugby World Cup. The practical significance of the chapter is that it shows some of the challenges and opportunities for development within a particular sport.

ARTICLE

Perhaps the biggest international sporting event of 2015 was the Rugby World Cup (RWC). This event has staked a claim to be the third biggest in the world, although other major events have also made similar claims. Before the tournament started, hosts England were considered as one of the favorites, although based on previous RWC competitions the winners were more likely to come from the southern hemisphere. Australia (1991 and 1999) and South Africa (2007) had claimed the three previous World Cups to have taken place in the northern hemisphere. New Zealand, the reigning champions, were the favorites with most bookmakers.

The evolution of the Rugby World Cup

The Rugby World Cup first took place in 1987, almost 100 years after the start of the modern Olympic Games, and almost 60 years after the inaugural Football World Cup. This was due, in part, to the fact that until 1995 rugby union was nominally an 'amateur' sport, although in some nations the payment of players was part of the game.

The 1987 event, co-hosted by New Zealand and Australia, was a low-key affair in which only invited nations took part. New Zealand claimed the first title, but it took until they hosted a World Cup for a second time in 2011 for the team to be victorious again. Staging the event there was a somewhat contentious decision, as Japan had put in a particularly strong bid to host in 2011. Since then, those governing rugby have taken time to embrace a more international outlook.

Awarding the 2019 finals to Japan was an important step forward, and taking the event to the USA in 2031 provides evidence of world rugby's work to expand the sport beyond a small core group of nations.

The men who took part in the first RWC were a variety of shapes and sizes. They came from varied occupational backgrounds, with players having to seek permission from their employers for time off to play in the tournament. Matches only took place during the day as few stadiums had floodlights, and there was very limited commercial involvement. Today, the leading rugby nations support full-time athletes, and many matches are scheduled for evening slots on prime-time television. These players are also now much bigger, fitter, and faster. Teams now come into the stadium with a support crew of dieticians, psychologists, analysts, and fitness coaches. Some leading players are paid large salaries, and tickets for the biggest matches become ever more expensive.

The game has always been controlled by a narrow core of nations (Harris, 2010). South Africa did not take part in the first two tournaments, but were controversially awarded the 1995 finals. The hosts went on to achieve a momentous victory, under the watch of new president Nelson Mandela, that has since been celebrated in the film *Invictus*.

In 1999 Wales were the hosts. The Millennium Stadium in Cardiff with its ultra-modern retractable roof, staged many matches (including the final), but games were also played in France and other parts of the UK. This had become par for the course as a small group of nations worked together to retain their grip on the governance of the sport.

Challenging the core

After the 2023 event in France, there are still only four nations who have ever lifted the trophy (Australia, England, New Zealand, and South Africa), and just five different nations (the above four and France) have appeared in the final. For any country outside of a very small group of the foundation nations to make it as far as the semi-final stages is rare. Argentina achieved third place in 2007 to challenge the hegemonic core (Wise & Harris, 2019), and also made it to the semi-finals in 2015 and 2023.

Argentina are still the exception here, though. The core nations of the rugby world still provide the majority of coaches at the World Cup. Many of the international teams have been coached by a New Zealander at the finals. New Zealand-born men have also represented a range of different nations at the event, although it should also be noted that New Zealand teams have often included players born in the surrounding Pacific Islands.

The sound of *Jerusalem* and *Swing Low Sweet Chariot* being sung by the fans at Twickenham in 2015 may have been quintessentially English, but some matches also took place at the Millennium Stadium in Cardiff. Wales were also a (kind of) host of England 2015, and getting through the tricky group stage meant that there was dancing in the streets of Cardiff, Conwy, and Caersws. England were defeated by Wales, and so became the first (and to date only) host nation to fail to make the knockout stages in the history of the tournament (see Harris, Wise & Vincent, 2021).

In 2015 South Africa may have been quietly confident about becoming the first three-time champions, although it was New Zealand that retained the trophy. South Africa have since gone on to win the last two tournaments (2019, 2023), and so southern hemisphere dominance of the event shows little signs of abating.

The future

Off the field of play there are changes afoot in the international game, with greater resources directed to support women's rugby, the inclusion of Rugby Sevens as an Olympic sport since 2016, and an Environmental Sustainability Plan with ambitious targets towards 2030 (World Rugby, 2021). Like all other sports, the COVID-19 pandemic had a significant impact on rugby union, and some national governing bodies experienced considerable financial difficulties.

The actor Richard Burton once suggested that rugby was a game of massive lies and stupendous exaggerations. Like many other major events, the RWC may not be quite as big as stakeholders like to claim. Yet what can't be denied is that the event is now unrecognizable from when the RWC started in 1987, and it is likely to develop further in the next decade.

MANAGERIAL IMPLICATIONS

The managerial implications of this chapter are to show that the sport of rugby union is looking more closely at the potential impact of the game across different places.

POLICY IMPLICATIONS

The policy implications of this chapter are to highlight the continued investment which needs to be made to develop rugby union beyond a narrow core.

RESEARCH IMPLICATIONS

The research implications of this chapter are that there is more work needed to look at developing international rugby union in different markets. This chapter also highlights the opportunity for future research to explore the internationalization of the sport as the RWC takes place in more nations.

QUIZ QUESTIONS

1. Is rugby union developing as a more global sport?
2. Who was the first host nation to fail to reach the knockout stages of a RWC?
3. Which country has best challenged the hegemonic core group of nations?

DEBATE QUESTIONS

1. Why have southern hemisphere nations dominated the RWC?
2. How big an influence do New Zealand coaches have on international rugby?
3. Highlight and describe when you think a fifth different nation will win a RWC?

ALIGNMENT TO UNITED NATIONS SUSTAINABLE DEVELOPMENT GOALS

Goal	How
1. No Poverty	
2. Zero Hunger	
3. Good Health and Wellbeing	Looking at the potential reach of the game across the world.
4. Quality Education	
5. Gender Equality	Increased investment in women's rugby.
6. Clean Water and Sanitation	
7. Affordable and Clean Energy	
8. Decent Work and Economic Growth	
9. Industry, Innovation, and Infrastructure	

Goal	How
10. Reduced Inequalities	Developing the sport beyond the narrow geographical core.
11. Sustainable Cities and Communities	
12. Responsible Consumption and Production	
13. Climate Action	
14. Life Below Water	
15. Life on Land	
16. Peace, Justice, and Strong Institutions	
17. Partnerships for the Goals	

REFERENCES

Harris, J. (2010). *Rugby Union and Globalization: An Odd-shaped World.* Basingstoke: Palgrave Macmillan.

Harris, J., Wise, N., & Vincent, J. (2021). The city and the country: Cardiff, England and the 2015 Rugby World Cup. *Journal of Sport & Tourism*, 25(4), 337–351.

Wise, N., & Harris, J. (2019). Challenging the core: The rise of Argentina in international rugby. In J. Harris & N. Wise (Eds.) *Rugby in Global Perspective: Playing on the Periphery.* London: Routledge.

World Rugby (2021). *Environmental Sustainability Plan 2030.* Dublin: World Rugby.

V EVENT-RELATED IDENTITY FORMATION

20 GLOBAL MIGRANT FESTIVALS

London Notting Hill Carnival versus the West-Indian American Parade Day

Nicole Ferdinand

AIM

This chapter aims to examine how migrant festivals and other events evolve from being local cultural celebrations into global events. The chapter suggests three strategies for the replication of migrant festivals on the path to globalization.

LEARNING OBJECTIVES

1. To define global festivals and events.
2. To explore the roles and meanings global events and festivals have for migrant communities.
3. To examine the various routes by which festivals leave their countries of origin to become international and then global celebrations.

DOI: 10.4324/9781003490326-26

THEORETICAL FOCUS AND SIGNIFICANCE

The theoretical focus of this chapter is on how the global festival is defined. Alongside concepts of globalization and glocalization, the concepts of hybridization and adaptation will also be explored. Strategies for understanding the replication of global migrant festivals are put forward. Identity politics amongst migrant communities continue to be of great relevance, especially with the rise of far-right movements that are currently targeting spaces where minority groups such as immigrants can find safety and a sense of belonging. It is perhaps more critical in recent years that the importance of these global festivals and events be understood and appreciated.

PRACTICAL FOCUS AND SIGNIFICANCE

The chapter will be of interest to the organizers of festivals already in the process of globalization, as well as those that have the potential to be globalized and internationalized. It will provide the organizers, as well as the other stakeholders, with a range of alternatives that can be explored in globalizing a festival. The chapter provides practical suggestions that festival organizers can use in replicating migrant festivals overseas, as well as a brief overview of the benefits and costs involved in utilizing different options.

ARTICLE

The terms 'global event' and 'mega-event' are often used interchangeably. Some may associate the former with large-scale sporting competitions like the Olympic Games. However, researchers recognize a broader range of events as global. Rojek (2012) identifies two types of global events: Cyclical events, such as St Patrick's Day and Chinese New Year's celebrations, and single-issue events, which leverage the power of celebrities and the media to raise awareness or funds for a cause. Arguably the most well-known example of a single-issue event is Live Aid, a globally televised event featuring musical performances to raise money for famine relief in Ethiopia. Richards and Columbo (2017), describe global music festivals as those that have global networks (for example artists and audiences) and cultures, and that exist in several key locations throughout the world.

The significance of global events extends to migrant festivals, which celebrate the cultures of immigrant communities. Among these festivals is the New York City St Patrick's Day Parade, originally an Irish celebration that has become world-famous (Marston, 2002). It has played a major role in turning St Patrick's Day into a worldwide tourism attraction, even in cities with little connection to the saint (Cronin & Adair, 2006, cited by Devine & Devine, 2022). Festivals like the St Patrick's Day Parade allow immigrant communities to showcase their cultures and take pride in their replication, but can also lead to commercial exploitation, with celebrations bearing little resemblance to their authentic roots.

To chart a path towards globalization, migrant festival organizers can examine the strategies employed by festivals considered to be 'globalized hubs' (Richards & Columbo, 2017) such as the London Notting Hill Carnival and other 'Trinidad-style carnivals' (Ferdinand & Williams, 2013).

It is unclear when carnival celebrations first emerged in Trinidad, though historical records suggest they began after the arrival of French slave owners in 1783. Early festivities were exclusive to upper-class slave owners and their associates, though slaves attached to plantations were eventually granted permission to hold celebrations (Hill, 1997). Over time, these events became imbued with African traditions, leading to the development of three distinct cultural forms that define the Trinidad Carnival. The oldest of these is the masquerade, which was introduced to Trinidad by French plantation owners. Calypso was developed by African slaves during the era of slavery (Martin, 1998). The steel pan and its accompanying music emerged much more recently, the widespread adoption of the instrument taking place only after 1945 (Dudley, 2007).

The London Notting Hill Carnival is a critical hub in the global festival network of Trinidad-style carnivals. This is quite a feat when one considers that the London Notting Hill Carnival was never meant to be a carnival at all. Its predecessor was the Notting Hill Festival, until 1964, when its founder, a British social worker, Rhuane Laslett, decided to add a steel band to the festival. This intervention caused the Trinidadian immigrants living in Notting Hill, the district of London from which the event gets its name, to spontaneously form a jumping and dancing procession behind the steel band. The Notting Hill Festival then became known as the Notting Hill Carnival, and later the London Notting Carnival (Ferdinand, 2013). Its influence can be seen in the numerous carnivals held throughout Britain, thanks to its introduction of static sound systems to carnival celebrations. This practice was pioneered by Jamaican DJs living in the UK back in 1975 (Gutzmore, 1982), and has played a significant role in the event's popularity. Over the years, the carnival has welcomed famous DJs, popular music artists, and even high-profile British politicians. However, it's not a carbon copy of the Trinidad carnival. Rather, it is a culturally hybridized form that embodies the concept of glocalization. Its significance lies in its ability to create a platform for the expression of diverse hybridized identities (Nurse, 1999). For instance, the carnival now features cultural expressions by groups from Brazil and Nigeria, whilst also showcasing a distinct Black British sensibility. It continues to evolve, staying relevant and meaningful for both participants and attendees. The London Notting Hill Carnival also has the distinction of being a Trinidad-style carnival that has gone on to inspire a carnival outside its country of origin. The event has been cited as a successful model for European cities, such as Rotterdam and Berlin, to engage residents from diverse cultural backgrounds, especially recent immigrants, and provide them with a platform to express their identities proudly (Noyes, 2007).

The largest of the Trinidad-style carnivals is in the United States, in New York City, and has attracted over three million visitors in a single year (Trotman, 2005). Originally rooted in celebrations held in Harlem during the 1920s, these festivities evolved into the New York Labor Day celebrations in 1947, and eventually gave rise to the West Indian American Parade Day. This event has inspired numerous other Trinidad-style carnivals in other American cities, typically featuring an American-style parade and celebrating a 'West Indian American' or 'Caribbean American' identity (Ferdinand, 2013). Trinidadians and/or a mix of Caribbean immigrants tend to be at the forefront of these festival organizations. The West-Indian American Parade Day and other Trinidad-style celebrations based in the United States, due to their proximity to Trinidad, are also critical festival hubs in the Trinidad-style carnival festival network. These events represent important sources of income for Trinidadian masquerade designers, steel bands, and calypso artists who export their cultural products, services, and expertise overseas to what has now become a year-round circuit of carnivals. However, there are also 'carnivalists' whose export markets will also include Europe, and most recently Africa, where Trinidad-style carnival-inspired celebrations can also be found (Ferdinand & Williams, 2013).

The London Notting Hill Carnival and West Indian Parade Day highlight three distinct avenues for migrant festival organizers to replicate successful events on a global scale. One strategy is the creation of a 'Fusion Festival', which, although not the original intention of the Notting Hill Festival, has undeniably contributed to its enduring appeal, by continuously introducing diverse cultural elements. The fusion festival approach has spawned another method for recreating migrant festivals: The 'Second Generation Festival'. Both the organizers of the Rotterdam ZoomerCarnival and the Berlin Carnival of Cultures have taken cues from the triumphs of the London Notting Hill Carnival as a model for celebrating diversity. The West-Indian American Parade Day originated from the earliest known Trinidad-style carnival celebrations to take place outside of Trinidad, in 1920s Harlem. It can be described as being 'Immigrant-Initiated', as there was no model of internationalization or adaption for the immigrant organizers to follow.

Each of the above strategies comes with its advantages and disadvantages. Adopting a fusion or second-generation approach allows organizers to build on an existing event which has proven successful in the past. However, this may result in expressions that are further removed from the original event compared to an immigrant-initiated celebration. The latter option provides the immigrant community with more control over the replicated festival, but requires more effort to establish. By learning from the experience of Trinidad-style festival organizers, migrant festival organizers, policymakers, and other stakeholders have the benefit of making more informed decisions about the costs and benefits of each approach.

MANAGERIAL IMPLICATIONS

Migrant festival managers interested in establishing a global festival need to carefully consider the advantages and disadvantages of different replication approaches in the context of their specific goals, resources, target audiences, and host countries.

POLICY IMPLICATIONS

Policymakers should recognize the importance of flexibility and adaptability in responding to the evolving needs and dynamics of migrant festivals. This includes being open to experimentation, innovation, and iteration in policy design and implementation to accommodate diverse replication approaches and support the long-term sustainability and success of migrant festivals.

RESEARCH IMPLICATIONS

Given that there a relatively few comparative festival studies, follow-on research from this chapter could undertake comparative studies on how other migrant communities mobilize around festival organizing initiatives, build social and economic capital, and assert cultural agency in the public sphere.

QUIZ QUESTIONS

1. Which of the following are terms that are used to describe global events?
   a) Mega-events;
   b) Major events;
   c) Celebratory events;
   d) All of the above.
2. Cyclical events and single-issue events are both described as annual celebrations.
   a) True;
   b) False.

3. Which of the following strategies for replicating migrant festivals offers the benefit of more control for immigrant festival organizers?
   a) Fusion festival;
   b) Immigrant-initiated festival;
   c) Second-generation festival;
   d) All of the above.

DEBATE QUESTIONS

1. Consider the role of both cyclical events, like cultural celebrations, and single-issue events, like fundraising concerts. How do these events shape perceptions of global issues and foster cultural exchange?
2. Discuss the implications of the commercialization and globalization of events, like St Patrick's Day, given their dual roles of promoting tourism and showcasing immigrant communities' cultures.
3. What are the key challenges faced by immigrant-initiated festivals, like the West-Indian American Parade Day, in establishing cultural traditions outside of their countries of origin?
4. In your opinion, which approach – fusion, second-generation, or immigrant-initiated – would be most effective in preserving the authenticity of migrant festivals while adapting them to globalized settings? Consider the balance between cultural preservation, community empowerment, and event accessibility in your response.

ALIGNMENT TO UNITED NATIONS SUSTAINABLE DEVELOPMENT GOALS

Goal	How
1. No Poverty	
2. Zero Hunger	
3. Good Health and Wellbeing	
4. Quality Education	
5. Gender Equality	
6. Clean Water and Sanitation	

Goal	How
7. Affordable and Clean Energy	
8. Decent Work and Economic Growth	
9. Industry, Innovation, and Infrastructure	
10. Reduced Inequalities	This chapter demonstrates how migrant festivals promote social inclusion which relates to target 10.2 of this goal.
11. Sustainable Cities and Communities	The chapter highlights the role migrant festivals play in promoting the inclusion of diverse residents and strengthening efforts to safeguard cultural heritage, which relate to targets 11.3 and 11.4 of this goal.
12. Responsible Consumption and Production	
13. Climate Action	
14. Life Below Water	
15. Life on Land	
16. Peace, Justice, and Strong Institutions	
17. Partnerships for the Goals	

REFERENCES

Devine, A.H., & Devine, F.G., (2022). Cultural contestation and masquerade politics: the challenge of trying to develop a cultural event in a divided city. *Event Management*, 26(5), 1113–1127.

Dudley, S. (2007). Creativity and the politics in the Steel band music of Ray Holman 1959-1972. In G. Green & P.W. Scher (eds.) *Trinidad Carnival: The Cultural Politics of a Transnational Festival* (pp. 161–177). Indiana University Press.

Ferdinand, N. (2013, August 26). Notting Hill Carnival is one of Trinidad's greatest exports. *The Conversation*. https://theconversation.com/notting-hill-carnival-is-one-of-trinidads-greatest-exports-17452

Ferdinand, N., & Williams, N.L. (2013). International festivals as experience production systems. *Tourism Management*, 34, 202–210.

Gutzmore, C. (1982). The Notting Hill Carnival. *Marxism Today*, 26, 31–33.
Hill, E. (1997). *TheTrinidad Carnival.* London: New Beacon Books Limited.
Marston, S.A. (2002). Making difference: conflict over Irish identity in the New York City St. Patrick's Day parade. *Political Geography*, 21(3), 373–392.
Martin, C. (1998). Trinidad Carnival glossary. *The Drama Review*, 42(3), 220–235.
Noyes, D. (2007). Cultural warming? Brazil in Berlin. In B. Fischer & H. Fehervary (eds.) *Cultural politics and the politics of culture* (pp. 55–76). Peter Lang International Academic Publishing Group.
Nurse, K. (1999). Globalization and Trinidad carnival: diaspora, hybridity and identity in global culture. *Cultural Studies*, 13(4), 661–690.
Richards, G., & Colombo, A. (2017). Creating network value The Barcelona Sónar Festival as a global events hub. In E. Lundberg, J. Ambrecht, T.D. Andersson & D. Getz (eds.) *The value of events* (pp. 73–86). Routledge.
Rojek, C. (2012). Global Event Management: a critique. *Leisure Studies*, 33(1), 32–47. https://doi.org/10.1080/02614367.2012.716077
Trotman, D. (2005). Transforming Caribbean and Canadian identity: contesting claims for Toronto's Caribana. *Atlantic Studies: Literary, Cultural and Historical Perspectives*, 2(2), 177–198.

21 COMMONWEALTH GAMES

Civic sponsorship of festive football in medieval and early modern Britain

Taylor Aucoin

AIM

To demonstrate the utility of sporting events to civic governments, institutions, and authorities in premodern Britain through the case study of football during Shrovetide (pre-Lent Carnival). It questions why many civic entities supported an ostensibly illegal sport which could be dangerous and disorderly, and thereby examines the social value of sport before the emergence of modern leisure markets.

LEARNING OBJECTIVES

1. To develop knowledge of festivals, sports and their relationship to one another in medieval and early modern Britain.
2. To examine the social and cultural value of sports like football to civic institutions in premodern Britain.
3. To critically consider the significance of leisure events in the premodern past.

DOI: 10.4324/9781003490326-27

THEORETICAL FOCUS AND SIGNIFICANCE

Theoretically, this chapter focuses on the social value of sport and leisure in premodern Britain, as examined through the case study of the civic sponsorship of Shrovetide football. Focus is on festive sporting events as forms of social control, and the late medieval and early modern concept of 'common wealth' or 'common profit'. Also considering the social/sociological impact of sporting and festive events in past societies in their own terms and context, eschewing binary interpretations of such events as either ritualistic or market oriented.

PRACTICAL FOCUS AND SIGNIFICANCE

Practically, this chapter focuses on the sporting and festive customs of Britain, specifically in terms of Shrovetide (Carnival) football in premodern cities, and what these can tell us of the social significance of sport, leisure and festivity in this society. It illuminates a little-known iteration of the global Carnival tradition (which still continues in some British communities to this day), and highlights an important aspect of football's history as a deep-rooted and intangible heritage of Britain and the English-speaking world.

ARTICLE

Sports and festivals are the dominant leisure events of the modern world. But while often thought of as distinct today, they have a close historical relationship extending deep into the premodern past. In medieval and early modern Britain, festivals, whether religious, agrarian, or political, were often the occasion of *ad hoc* or formally organized public competitions. Perhaps no other festival was more associated with sport than the pre-Lent Carnival, known as Shrovetide in England and Fastern's Eve in Scotland. Today, pancakes have become the chief focus of Shrove Tuesday in the UK (Aucoin, 2021), but during the medieval and early modern periods, a spirit of communal play and competition pervaded almost every aspect of the day and its customs (Aucoin, 2019; Hutton, 1996, pp. 151–168).

Yet football stood apart from other Shrovetide games in its widespread and long-standing popularity. As players from the Scottish Borders town of Duns reported in 1686, it was 'an ancient custom throughout all this kingdom to play at football upon Fastens Eve' (Paton, 1930, p. 146). And indeed, Shrovetide ball games are documented from the 12th century onwards, in cities, towns and villages throughout the British Isles, with several annual matches surviving today in England and Scotland (Hornby, 2008) (see Figure 21.1). Despite legal bans on

Figure 21.1
Annual Shrove Tuesday Football Match begins in Atherstone, England (2015). Image credit: Taylor Aucoin.

football in pre-modern Britain, many Shrove Tuesday matches benefited from the support of those in charge, like the bailiff and elders of Duns. Why did some civic institutions and leaders embrace this game in the face of prohibition, and what can this tell us about the social value of football, sport and festivity in the past?

'Football' in this premodern sense refers to a loose family of games where players contested a ball with hands and/or feet, usually towards a goal. As ancestors to modern codes like association, rugby, or American football, 'folk football' matches varied considerably in the manner of play. Some games featured small and evenly numbered teams playing within a defined space, like a field or street. Others saw scores, or even hundreds, of participants fighting to advance a ball through streets and countryside, to far flung goals like mills, streams, or even the church (see Figure 21.2). Either form of football could be seen during Shrovetide, with teams organized along various communal lines such as town and country, parish versus parish, or married men against bachelors.

Authorities frequently viewed football unfavorably, due to its destructive and violent potential. Medieval royal prohibitions deemed it 'vain, unthrifty and idle', while Puritans considered it 'a bloody and murdering practise' (Marples, 1954, p. 28). Nonetheless, others in power obviously saw potential in the sport, to judge from its festive sponsorship in many urban communities. Tudor Chester provides a detailed and prototypical example. Every Shrove Tuesday in the early 16th century, the Merchant Drapers' Company received a football from the Shoemakers' Company, a wooden ball from the Saddlers' Company, and a small silk ball from

Figure 21.2
Alexander Carse, The foot-ball play (c.1830). Depicts a folk football match in a Scottish Border village. Image in the Public Domain.

each city freeman married within the last year. As the mayor looked on, the Drapers tossed up the balls (which doubled as prizes) for the craftsmen and crowd to play from the common field to the city's Common Hall (Baldwin *et al.*, 2007, pp. 75–77, 326–331).

The particulars of Chester's Shrovetide sponsorship were mirrored throughout the British Isles. Craftsmen and guilds played key roles as participants and providers of the ball. On Shrove Tuesday 1373, skinners and tailors played in the streets of London (Aucoin, 2019, pp. 109–110), while butchers fought over the ball in Jedburgh 1706 (Hornby, 2008, p. 114). The Skinners' and Shoemakers' companies paraded the ball to the match between married and bachelor freemen in late 18th-century Alnwick (Kitching, 2011). Indeed, leather-workers such as shoemakers were especially important: They crafted Shrovetide footballs in 15th-century London, 16th-century Glasgow and 17th-century Carlisle (Aucoin, 2019, pp. 93–147). When the bailiff of Duns confiscated the drum used to summon players to the annual Fastern's Eve ball game in 1724, it was shoemaker (and ball maker) William Home who led a riotous attempt to retrieve the instrument (Hornby, 2008, p. 22).

Newlyweds also provided the ball in many communities. Like in Chester, recently married freemen of Dublin had to present a ball to city magistrates every Shrove Tuesday during the 15th and 16th centuries. Newlywed members of trade guilds in Perth, Scotland, and the Corfe Castle Company of Marblers in Dorset, also paid a Shrovetide 'football due', while a similar custom seems to have existed in medieval London. These were part of a more widespread folk tradition, where newly married couples owed a 'bride ball' or 'ball money', as a sort of life insurance payment for the potential risk which a marriage placed upon the wider community, should a wife be widowed or children orphaned. Since weddings were customary during Shrovetide (and prohibited in Lent), it was an ideal time to collect such dues (Aucoin, 2019, pp. 139–143).

Behind all this, civic governments might collect the 'wedding balls', hire musicians to pump up the crowds, or pay for equipment. Over time, authorities in most major cities did cease their support of Shrovetide football. Some cities like St Andrews simply banned it; in 1537 the burgh provost and university dean cancelled the annual match because of its 'many ills' and 'disorder' (Dunlop, 1964, pp. 380–381). Others 'reformed' the games into less dangerous entertainments, like foot and horse races in 1540 Chester, or a public display of the city fire-engine's capabilities in 1725 Carlisle (Aucoin, 2019, pp. 93–147). Attempts to ban or reform were not always successful – the Duns game has survived to the present day, despite the previously mentioned efforts to stop it in 1724 (Hornby, 2008, pp. 132–137). Nonetheless, officially sanctioned Shrovetide ball games were mostly confined to smaller market towns and villages by the middle of the 18th century. Yet the question remains: Why did official support for a disorderly and 'unlawful' game linger as long as it did?

Partially, festive sponsorship gave officials the opportunity to somewhat contain a rowdy game that might happen with or without their consent. Certainly, outright bans were rarely effective, to judge from repeated mayoral ordinances 'against football play at Shrovetide' in the streets of Elizabethan London (Aucoin, 2019, p. 104). Yet, the appeal of patronage went beyond social control. The often-exclusive participation of guild or burgh members (known as 'freemen') in Shrovetide ball games reaffirmed corporate status, with its privileges and obligations. These obligations could include football itself. In January 1590, the shoemaker John Neil was made a 'burgess' or freeman of Glasgow in exchange for supplying 'six good and sufficient footballs' every Shrove Tuesday during his lifetime (Marwick, 1914, p. 149).

Failure to participate in or furnish football, via payments of the 'wedding ball' for example, could result in imprisonment, heavy fines, or the forced closing of a craftsman's shop. The goods of Robert Dykes, a maltman of Rutherglen, Scotland were distrained in 1626 because he failed to join the rest the burgesses (i.e., freemen) on the town green for the annual Shrovetide match (Brochard, 2022, pp. 67–68). Such harsh penalties convey the worth of Shrove Tuesday football to these pre-modern communities. To them football was not a 'vain and idle' game, but an 'ancient and laudable custom' of 'goodly feats and exercise' (Aucoin, 2019, p. 95). Rather than 'unthrifty', its value equated to the 'use and benefit of the Company' (Magoun, pp. 104–105) and the advantage of 'the common wealth' (Baldwin *et al.*, 2007, p. 331). Fines paid in lieu of the Shrovetide ball in Dublin and Chester, for example, went towards 'the use of the said City' (Baldwin *et al.*, 2007, pp. 494–495) or 'town works where it [was] most needful' (Gilbert, 1889, p. 290). Shrovetide football thus reflected ideals of common wealth, common profit, or common good which civic officials and institutions deemed well worth preserving (Harry, 2019; Burgess & Knights, 2011): Such events allowed them to publicly reaffirm and signal their civic privileges, while simultaneously fulfilling the communal obligations which these entailed.

POLICY IMPLICATIONS

The social significance of football (in its many forms) in Britain and the Anglosphere did not emerge solely from a 'civilizing burst' of the 19th century and its codification of rules. Indeed, the arguments in this article suggest football has been 'more than a game', for much longer – an intangible heritage worthy of UNESCO which policy makers could consider promoting as such.

RESEARCH IMPLICATIONS

Economists and sociologists have often contrasted the modern leisure market with a premodern past in which leisure time was preferred over consumerism, and leisure events themselves were often ritualistic, violent, and informal. This research complicates such assumptions, and suggests further work is needed on the social impact and significance of sporting and festive events in premodern societies, the latter clearly exhibiting a complexity which neither ritual nor market value can fully define.

QUIZ QUESTIONS

1. How could football and other sporting events reflect or reaffirm identities in premodern Britain?
2. In what ways did civic institutions and authorities participate in or sponsor football in medieval and early modern Britain?
3. What were the potential reasons for civic support of an ostensibly illegal sport?

DEBATE QUESTIONS

1. Do you think authorities sponsoring Shrovetide football could be an effective means of social control?
2. Were authorities more likely to support Shrovetide football as a social control on potential disorder, or as an event which promoted their exclusive position within the urban hierarchy?
3. Do you think players and promoters of civic football were genuinely interested in furthering the 'common wealth' or 'common profit' of the urban community, or more concerned with preserving their own civic privileges? Were the two mutually exclusive?

ALIGNMENT TO UNITED NATIONS SUSTAINABLE DEVELOPMENT GOALS

Goal	How
1. No Poverty	
2. Zero Hunger	
3. Good Health and Wellbeing	
4. Quality Education	
5. Gender Equality	
6. Clean Water and Sanitation	
7. Affordable and Clean Energy	
8. Decent Work and Economic Growth	
9. Industry, Innovation, and Infrastructure	
10. Reduced Inequalities	
11. Sustainable Cities and Communities	
12. Responsible Consumption and Production	
13. Climate Action	
14. Life Below Water	

Goal	How
15. Life on Land	
16. Peace, Justice, and Strong Institutions	
17. Partnerships for the Goals	

REFERENCES

Aucoin, T. (2019). *'When the Pancake Bell Rings': Shrove Tuesday and the Social Efficacy of Carnival Time in Medieval and Early Modern Britain*. [Doctoral thesis, University of Bristol]. Explore Bristol Research Portal. https://research-information.bris.ac.uk/en/studentTheses/when-the-pancake-bell-rings

Aucoin, T. (2021). The politics of pancakes. *History Today*, *71*(2), 22–24. www.historytoday.com/archive/history-matters/politics-pancakes

Baldwin, E., Clopper, L.M. & Mills, D. (Eds.). (2007). *Records of Early English Drama: Cheshire including Chester*. (Vols. 1–2). University of Toronto Press. https://archive.org/details/cheshireinclreed01clopuoft

Brochard, T. (2022). Sports in Scottish burgh and notarial records, 1500–1700, Part 2. *Scottish Archives, 28*, 50–71.

Burgess, G. & Knights, M. (2011). Commonwealth: The social, cultural, and conceptual contexts of an early modern keyword. *The Historical Journal*, *54*(3), 659–687. https://doi.org/10.1017/S0018246X11000203

Dunlop, A.I. (Ed.). (1964). *Acta Facultatis artium Universitatis Sanctiandree 1413 – 1588*. (Vols. 1–2). Scottish History Society. https://digital.nls.uk/scottish-history-society-publications/browse/archive/128281391

Gilbert, J.T. (Ed.). (1889). *Calendar of the Ancient Records of Dublin in the Possession of the Municipal Corporation*. (Vol. 1). Dollard. https://archive.org/details/calendarofancien01dubl_0/page/290/mode/2up

Harry, D. (2019). *Constructing a Civic Community in Late Medieval London: The Common Profit, Charity and Commemoration*. Boydell & Brewer. https://doi.org/10.1017/9781787444751

Hornby, H. (2008). *Uppies and Downies: The Extraordinary Football Games of Britain*. English Heritage. https://archive.org/details/uppiesdowniesext0000horn

Hutton, R. (1996). *The Stations of the Sun: A History of the Ritual Year in Britain*. Oxford University Press. https://doi.org/10.1093/acprof:oso/9780198205708.001.0001

Kitching, G. (2011). 'From Time Immemorial': The Alnwick Shrovetide Football Match and the Continuous Remaking of Tradition 1828–1890. *International Journal of the History of Sport, 28*(6), 831–852. https://doi.org/10.1080/09523367.2011.557907

Marples, M. (1954). *A History of Football*. Secker & Warburg.

Marwick, J.D. (Ed.). (1914). *Extracts From the Records of the Burgh of Glasgow*. (Vol. 1, 1573–1642). Scottish Burgh Records Society. https://archive.org/details/extractsfromrec00renwgoog/page/n3/mode/2up

Paton, H. (Ed.). (1930). The Register of the Privy Council of Scotland, Third Series, (Vol. XII). H.M. General Register House. https://hdl.handle.net/2027/mdp.35112103825529

22 THE SUPER BOWL
The risk of inauthentic brand storytelling

Lucy Gill-Simmen and Ling Xiao

AIM

This chapter aims to highlight the importance of authenticity when brands seek to tell their stories. Many brands are jumping on the social justice bandwagon, and this has left consumers confused and lacking trust in the brand.

LEARNING OBJECTIVES

1. Explain the importance of brand authenticity.
2. Analyse the consequences of inauthentic storytelling.
3. Show how to develop trust using immersive digital narratives.

DOI: 10.4324/9781003490326-28

THEORETICAL FOCUS AND SIGNIFICANCE

Theoretically, this chapter focuses on the authenticity of storytelling and digital narrative transportation as a method to instill trust and belief. With so many brands being accused of green-washing and 'wokery', it makes sense for brands to identify ways in which they can tell their stories which are authentic and meaningful.

PRACTICAL FOCUS AND SIGNIFICANCE

Practically, this chapter focuses on how brands can adopt particular storytelling methods to portray who they are in a meaningful and authentic way. If brands get their messaging wrong, this can have serious consequences for brands and their relationships with consumers, which at times may be difficult to repair.

ARTICLE

Theoretical underpinnings of authentic brand storytelling

The concept of authenticity in branding is rooted in various theoretical frameworks from marketing, psychology, and communication. Self-congruity theory posits that consumers prefer brands that match their self-concept and values (Sirgy, 1982). When brands tell stories that resonate with consumers' identities, it enhances brand identification and loyalty. Immersive stories can engross audiences, shaping their beliefs, attitudes, and intentions, as explained through the process of narrative transportation (Green & Brock, 2000). By crafting compelling brand narratives, companies can transport consumers into their world, and forge deeper emotional connections. The elaboration likelihood model (Petty & Cacioppo, 1986) suggests that audiences process persuasive messages differently, depending on their motivation and ability. Authentic, emotionally engaging brand stories are more likely to be processed through the central route, leading to lasting attitude change, compared to peripheral cues like celebrity endorsements or flashy visuals.

By understanding these theoretical principles, brands can create more authentic, impactful storytelling that truly connects with their target audiences.

Brand authenticity

Brand authenticity has become ever more important in our digitally-connected world (Napoli, Dickinson, Beverland & Farrelly, 2014). Recent scandals involving brands like Peloton and The Honest Company show how quickly inauthentic stories and claims can damage trust (Chaudhuri & Holbrook, 2001). Audiences can soon sense falsehoods and become cynical, diminishing brand trust, and affecting loyalty. It is not only external audiences that sense this, but also the employees, once they lose trust, this can further damage the brand. According to earlier research, employees who believe in the brand will go out of their way to do good (Gill-Simmen, MacInnis, Eisingerich & Whan Park, 2018). So, when brands appear to 'bang the social justice drum' on the outside, and employees are feeling a lack of equality on the inside, this can lead to distrust (Portal, Abratt & Bendixen, 2019).

When brands go too far

Consumers prefer brands whose values align with their own (Michel, Torelli, Fleck & Hubert, 2022). With reducing harm to the environment and standing up for social issues as examples of consumer expectations of the brands they purchase, some brands may be tempted to jump on the bandwagon as a matter of principle.

After all the hype surrounding Kendall Jenner's farcical ad with Pepsi, which not only downplayed the criticality of black violence, but also glamourised it, one would think the sector would have learned a lesson. Yet, not long after, Gillette, in its attempt to play the corporate social activist card, launched its 'is this the best a man can get' campaign. This fuelled anger amongst some consumers, who were sceptical of its motives. Others felt the brand sent messages suggesting that the majority of men engage in toxic behaviours.

Burger King too fell foul of trying to promote social causes, and faced backlash for its mental health awareness campaign (Graham, 2019). Accused of clouding serious topics with playful language, authenticity was brought into question. Consumers started wondering why brands were becoming so righteous.

More recently, Budweiser turned the adage 'there's no such thing as bad publicity' on its head. Sales of Bud Light plunged 25% in response to its promotion featuring transgender influencer, Dylan Mulvaney. This led to a boycott of the brand by angry conservative consumers accusing the brand of going 'woke' (BBC News, 2023). So damaging was the consumer response that Bud Light's marketing vice-president, Alissa Heinerscheid, and vice-president of marketing for its mainstream brands, Daniel Blake, were forced to take a leave of absence.

When brands fail to align their behaviours with their espoused values, this too can wreak havoc with a brand's reputation. The consumer base ends up feeling alienated by the brand's perceived hypocrisy and inauthenticity. Victoria's Secret recent rebrand failed in its attempts to become more inclusive and an advocate for women. Instead, following the launch of 'the Tour "23"' women were left feeling inferior. The reason for this was a combination of a lack of market research, and a failure to listen to the fans of the brand.

Lessons learned and transportation into narrative worlds

The Super Bowl is renowned for its commercials, with ad breaks often taking centre stage over the game. Some brands are known for using this stage to signal virtue or promote their purpose. But with this comes the risk of inauthenticity.

With the 2024 Super Bowl LVIII complete and highly coveted 30-second slots sold for $6.5 to $7 million, brands want to make sure they do not go down as yet another brand chasing social causes to look good.

We suggest rather than preaching values, or grasping at emotional connections without context, brands should use the power of narrative transportation to convince viewers of their underlying purpose. Research shows that narrative transportation increases reader identification with characters, shifts attitudes and beliefs, and creates more lasting memorability than straightforward information delivery (Green, 2021).

Unlike explicit messaging, which can feel inauthentic, getting lost in a story can inspire emotions and shape beliefs in a subtle, organic way, transforming attitudes, beliefs, and moods (Green, Brock & Kaufman, 2004). When considering Apple's 1984 commercial introducing the Macintosh – it did not talk about product features but rather created a hero narrative against conformity and totalitarianism.

In a similar vein, Coca-Cola's famous 1971 Hilltop ad united people through the uplifting experience of drinking a soda at a time when America was experiencing a dark period in the country's history during the Vietnam War. These are the types of narrative advertisements that resonate, rather than targeting consumers with a supposed values-based message.

Validating authenticity of narratives using digital immersive storytelling

In our research, we go further. We propose immersive digital storytelling techniques as highly novel methods for brands to craft and validate the authenticity of their narratives. Immersive storytelling transports consumers and employees into a world which is real (Xiao & Gill-Simmen, 2024). Interactive digital media enables more participatory story experiences between brands and audiences. Working with a company to showcase their sustainability efforts transparently, we created an immersive storytelling experience using extended reality technology where the founder of the company takes the audience on a walk through a forest the company purchased to help offset their carbon emissions. This visceral storytelling immerses the viewers via a VR headset in the experience (see Figure 22.1), eliciting positive

Image source: Authors.

Figure 22.1
Immersive VR experiences can validate the authenticity of a brand's sustainability initiatives.

responses. There's no doubt in their mind, this is real. It emotionally engages consumers with a real-life story, thus avoiding allegations of 'greenwashing' plaguing major brands like Google and Amazon (BBC News, 2022).

By showing rather than telling, this gives consumers a deeply authentic experience of the brand's causes. They can see for themselves what the company is doing, rather than relying on messages from traditional advertising.

In conclusion, brands must tread carefully when trying to capitalise on social issues through their advertising. Inauthentic attempts at virtue signalling can quickly backfire, damaging brand trust and loyalty. Instead, it is recommended to use the power of narrative transportation and immersive digital storytelling to engage audiences with authentic, emotionally resonant brand stories. By creating experiences that allow consumers to walk in a brand's shoes and see their purpose and values in action, companies can build lasting connections, and avoid the pitfalls of superficial woke-washing.

MANAGERIAL IMPLICATIONS

Managers should seek ways to tell their brand stories in a transparent and authentic manner, and in a way which resonates with consumers.

POLICY IMPLICATIONS

Policymakers should consider the need for guidelines or regulations on authentic brand storytelling and/or advertising. They should also seek to address greenwashing and misleading environmental claims, and protect consumer interests and prevent misleading marketing practices.

RESEARCH IMPLICATIONS

Researchers should consider ways in which companies execute brand storytelling and identify ways in which SMEs, for instance, may work with limited budgets to execute authentic brand storytelling campaigns.

QUIZ QUESTIONS

1. Why has brand authenticity become so important in today's society?
2. What are the implications for brands that are inauthentic?
3. What are some examples of brands that have gone too far with their brand storytelling?
4. How might narrative transportation help brands in their plight to communicate their messages?
5. What technique can brand's use to transport consumers into their brand narratives?

DEBATE QUESTIONS

1. Should there be stricter regulations or guidelines on what claims brands can make in their marketing campaigns to prevent instances of inauthenticity or exaggeration?
2. Are immersive digital storytelling techniques like extended reality a solution to increase brand authenticity, or do they raise new ethical concerns about manipulating consumer perceptions?
3. To what extent should brands be held accountable for aligning their internal practices and employee treatment with the values they promote externally through marketing?
4. Is it ever appropriate for brands to take a stance on social or political issues in their advertising, or does this inherently risk being perceived as inauthentic or exploitative?
5. Should there be independent third-party audits or certifications to validate brands' claims about sustainability, diversity, and other socially responsible practices?

ALIGNMENT TO UNITED NATIONS SUSTAINABLE DEVELOPMENT GOALS

Goal	How
1. No Poverty	
2. Zero Hunger	
3. Good Health and Wellbeing	
4. Quality Education	The article could be used as a case study in a classroom to teach students about ethical and responsible behaviour.
5. Gender Equality	
6. Clean Water and Sanitation	
7. Affordable and Clean Energy	
8. Decent Work and Economic Growth	The article highlights the importance of brands aligning their internal practices and employee treatment with the values they promote externally, which relates to promoting decent work environments and sustainable economic growth.
9. Industry, Innovation, and Infrastructure	The article proposes using innovative immersive digital storytelling techniques like extended reality for authentic brand narratives. This aligns with promoting innovative and sustainable industrialisation practices and fostering innovation in marketing and advertising.
10. Reduced Inequalities	
11. Sustainable Cities and Communities	By advocating for authentic and transparent brand narratives, the article indirectly supports sustainable consumption patterns and lifestyles, which contribute to sustainable communities.

Goal	How
12. Responsible Consumption and Production	The article emphasises the importance of brand authenticity and transparency, which aligns with responsible marketing practices and preventing greenwashing (making misleading environmental claims).
13. Climate Action	The article provides an example of how an SME adopted digital immersive storytelling to communicate its story to consumers.
14. Life Below Water	
15. Life on Land	
16. Peace, Justice, and Strong Institutions	
17. Partnerships for the Goals	The article suggests potential partnerships between brands, researchers, and policymakers to develop guidelines, regulations, and certifications for authentic marketing practices. This aligns with strengthening the global partnership for sustainable development through multi-stakeholder collaborations.

REFERENCES

BBC News. (2022, February 7). Climate change: Top companies exaggerating their progress – study. www.bbc.co.uk/news/science-environment-60248830

BBC News. (2023, August 3). Bud Light boycott over trans influencer Dylan Mulvaney hits beer giant's sales. www.bbc.co.uk/news/business-66398296

Chaudhuri, A., & Holbrook, M.B. (2001). The chain of effects from brand trust and brand affect to brand performance: the role of brand loyalty. *Journal of Marketing*, 65(2), 81–93. https://doi.org/10.1509/jmkg.65.2.81.18255

Gill-Simmen, L., MacInnis, D.J., Eisingerich, A.B., & Whan Park, C. (2018). Brand-self connections and brand prominence as drivers of employee brand attachment. *AMS Review*, 8(3), 128–146. https://doi.org/10.1007/s13162-018-0110-6

Graham, M. (2019, May 3). Burger King faces backlash after linking ad campaign to mental health, showing the risks of cause-based marketing. *CNBC*. www.cnbc.com/2019/05/03/burger-king-faces-backlash-after-linking-ad-campaign-to-mental-health.html

Green, M.C. (2021). Transportation into narrative worlds. In L.B. Frank & P. Falzone (Eds.), *Entertainment-education behind the scenes: Case studies for theory and practice* (pp. 87–101). Palgrave Macmillan. https://doi.org/10.1007/978-3-030-63614-2_6

Green, M.C., & Brock, T.C. (2000). The role of transportation in the persuasiveness of public narratives. *Journal of Personality and Social Psychology*, 79(5), 701–721. https://doi.org/10.1037/0022-3514.79.5.701

Green, M.C., Brock, T.C., & Kaufman, G.F. (2004). Understanding media enjoyment: The role of transportation into narrative worlds. *Communication Theory*, 14(4), 311–327. https://doi.org/10.1111/j.1468-2885.2004.tb00317.x

Michel, G., Torelli, C.J., Fleck, N., & Hubert, B. (2022). Self-brand values congruity and incongruity: Their impacts on self-expansion and consumers' responses to brands. *Journal of Business Research*, 142, 301–316. https://doi.org/10.1016/j.jbusres.2021.12.032

Napoli, J., Dickinson, S.J., Beverland, M.B., & Farrelly, F. (2014). Measuring consumer-based brand authenticity. *Journal of Business Research*, 67(6), 1090–1098. https://doi.org/10.1016/j.jbusres.2013.06.001

Petty, R.E., & Cacioppo, J.T. (1986). The elaboration likelihood model of persuasion. In J. Seiter and R. Gass (Eds.), *Communication and persuasion* (pp. 1–24). Springer. https://doi.org/10.1007/978-1-4612-4964-1_1

Portal, S., Abratt, R., & Bendixen, M. (2019). The role of brand authenticity in developing brand trust. *Journal of Strategic Marketing*, 27(8), 714–729. https://doi.org/10.1080/0965254X.2018.1466828

Sirgy, M.J. (1982). Self-concept in consumer behavior: A critical review. *Journal of Consumer Research*, 9(3), 287–300. https://doi.org/10.1086/208924

Xiao, L., & Gill-Simmen, L. (2024). Meeting Net-Zero: Zero-Sum Or Win-Win For SMEs? A Novel Approach To Marketing A Brand's Purpose Through Immersive Digital Storytelling. https://dosrhul.org/2024/01/26/meeting-net-zero-zero-sum-or-win-win-for-smes-a-novel-approach-to-marketing-a-brands-purpose-through-immersive-digital-storytelling/

23 SOCIALLY RESPONSIBLE LIVE MUSIC

Do fans/consumers care?

Gary Sinclair, Todd Green, and Julie Tinson

AIM

Explore how fans/consumers perceive socially responsible music events.

LEARNING OBJECTIVES

1. Understand the historical relationship between live music and socially responsible initiatives.
2. Critically engage in the nuances of socially responsible music consumption.
3. Understand what makes an effective/ineffective pairing of live music and a social cause.

DOI: 10.4324/9781003490326-29

THEORETICAL FOCUS AND SIGNIFICANCE

This chapter references literature on hedonic socially responsible consumption and the impacts of corporate greenwashing. It adds nuance to the presumption that pairing a socially responsible message with a hedonic product (music) will have a positive impact. We explore the complexities of consumer experiences in this regard.

PRACTICAL FOCUS AND SIGNIFICANCE

Stakeholders responsible for delivering live music events must place strong emphasis on how the production fits with the social cause, and how authenticity in engagement can be articulated both in the event and the communication about the event. Live music is historically a powerful agent of social change. Understanding how that can work in a hypercommodified era of live music is significant. Furthermore, it is something that is important for music fans.

ARTICLE

Live music events have taken on an increasing economic importance in the digital era (Mortimer *et al.*, 2012) and post COVID-19 (Guarisa *et al.*, 2023). This is in part a reaction to the piracy crisis of the early 21st century, but also a response to an increasing consumer demand, the globalization of the music audience, and technological and logistical leaps that have led to accelerated innovation and a hyper efficient and hyper-commercialized international live music product. The numbers support this. For example, Live Nation, the company that owns Ticketmaster, reported that 2023 was its biggest year ever for ticket sales and attendances (Live Nation, 2024). The company's total revenue also went up by 36% to $22.7 billion (Live Nation, 2024). Taylor Swift's Eras tour generated more than a billion dollars in ticket sales (Dellato, 2023). Business is booming. How much of this goes to artists is another story.

Although global arena tours from mega acts like the Rolling Stones have essentially existed since the late 1960s, the commercial scope and emphasis of such events was nowhere close to the apex it has reached today. For example, the first Glastonbury Festival in 1970 cost £1 for entry and it had only reached £28 by 1989. It was £355 in 2024. We make this point, not to necessarily complain about ticket prices – there are plenty of outlets in which to do that – but to illustrate how the emphasis of such events has somewhat shifted from organic countercultural movements that used the music event to champion social justice and political resistance, to commercial events, some of which place an emphasis (or make room for) such social issues.

Iconic moments where artists challenge societal norms through their music, like Jimi Hendrix's legendary guitar solos against American imperialism at Woodstock, have seemingly become rare. Instead, festivals predominantly promote commercial interests and aspirations. There is an argument that attending live music events no longer embodies the countercultural rebellion it once may have. There is, of course, a market for the social and countercultural aspect of live music consumption. Glastonbury is a good example of that. It has the identity, it has (apologies for the use of the upcoming dirty word), the brand.

But why should live music events be a space in which it is expected that social issues are championed? Music and the arts are commonly seen as potent tools for promoting social responsibility, due to their ability to evoke profound emotional responses. Musicians are role models that have significant influence. The history of Rock 'n' Roll is illustrative of that. Events such as Live Aid can stir up powerful feelings and bring certain issues to the forefront of the public's consciousness. Live music events have the possibility to transform society. If we take that as a given, we are still left with the question of what the music fan/consumer thinks about events being used to promote socially responsible causes. The remainder of this chapter draws from our research in answering this questions.

The irony is that the behavior of musicians, like every other high-profile person or entity in today's world, is under greater scrutiny than ever. As is the case for most businesses, they typically require some sort of positioning on social issues. It should be easier for musicians to tie their 'product' with a cause, because it is a type of hedonic consumption. Research suggests that consumers respond more favorably to hedonic offerings compared to utilitarian offerings in this context (Strahilevitz & Myers, 1998). However, our study (Green *et al.*, 2016) indicates a more complicated relationship between consumers and socially responsible hedonic products. Drawing from interviews with music consumers,we can see that many of them respond negatively when their favorite artists use their live platform to preach about socially responsible issues. Some fans view music as a means of escaping from their daily lives, and often express a preference for avoiding socially responsible activities while attending live music events. Interestingly, some of the participants specifically argued that they had to think through issues of social responsibility so frequently in their everyday lives, in the consumer decisions they had to make, that they didn't want to be faced with these issues in their leisure time.

Moreover, consumers scrutinize the authenticity of artists or organizations involved in socially responsible actions, and tend to disregard musicians who seem to engage in social causes solely for self-serving purposes, such as boosting record sales. This represents a broader trend of increasing consumer cynicism. Teichmann *et al.* (2024) cite how consistent corporate greenwashing has diminished consumer trust. This greenwashing is replicated in the case of musicians and live music events. Many artists speak out about climate change, yet undertake large international tours that are responsible for significant carbon emissions. Hence, it is not simply a case of pairing the music product with a social cause. To effectively resonate with an audience, there must be a sense of authenticity and it has to be managed. Otherwise, as our findings illustrate, fans will ignore, or worse, rebel against the socially responsible message.

The focus on authenticity aligns with prior studies on music consumption, indicating that fans differentiate artists (and themselves) based on displays of legitimacy and their interactions with mainstream media (Thornton, 1995). Thus, the crucial strategy for promoting socially responsible behavior is to connect with consumers on this level, utilizing the same creative and authentic methods that initially attracted them to the music. What does this look like when it comes to an issue like climate change? Performers such as Jack Johnson and Coldplay have pledged to make their tours more environmentally friendly (Aswad, 2023), and worked actively with non-profits to enact various initiatives such as removing plastic cups, carbon offsetting, the use of electric vehicles in transportation, and through incentivizing fans to adopt more sustainable behaviors when attending gigs, by offering them discounts for tickets and merchandise. What is clear is that the message must connect with the actual product, the message must be communicated through the music and the experience of the live event. However, that is more complicated than it seems, and fans must truly perceive the message to be authentic to buy in.

MANAGERIAL IMPLICATIONS

Think deeply about how the live act pairs with the social cause. Implement actions beyond surface level connections that tap into the emotional and identification characteristics of the music experience.

POLICY IMPLICATIONS

Regulations that address the carbon emissions of live music industry and potential greenwashing of events must be developed further.

RESEARCH IMPLICATIONS

Not much research on this subject has followed our 2016 study. We would suggest a quantitative (survey or experimental) study that captures a wider sample of music fans to identify specifically what social issues are important to them, and the most effective ways such issues can be engaged with in live music event contexts.

QUIZ QUESTIONS

1. Why is the live music industry booming?
2. How and why has the concept of music as counterculture evolved since Woodstock?
3. Hedonic goods paired with a socially responsible message are more impactful than utilitarian goods. Discuss.
4. Identify examples of live music events that are associated with meaningful social change.
5. What are some reasons consumers tune out from social messages at concerts?

DEBATE QUESTIONS

1. Do musicians have a responsibility to promote socially responsible causes?
2. Does commercial involvement in these events negate any sense of authenticity in musicians promoting social causes?
3. Does promotion of social causes reduce the level of enjoyment at a live music event?

ALIGNMENT TO UNITED NATIONS SUSTAINABLE DEVELOPMENT GOALS

Goal	How
1. No Poverty	
2. Zero Hunger	
3. Good Health and Wellbeing	
4. Quality Education	
5. Gender Equality	
6. Clean Water and Sanitation	
7. Affordable and Clean Energy	
8. Decent Work and Economic Growth	

Goal	How
9. Industry, Innovation, and Infrastructure	
10. Reduced Inequalities	
11. Sustainable Cities and Communities	
12. Responsible Consumption and Production	It considers the intricacies of socially responsible live music consumption and production.
13. Climate Action	It considers best practice for promoting pro-climate action in the live music industry
14. Life Below Water	
15. Life on Land	
16. Peace, Justice, and Strong Institutions	
17. Partnerships for the Goals	

REFERENCES

Aswad, J. (2023, June 5th). Coldplay's 'Music of the Spheres' Tour Drastically Reduces Band's Carbon Footprint, Sets New Standards in Sustainability. *Variety*. https://variety.com/2023/music/news/coldplay-tour-carbon-footprint-sustainability-green-1235632704/

Dellato, M. (2023, October 15th). The top-earning summer concert tours of 2023. *Forbes*. www.forbes.com/sites/marisadellatto/2023/10/13/the-top-earning-summer-concert-tours-2023-taylor-swift-beyonce/

Green, T., Sinclair, G., & Tinson, J. (2016). Do they know it's CSR at all? An exploration of socially responsible music consumption. *Journal of Business Ethics*, 138(2), 231–246. https://doi.org/10.1007/s10551-015-2582-8

Guarisa, M.L.Z., Figueiredo, J.L., & Machado, A.F. (2023). The show must go on: proposals to measure the economic value of Grassroots Music Venues. *Cultural Trends*, 1–18. https://doi.org/10.1080/09548963.2023.2193874

Live Nation. (2024, February 22). Live Nation Entertainment reports full year and fourth quarter 2023 results. www.livenationentertainment.com/2024/02/live-nation-entertainment-reports-full-year-and-fourth-quarter-2023-results/

Mortimer, J.H., Nosko, C., & Sorensen, A. (2012). Supply responses to digital distribution: Recorded music and live performances. Information Economics and Policy, 24(1), 3–14.

Strahilevitz, M. & Myers, J.G. (1998). Donations to charity as purchase incentives: How well they work may depend on what you are trying to sell. *Journal of Consumer Research, 24*(4), 434–446.

Teichmann, F.M.J., Wittmann, C., Boticiu, S.R. & Sergi, B.S.S. (2024). Can the consumer perception of corporate social responsibility be saved? An examination into the effects of corporate greenwashing on the consumer and financial market. *Journal of Financial Crime, Volume ahead-of-print* (Issue ahead-of-print). https://doi.org/10.1108/JFC-11-2023-0303

Thornton, S. (1995). *Club cultures: Music, media and subcultural capital.* Cambridge: Polity Press.

24 CONCLUSIONS AND RECOMMENDATIONS

Mike Duignan

'Event and Economic Development' comprehensively explores the transformative power of events as catalysts for economic growth, cultural expression, and urban and national development. Through diverse case studies, it illustrates how events can serve as strategic tools for nation branding, community revitalization, and global influence, while also examining the challenges and ethical considerations they present. From mega-sporting events like the FIFA World Cup and the Olympics, to localized cultural festivals such as Dark Mofo and Día de los Muertos, the book underscores the multifaceted impact of events and their role in shaping societies.

Mega-events are a central theme, particularly their use by emerging nations to project soft power, enhance global visibility, and attract foreign investment. Nations such as Qatar, South Africa, and Brazil have leveraged events like the FIFA World Cup and the Olympics to showcase their cultural heritage, modern infrastructure, and political stability. For instance, Qatar's hosting of the 2022 FIFA World Cup positioned the nation as a global hub for sports, while navigating criticisms around human rights and accusations of sportswashing. These events demonstrate the strategic value of mega-events in nation branding, yet they also highlight significant risks, including escalating costs, uneven local benefits, and controversies surrounding governance and ethical considerations. Despite these challenges, the legacy of such events often extends beyond economic gains, influencing public diplomacy and shaping national identity.

On a regional scale, festivals such as Dark Mofo in Hobart and Banyuwangi's cultural events in Indonesia, demonstrate how localized celebrations can drive urban renewal and economic resilience. These festivals have successfully capitalized on unique cultural and environmental contexts to attract tourism, foster community pride, and stimulate local economies. Dark Mofo, for example, trans-

LEARNING OBJECTIVES

DOI: 10.4324/9781003490326-30

formed Hobart's winter tourism by embracing the city's gothic aesthetic and engaging the local community. Similarly, Banyuwangi's festival-driven strategy boosted regional tourism fivefold, showcasing how carefully curated cultural programs can serve as a foundation for sustainable development. These examples reveal the potential of smaller-scale events to create lasting economic and social impact while emphasizing the importance of aligning events with local identities and broader development goals.

Cultural events also highlight the tensions between authenticity and commercialization. Día de los Muertos serves as a compelling example, balancing its deep cultural significance with its widespread appeal, fueled by commercialization through tourism and media. While some lament the dilution of traditional practices, the economic dimension of such events has been instrumental in sustaining their relevance across generations. Similarly, the commodification of Electronic Dance Music (EDM) culture, explored in this book, reflects a broader shift in cultural movements as they transition from countercultural roots to commercialized industries. These chapters underscore the need for event organizers to navigate the fine line between economic viability and preserving cultural authenticity.

Urban transformation is another significant theme, with events playing a pivotal role in reshaping cities and addressing long-term development challenges. The Commonwealth Games in Birmingham exemplify how strategic urban planning can leverage events to create sustainable infrastructure and improve livability. By embedding the Games within a broader urban strategy, Birmingham demonstrated the potential for events to drive positive change beyond their immediate timelines. However, these efforts also reveal the limitations of events as standalone solutions to systemic issues. While events can provide temporary boosts to tourism and local economies, their long-term success depends on integrating them into comprehensive development plans that prioritize inclusivity and sustainability.

The book also addresses the ethical dimensions of events, particularly in sponsorship and public health. Chapters analyzing events like Euro 2024 examine the implications of partnerships with industries promoting unhealthy products such as junk food, alcohol, and gambling. These sponsorships, while lucrative, raise significant public health concerns and ethical questions about the priorities of event organizers. This theme is further explored in discussions about community displacement and gentrification driven by food-based cultural events. The commodification of ethnic neighborhoods into trendy food destinations, while economically beneficial, often marginalizes local communities, replacing authentic cultural expressions with curated experiences for affluent newcomers.

Climate resilience and sustainability are critical concerns throughout the book, particularly for mega-events like the Olympics. Rising costs, environmental impacts, and declining public support for hosting bids have prompted initiatives such as the International Olympic Committee's 'New Norm', which aims to make events more cost-effective and environmentally friendly. Brisbane's approach to the 2032 Olympics, emphasizing temporary venues and regional integration, offers a potential model for sustainable event hosting. However, the book cautions that achieving meaningful legacies requires careful planning and long-term commitment from stakeholders.

Technological advancements and the evolving media landscape also play a pivotal role in shaping event narratives and engagement. Social media has revolutionized how events are experienced, enabling alternate storytelling and amplifying voices beyond traditional broadcasters. The 2024 Paris Olympics, for instance, highlights how digital platforms can enhance global reach, while complicating the control of narratives and legacies. This dynamic underscores the growing importance of media strategies in ensuring events achieve their intended impact.

Ultimately, the book argues that while events possess unparalleled potential to unite people, stimulate economies, and celebrate cultural identities, their success depends on striking a delicate balance between economic ambitions and ethical responsibilities. Event organizers must address challenges such as commercialization, community displacement, and environmental sustainability, while ensuring that events deliver meaningful and inclusive benefits. By examining these issues through diverse case studies, the book provides a nuanced understanding of the power of events as tools for development and social transformation. It serves as a valuable resource for policymakers, planners, and scholars seeking to harness the transformative potential of events for the greater good.

INDEX

FSC
www.fsc.org
MIX
Papier | Fördert gute Waldnutzung
FSC® C083411

Kolibri 360 GmbH
Ferdinand-Jühlke-Straße 7
99095 Erfurt, Deutschland
produktsicherheit@kolibri360.de